N

iversity

Central Tehran

Street names in brackets are no longer current;
post-revolutionary names are not known.

Motahari

bassy

Canadian Embassy

oosevelt)

(Abbasabad)

THE
CANADIAN
CAPER

THE CANADIAN CAPER

Jean Pelletier &
Claude Adams

WILLIAM MORROW AND COMPANY, INC.
New York   1981

Library of Congress Cataloging in Publication Data

Pelletier, Jean, 1948-
   The Canadian caper.

   Includes bibliographical references.
   1. Iran Hostage Crisis, 1979-   I. Adams,
Claude. II. Title.
E183.8.I55P44 1981   973.926   81-38365
ISBN 0-688-00756-2   AACR2

Printed in the United States of America

First U.S. Edition

1 2 3 4 5 6 7 8 9 10

A PEPPERMINT DESIGN/RICHARD MILLER

To Jean-David and Meredith

"...The possibility of a future crisis situation cannot be totally ignored and for this reason, contingency plans to deal with an emergency are necessary....United States personnel in Iran could become, in a sense, hostages."

From a 1976 Senate subcommittee staff report on United States military co-operation with the Shah of Iran

CONTENTS

THE CANADIAN CAPER

1

*I*N *THE* *CONFERENCE* *ROOM* at Honolulu's posh Sheraton Waikiki, Ken Taylor, drink in hand, surreptitiously glanced at his wristwatch. The convention of North American publishers was fast coming to a close, and Taylor would be the last to speak. He could feel a headache building: the dry martini tasted flat, and the cigar smoke was becoming oppressive. Taylor was starting to feel like a wind-up doll who's told the same story and gone through the same mechanical motions once too often. There was a tap on his shoulder — more introductions, and more handshakes. He rearranged his expression, smiled, and launched into another discussion.

Since early February, Taylor had logged more miles than he cared to number, appearing before more groups than he could possibly remember. Those months in Tehran had been hectic, sure, but even there his life had followed a certain order. He had operated on adrenal energy; the need for caution and deliberateness and precision had kept him alert. Life on the razor's edge had had a certain exhilaration to it. He had done his job well, and the last weekend in January, when he had tidied up his affairs and bade his last farewell to Tehran, would always be the high point of his life. The details were still vividly etched in his mind.

Since then, he had played the part of the peripatetic hero, basking in the glow of the celebrity, the toast of North America. What had the tabloids called him? A latter-day Scarlet Pimpernel. And here he was in Honolulu, next stop

Los Angeles, next stop...only his secretary in Ottawa knew for sure.

"...hostages will surely become an albatross around the neck of Khomeini, don't you agree, Mr. Ambassador?"

"Uh, I'm sorry," Taylor said, looking into the face of the publisher from — damn, what did his lapel-sticker say — Miami. "Oh, yes, of course. A good analogy" — I must stop daydreaming! — "the conditions of their release will impose a lot of pressure on the Majlis which..."

And so on. Once started, he could roll out the lines with ease. He could build convincing analyses of the confused Iranian political situation, and his brief sketches of the nation's leaders were always well received. Two or three times this evening he had also been prevailed upon to tell the story of the "exfiltration" — the sanitized version, of course, staying well away from the sensitive areas, lightly glossing over details like the false passports and the visas and the fall-back contingencies. Occasionally, the questions would cut too close to the classified bone, and he would have to back off. Usually, his listeners were unaware that they were not being told the whole story.

At 9:30 p.m., Taylor sought out the organizers of the convention and said he had to leave. Their thanks were sincere. "The panel discussion this afternoon was terrific," they told him. "Splendid. We can't tell you how much..." etc. He left the convention room and allowed himself a long exhalation of relief.

In the lobby, Taylor saw his wife, Pat, emerge from the elevator, clutching the car keys in her right hand. Her face was drawn. "Ken," she said, "it's just come over the television news. It finally happened. The Americans have sent in a team to free the hostages. They flew into the desert and landed. But they had to abort."

"Jesus!" Taylor breathed. "So they finally did it. After all these months, and sending up all this smoke. But why did they abort?"

"They didn't say. But it looks bad, Ken. ABC has called from Honolulu, from L.A., from Detroit. They want a comment from you. I have the numbers. Shall we go back up...?"

"No," Taylor said. "Let's get the car. There should be more news coming over the radio. Anyway, I need time to think."

While Taylor drove their rented Chevy through the cool Hawaii evening to meet friends at the airport, his wife twirled the dials of the dashboard radio. Bit by painful bit, the story came in: Half a dozen helicopters and two giant Hercules transports had slipped into Iranian airspace and unloaded their human cargo on a desert landing-strip south of Tehran. But, for some reason, the mission had been called off. And there were reports of fatalities, rumours of a debacle.

Taylor gave his wife a sidelong glance. "My God, they never even progressed beyond the first staging area. After all that planning, all that work.... Khomeini will have a field day with this. What in hell could have gone wrong?"

It was early morning in the Dasht-e Kavir — Great Salt — desert of central Iran. Wisps of smoke curled into the chill air; everything else was as still as death. Only minutes before, the armed men, hollering in a half-dozen American accents, had clambered aboard two transport aircraft and flown away into the still night, heading east in the direction of Cairo. In one of the transports, Colonel Charlie Beckwith, the field commander of the Eagle Claw commando raid, sat quietly shaking his head. The enormity of what he and his men had just experienced had not quite filtered through. His men left him to his black thoughts.

Beckwith, a Vietnam veteran, had seen his share of botched missions, but there had been nothing, anywhere, to compare with this. Eight helicopters, two transport planes, and ninety men — the tightest, best-trained, and best-equipped commandos ever assembled by the American military — had made up the strike force flown into Iranian airspace under cover of darkness. But a vicious sandstorm and mechanical problems had cut the chopper force down to five, and Beckwith had made the toughest decision of his life: the raid had to be called off. So finely tuned was the operation that five Sea Stallion helicopters would not have been enough. The margin of safety was gone. Beckwith refused to risk his men. The word went to Washington: "Mission aborted", and President Carter concurred.

Then came the horror. As the aircraft were refuelling in the darkness, one of the choppers veered and crashed into the side of a stationary C-130 transport. An immense ball of flame lit up the desert, and screams pierced the night. Like a monstrous flashbulb, the flare burned the image into Beckwith's mind. Eighty-two men, now panic-stricken, suffocated by the stench of death, rushed into the remaining Hercules. The plane screamed down the runway, rose several yards, dropped to the tarmac with a sickening bump, and then lifted clear into the sky.

Left behind were eight dead Americans and five helicopters, standing vigil for the fallen. One body lay in the sand, charred black, indistinct like a piece of sculpture that had toppled and was melting. An arm was outstretched. Only the victim's helmet was intact, reflecting the dying flames of the twisted hulks of metal that lay beyond.

In the thin light of dawn, a line of Iranian troops approached this apocalyptic scene with weapons at the ready. Flying low overhead, jet fighters with the markings of the Iranian air force strafed the wreckage, just in case some of the raiders had been left behind. Once the aerial attack was over, the troops moved in, sidestepping two or three bodies. Their first mission was to disable the remaining choppers, and they set about the task with enthusiasm. They were fatally sloppy. One soldier was killed and two others injured in an explosion. An officer began shouting harsh orders in Farsi. The helicopters were to be carefully searched, and all American matériel collected. After that, the bodies of the dead Americans were to be "bagged". Within hours, Iranian authorities would begin piecing together the failure of the Eagle Claw mission amid the desolation of Dasht-e Kavir.

The world would gasp.

The next morning, as Ken and Pat Taylor were sitting in their hotel room watching U.S. Defense Secretary Harold Brown explain the disaster, Iran's government had already begun to crow over the spilled American blood. A prominent ayatollah, known as Khalkhali, or "Judge Blood", noted grimly that "Iran may not have good radar, but Allah's is far better than anything the Americans may have."

In a room at Iran's foreign ministry in Tehran, Sadeq Ghotbzadeh, one of the Ayatollah's closest lay lieutenants, was inspecting the fragments collected from the American staging-area in the Dasht-e Kavir. Pulled out of the sand and from amid the still-warm wreckage, these had been flown directly to Tehran, under orders from Ghotbzadeh's office. One of the first things the minister noticed was a plastic-covered sheet of paper that, on brief inspection, turned out to be an aerial map of the city. An intelligence officer pointed to a number of circles drawn on the map. The circles, the officer noted, were numbered and keyed to a list headed by the words "Extraction Helo LZs". Under this cryptic heading appeared the words "Bus Stop 1: Stadium; Bus Stop 2: Racetrack", and so on. Twelve "bus stops" were listed. The intelligence officer explained: "We believe that the 'bus stops' were alternate landing sites for American helicopters, should they not have been able to land near the American embassy."

Ghotbzadeh nodded and shook his head in wonder. He admired the professionalism displayed in the finely detailed map. The Americans had some efficient agents working for them in Tehran, he was forced to admit.

He would have liked to know who they were.

Kenneth Taylor and his wife boarded a TWA flight at Honolulu airport, en route for Los Angeles and another hero's welcome. As he settled into his first-class-compartment seat, Taylor's thoughts were called back to a rainy Sunday in November and a chanting mob in an ancient city that he would probably never see again.

2

*T*HEY'RE COMING OVER THE WALL."
The secretary at the window on the second floor of the visa building was wide-eyed and stammering in fear. "Look, over there," she said in Farsi-accented English. At his desk, littered with visa applications and scraps of telexes, consular attaché Mark Lijek jerked back his chair and sprang to his feet.

It was late morning, Tehran time, on an overcast November the fourth.

Lijek, a boyish, short, mustachioed Californian, who'd arrived in Iran only three months earlier, strode across the room and leaned over the Iranian secretary's shoulder. What he saw, only forty yards away, chilled him. "Jesus in heaven," he whispered. Although the window permitted a view of only a fraction of the compound, he could see dozens of youths swarming over the ten-foot compound wall, screaming and waving banners. Some had already penetrated the grounds, and they were rushing towards the main gates, to open them from the inside.

Lijek's first scrambled thought was: "Nobody's trying to stop them." He was aware of someone standing beside him. It was Kim King, a footloose twenty-seven-year-old American tourist and frequent visitor to the embassy's consular offices, who was straining for a look. Beyond the wall, the two men and the girl could see a seething mass of people on Taleghani Street, the southern perimeter of the American compound. "Jesus, we have company," King wisecracked. In the turmoil just outside the gates, they could see clusters of Revolutionary

Guards, in their shabby, unbuttoned fatigues, carrying submachine guns. Lijek knew that members of this militia, the most zealous of the revolutionary cadres, commanded a fearful respect among the populace. But, dammit, he thought, the guards were doing nothing to stop the street roughs — some in their early teens — from clambering over the walls. And where were the local police guards, Lijek wondered. Where were the damn embassy Marines?

King tapped the windowpane with his finger. "Aren't these supposed to be bulletproof?" he asked Lijek.

"Yeah, they're supposed to be," the attaché answered distractedly. "'Course, they've never been tested." He was beginning to resent King's flip attitude.

"Well, we'll soon find out, won't we?" King replied.

Lijek turned away from the window, and surveyed the scene in the working area behind him. Normally the loudest sound was the clatter of typewriters, or low conversation as someone strolled from one desk to another. Now the scene was one of frantic activity. He could see a dozen of his colleagues rushing back and forth between the two windows that overlooked the courtyard of the embassy grounds. They were shouting at one another. A few were wild-eyed, running their hands feverishly through their hair, close to shock. I'm getting close to that state myself, he realized.

His wife Cora appeared, and he put his arm around her. Poor Cora. She had joined him in Tehran just two months earlier and was working as a clerk in the consular building. Withstanding a spontaneous attack by a bunch of crazed fundamentalist fanatics had not been part of her job description.

Lijek walked the few steps to the waiting-room area, only yards away from his desk. There, about twenty Iranians, who had been waiting for their visa applications to be processed, were huddled in a terrified group. Lijek heard moans and wails and some mumbled prayers. He understood little Farsi, but he could sense the collective panic. One man sat cross-legged on the floor, away from the group, babbling to himself. Another man approached him, waving his arms, pointing out the window and uttering a stream of garbled words. Lijek could only shrug and say placatingly: "Settle down. Things will be all right soon. Settle down." The Iranian gave him a look of blank incomprehension.

These people had good reason to worry, Lijek knew. They understood better than he the fanaticism and seething rage of the militants swarming over the walls outside. And here these Iranians were, trapped in the very lair of the American "devils" that the revolutionaries were seeking to exorcise, on the very day that the avenging hordes descended.

But Lijek could spare little time for these sympathetic reflections. He turned and hurried down the hall.

Without knocking, he rushed into the office of Bob Anders, the heavy-set, easygoing, grey-haired consular chief, who was talking excitedly into a telephone. Anders looked up at him, shrugged, and pointed to a chair. After replacing the receiver, he said: "That was Security over at chancery. They're trying to raise the Iranian foreign ministry and get some police or troops or anybody the hell over here." Anders ran his hand through his close-cropped hair. "They're also on the hotline to State [the U.S. State Department]. Jesus, Mark, can't we settle down those people out there? All that weeping and wailing isn't making things any easier on everybody's nerves."

Anders knew there was some hope for the occupants of the consular building — a slim one, but it was something to hang on to. Earlier in the day, when the marching students had begun to course into the street toward the embassy grounds, the building's doors had been locked, as a precaution. Should the militants approach and try the doors, they might assume the building was deserted, closed for business. It would give the Americans a few precious hours.

It was just before 3 a.m., Washington time, and the city slept. Many of the public buildings, like President Jimmy Carter's White House, were floodlit, but most of the city and government buildings were dark and silent. At the State Department building on C Street, however, the lights were burning, and major events were unfolding.

As soon as the Tehran call came in, the overnight duty officer at the operations centre, which handles cable and telephone traffic from 284 U.S. posts around the world, knew he had a top-grade crisis on his hands. Elizabeth Ann Swift, deputy political consul at the embassy in Tehran, was on the "box". Swift was fighting to keep her cool, but the duty officer had a good ear for the nuances in a human voice, even over a 7,000-mile telephone hookup. And Swift was on the edge of panic. Hundreds of Iranians, she said, were pouring into the compound; the local police guards had disappeared into the crowds, and the Marines were barricading the nerve centre of the American mission, the chancery building. It was bad, she said, as bad as it could possibly be. She wanted instructions. "Stay on the line," the duty officer ordered.

He turned to the staffer at the main telephone console with its 120 buttons. "Get me Newsom right away," he barked. Within seconds, she had roused David Dunlop Newsom, U.S. undersecretary of state for political affairs and the highest-ranking foreign-service officer in the department. Newsom had been dragged out of a deep sleep, but the first urgent words from the duty officer swept the cobwebs out of his consciousness. "The embassy in Tehran is being overrun," the man said, "and we have a political officer on the line. You'll want to talk to her. It sounds bad."

"I'll be over right away," Newsom said hurriedly and hung up.

The duty officer reflexively glanced up at the row of six clocks on the wall of the operations centre. They gave the precise local time and the time in Tehran, Greenwich, Paris, Seoul, and El Salvador. Behind him, an array of tickers and teletypes, linked with every world capital from Singapore to Santiago, sat mute, as if paralysed into silence by a crisis that superseded all others. The duty officer gave instructions to the staffer at the console to pull together a fresh shift of people. Throughout Washington and the nearby Virginia and Maryland suburbs, telephones began ringing in the night, and sleepers were yanked from their beds.

Inside the embassy grounds, one of the invaders who had clambered over the wall pulled away from the main group and ran toward the gate. From the belt of the embassy guard he tore a set of keys, and slipped one into the padlock holding together a chain that secured the main gate. It was like the opening of a dam. He cried out in triumph as the mob, screaming "*Allah Akhbar* ['God is Great']," pushed open the barrier and poured across the parking lot, waving enormous banners and posters of the Ayatollah Khomeini. Meeting no resistance, within seconds they had smashed their way into the two-storey ambassadorial residence, a plush, tree-shaded layout with high-ceilinged salons and graceful terraces surrounding a swimming pool.

While the residence was an easy conquest, the nearby chancery was a different matter. This was the citadel within the walls, a stuccoed building with armour-plated doors, grillework, checkpoints, and closed-circuit TV cameras that fed a bank of monitors in the Marine-guard offices behind the doors. The chancery housed the embassy's vital communications equipment, the vaults of highly sensitive documents, and the offices of the key embassy personnel. And five dozen frightened occupants.

In front of the chancery doors a detachment of U.S. Marines stood in combat gear, facing the swelling crowd. At a shouted command the Marines lobbed tear-gas grenades in unison into the crowd. For a moment or two, the main phalanx of the mob retreated. "Okay, inside and lock her up," shouted an officer. "And get everybody upstairs." A half-dozen Marines dashed into the chancery and electronically closed the armoured doors. For the time being they were sealed off from the mob.

It is a popular fiction that the Marines stationed at an embassy, any embassy, are there to repel an attack. True, they carry .38-calibre sidearms and have access to pumpguns that fire buckshot, to tear gas, to gas masks, and to some high-powered rifles that are kept well out of sight — but they are not equipped to fight off a mob. Indeed, they have strict orders to take only *defensive* action to buy time — minutes, perhaps hours — to allow embassy staff to destroy the most sensitive papers. Only if an embassy staff member's life is clearly in danger can a Marine shoot to kill. His orders are: fire warning shots, look as menacing as possible, and retreat. It is a strict rule of international diplomacy that only the host country can use brute force to protect an embassy. The embassy Marines had done their job; now it was up to the Iranian government to come to the Americans' defence.

After retreating into the chancery, the Marines herded about sixty American staffers and five Iranian workers up to the second floor. In a crisis, and this clearly was one, the second floor could be sealed off from the ground floor. Here, senior embassy officials were on the telephone to Bruce Laingen, the American chargé d'affaires and Washington's top man in Tehran, who had sped to the Iranian foreign ministry earlier that morning while the students were advancing toward the embassy.

Laingen had been afraid that this might develop into more than just another common-or-garden-variety anti-American demonstration, and now, as he listened over the telephone line to the hysterical shouts of the students, he knew his fears had been realized. "Okay," he barked over the phone to his staff, "proceed to destruct. I'm trying to get Yazdi [Iranian foreign minister Ibrahim Yazdi] to send in the military, but there are some snags. And it sounds like we can't delay any longer. Get the shredders working, now!"

This signal sent a small group of Marines and staffers into the chancery vault, where they began to make confetti out of every bit of classified material they could lay their hands on. It was a monstrous job: it would take many hours, perhaps days, to shred the mounds of paper. But they couldn't stop to think about the futility of what they were doing.

It was now early afternoon.

In Washington, a hastily and carelessly dressed David Newsom strode into the operations centre on the seventh floor of the State Department building and picked up the hotline to Tehran. Consul Elizabeth Ann Swift told him in clipped sentences that the embassy staff didn't think they could hold out much longer. "Laingen has given the order to destruct," she said, "and we're working at it. But we can't seem to raise the local authorities."

"What about the local police guards?" Newsom asked, referring to the fifteen Tehran police officers who had been stationed at the embassy gates since the summer before.

"They seem to have melted into the crowds just after the attack began," Swift said. "And the place is crawling with Revolutionary Guards. Hold on a sec. I'm just getting some more bad news." An aide had rushed to tell her that embassy security officer Mike Holland and four Marines had just surrendered to the mob. The invaders, aware that with every passing minute the shredders were chewing their way through the embassy documents, had yelled out a warning: "Throw down your guns, and you won't be harmed. Resist any longer, and you'll die." The Marines knew the game was up; the crowd had already begun to penetrate the chancery by cutting through the bars over a ground-level window. Any further resistance would surely trigger a bloodbath.

In the courtyard, the Marines tossed down their guns. One of the leaders of the militant students tore off their gas masks and snarled in broken English: "Your turn to breathe some of the gas." The Marines were bound and herded across the compound.

With his ear to the telephone receiver, Newsom gathered that it would be some minutes before the students managed to break through to the second floor, and maybe another hour before they located the vault and the paper-destroyers inside. He looked thoughtfully out of the window. The first glimmer of dawn was breaking through the sky to the east of Washington. Before sunrise, the United States would have lost an embassy.

On the second floor of the U.S. embassy consular building, attaché Joe Stafford, twenty-nine, and his tall, black-haired wife, Kathleen, stood with their arms around one another. It had been only minutes since the attack on the embassy had begun, but for Stafford the minutes had dragged interminably. He had little hope that the militants would long ignore this part of the compound, but Stafford, a serious, quiet man whose father was vice-president of Occidental Petroleum, a major oil company, knew little about the frenzied psychology of a mob. In his daily routine of processing the visa applications of westernized Iranians eager to escape possible retribution at the hands of the Ayatollah's fanatically anti-American regime, he was isolated from the cutting edge of the revolution. (What Stafford also didn't know was that because the consular building ground floor was empty, having just been renovated and freshly painted, the invaders had decided to ignore it, wrongly believing the whole building to be deserted.)

Sweating with fear, expecting to face the barrel of a submachine gun any minute, Stafford turned questioningly to his boss, consular chief Bob Anders. "Take it easy, Joe," his superior said reassuringly. "We're trying to rouse the authorities to send in the troops. They should be here soon. Why don't you and Kathy go over and try to comfort the Iranians in the waiting room?"

Anders was interrupted by the abrupt appearance of an American Marine who was yelling into a walkie-talkie. "This is sector L," the Marine barked. "We have more than a dozen of our people here. And a few dozen natives. Out." Anders, the Staffords, the Lijeks, and Kim King huddled around the Marine, whose nametag read Sgt. James Lopez. He was wearing glasses and looked to be in his mid twenties.

Lopez was straining to make out a high-pitched reply coming over the walkie-talkie. King pointed to the .38 special that the Marine carried in his hip holster. "Are you guys handing out weapons? I think I know how to use — "

But he was interrupted by Bob Anders. "Sergeant, what is the situation out there?"

"Sir, it looks pretty bad," Lopez answered. "I think we'd all better get ready to file downstairs, walk toward the chancery, and give ourselves up."

"Now wait a minute, sergeant. Give ourselves up?"

Anders said. "But the militants don't even know we're here, for God's sake."

"I think it's only a matter of time, sir," Lopez answered. "Unless you have a better idea."

"Well," Anders replied brusquely, "getting the hell out of this building, for one thing. Why not try the street exit?"

Kim King broke in once again to ask about the gun. Lijek and Anders turned to face him, growing increasingly angry. Lopez shot back: "Look, buddy. This is the only weapon I got, and even *I* can't use it."

"What do you mean, *you* can't use it?" King sputtered.

"Orders," said the Marine. "We can't just go plugging people. It's called passive resistance. And lemme tell ya another thing. When we get out of here, we don't do nothing to get 'em excited. We do what they say, if they get us. Don't do anything to get 'em pissed off. Understand?"

King quipped: "Well, if I'm gonna give my blood, I'd just as soon give it to a blood bank, thank you very much." The Marine didn't answer. The walkie-talkie squawked again, and he spun on his heels and headed down the stairs.

Henry Lee Schatz stubbed out his cigarette and buzzed his secretary. "Can you go over and collect the mail at the chancery?" he asked. The girl, a young Iranian who'd been with him a month, said she was on her way.

Schatz could hear the mob noise outside his office, located in a building just a few minutes' walk from the American compound. As an American agricultural attaché, he did not rate office space in the already crowded chancery, so they had assigned him a cubicle in a building leased by the Swedes. Schatz, a tall, wide-shouldered Idaho bachelor, with an ingratiatingly casual manner, didn't mind working apart from the rest of the American mission in the city. It was less distracting here, and besides, he was only a brief stroll away from the compound. Not far enough, however, from the damn street noise, he mused.

Schatz turned back to his paperwork: columns of numbers about crop yields, export figures, and short-term projections of Iranian grain consumption. Suddenly, his secretary rushed panting into the office.

"Mr. Schatz," she cried breathlessly, "they've broken into the embassy. Hundreds of them. They're all over the street. They —"

"Wait a minute," Schatz said. "Slow down. *Who* has broken into the embassy?"

"The students from the university. They're all over the place. Somebody down on the street told me they climbed over the walls. They've taken down the American flag and they're burning it!"

His stomach in a knot, Schatz rushed back to the window and saw the hordes spilling through the main gate and over the walls. For a few seconds he took in the scene of pandemonium; then he picked up his papers and locked them in the filing cabinet.

He called in his staff. "Look, I'm leaving now," he said. "If anybody comes in here asking for me, say I've left, you don't know where I am, and you don't know when I'll be back. Nothing more."

He shook their hands, and wished them luck.

No need to start shredding or burning, he thought. He knew that if this was the real thing, if the right-wing mobs were indeed taking over, then his office would eventually be ransacked and all the documents removed. Big deal. Agricultural statistics would hardly stoke the fires of the revolution, or jeopardize American interests, he mused sardonically.

His next moves were reflexive. Diplomatic staff in foreign capitals are under standing orders in case of crisis: turn all the locks, destroy anything that might be even remotely sensitive or incriminating, hightail it to the nearest friendly embassy, and under no circumstances leave a trail if you can avoid it. That meant no contact with foreign nationals while in flight.

Luckily Schatz didn't even have to leave his office building to find a refuge. He was on speaking terms with a handful of Swedish diplomats, and there was little question in his mind that they would shelter him. First he decided to make a quick sortie to his apartment to gather up a few belongings — just enough to fit into a rucksack. He was not unduly worried as he strolled through the Iranian crowds. Unlike the American consulate staff, he had few professional contacts with Iranian citizens; the people he dealt with were low- and middle-echelon bureaucrats. He speculated that the Iranian militants would surely have better things to do in their first day of occupation than to go on a scavenger hunt for information on the whereabouts of an obscure agricultural attaché.

Within hours, Schatz was on safe ground with his new-found Swedish hosts. He had regretted leaving behind his valuables at the apartment: thousands of precious dollars' worth of stereo equipment, his collection of ivory carvings, and most of his wardrobe. It would all likely be sucked into the vortex of the revolution in the coming days, part of the flotsam and jetsam of the American presence in Iran.

Inside the compound, the surrender of the Marines had fired the militants' confidence. The students occupied the ground floor of the chancery, and groups of them stood marvelling at the television circuitry in the Marine guardroom. So far, everything had gone smoothly and without bloodshed. A fundamentalist student who called himself "Brother Ali" shouted for order and pointed to the staircase leading to the second floor.

"Follow me," he screamed in Farsi. "The American spies are upstairs. Long live Khomeini."

Dozens of students fell in behind him and raced up the staircase. It had all been so easy, and the best part was just ahead.

Inside the consular building, they could hear the sound of footsteps on the roof. Heads were turned upwards, and all conversation stopped. Though the sounds were faint, they were like an incessant drumbeat to the listeners, coming closer, ever closer. King turned to Lijek and asked if there were any open vents from the roof into the second floor. "You know," he said, "they could just drop a little hot number down on us, and it would be lights out."

"Cut it out, will you, " Lijek responded irritably.

He was losing patience with King, who was sticking to him like glue. He wished the guy would go away and pester somebody else with his wisecracks.

The panicky Iranians in the waiting room were beginning to calm down, Lijek noticed. Bob Anders had done his "big father" number on them, and the Iranians responded to his soothing words even though they could understand little English. A secretary was passing around a bowl of hard candy, and Lijek could hear them crunching nervously on the sweets.

Back at the windows, Lijek and King heard a series of pistol shots. They saw students carrying giant banners bearing the portrait of the Ayatollah Khomeini. Over and over again, they heard shouts of "*La Illah Illallah* ['There is no God but Allah']." The hard truth was sinking in. This was it. Christ, they were in the middle of a *jihad*, a holy war.

Just then Lopez raced back into the room, carrying what King quickly identified as a shotgun that fired tear-gas cannisters. The Marine explained in clipped monosyllables that this would be the most effective weapon under the circumstances. "Bust up a crowd in no time," he explained. "You don't kill anyone, just change the atmosphere." He allowed himself a tight grin.

Within minutes, the weapon was to prove its usefulness. A secretary burst in to say that she had heard the sound of breaking glass in a nearby men's lavatory. The Marine raced down the hall and through the door marked "Men". King and Lijek saw him fire two cannisters into the room, wait a few moments while the noxious fumes spread, and then quickly close the door.There were tears in his eyes. "Caught a whiff," Lopez sniffled. "We'd better secure this door fast."

King and two other Americans found a metal coat-hanger and twisted it around the doorknob. Then they fastened the end of the wire to the knob of the adjacent women's washroom. King offered to stand guard. Later the irony would strike him: all hell was breaking loose, the power balance of the Middle East was being altered on a few acres of American embassy soil, and here was a party of frightened Americans trying to stem the floodtide of revolution with a few inches of wire twisted around a bathroom door.

Behind his desk at the Canadian embassy, about a kilometre to the north, Ambassador Ken Taylor was sipping coffee and leafing through the weekend papers. His shirt collar was open, and his sports jacket was thrown over a nearby chair. His muscles throbbed with a dull ache from the vigorous tennis game he'd played the day before.

Taylor glanced at an editorial in the independent English-language Tehran *Times*. It was an exhortation to the city's students, warning them not to become too absorbed in politics. The tone of the piece was similar to what he would have expected from his hometown newspaper, the Calgary *Albertan*. "A time will definitely come," the editorialist had written, "when politics and other fields of national life will be open to the students and they will be free to take part in these activities. Until such time, the students should refrain from taking part in demonstrations as, in the final analysis, it is the students themselves who will lose...."

Taylor sighed. One might as well tell the mullahs to think but of paradise or wish the Tehran traffic jams away. He was a bit astonished that any educated person in revolutionary Iran could indulge in such feather-headed bunk. Turning the page of the broadsheet, he skipped the horoscope, the poems of Persian antiquity, and the fifth excerpt from the memoirs of Henry Kissinger.

Shortly after 11 a.m. his desk telephone rang. It was a clerk from downstairs whose functions included monitoring the local radio. "Mr. Ambassador," the clerk said, "I'm sorry to bother you, but I've just picked up something on the box. I can't make it all out, but they're saying something about the

American embassy, something about a victory over the devils, how Carter will tremble. Could just be more of the rhetoric we've been hearing for the last few weeks, but it might be worth checking out."

"Thank you," Taylor said. "I'll do that. Keep monitoring. Let me know anything more substantial."

The ambassador cleared away the newspapers and buzzed his secretary, Laverna Dollimore. "Laverna, get me the Swedish ambassador."

Within seconds, Kaj Sundberg was on the line. His embassy virtually overlooked the American compound. "Kaj," Taylor said. "We've just picked up something on the local radio about the American embassy. Is there anything—"

"It's true," Sundberg interrupted excitedly. "The worst has happened. Hundreds of students are inside the compound. The size of the mob is incredible. I don't see how the Americans can hold out much longer."

While Sundberg provided a few more colourful details, Taylor felt fear ripple through him. He rang off and leaned back in his leather chair. After only a few minutes' thought he picked up a pen and began scribbling the words of a telex to Ottawa.

"The power's gone."

For the first time Bob Anders could feel real panic race throughout the group. In the darkened room, he sensed bodies stiffening and hearts pounding. He reflexively reached for a nearby light switch and flipped it — nothing happened. The Lijeks, the Staffords, Kim King, the handful of other Americans in the room, and the twenty Iranians, all turned to Anders. "Somebody must have gotten to the power plant," he said, trying to sound calm.

"Doesn't that mean all the doors are electronically locked?" an unidentified voice asked.

"Yeah," Anders said. "But only from the outside. We can still get out."

Kim King struck matches one after another until Sergeant Lopez reappeared in a doorway with a flashlight. He flicked the beam over the faces in the office area and walked towards Anders.

"All right, we're on our own," the Marine said. "I'm not getting an answer on the walkie-talkie. They must have nabbed the rest of the guys. So now we go by the book."

"The book?" King asked, taking the flashlight and shining it on the ceiling to shed more light.

"That's right. Routine procedure. Now I want everybody away from the windows, stay out of sight, and gather over there at the back of the room. So far, they've been busy elsewhere. They've overlooked us. Now what we have to do is evacuate the building. We go down the stairs in groups of two —"

"You've got to be kidding," King broke in. "What's with all this kindergarten formation business?"

"Knock it off," the Marine shouted. "This ain't the time to argue. Now we have to do this right, because we only get one chance."

As they formed up to leave the building, the Americans and Iranians began anxiously discussing where they would go once they had fled the compound. King suggested the British embassy, eight blocks away. They would surely be given haven there. An Iranian woman pleaded: "I don't think I could find it." She turned to the people around her, and they also shrugged in ignorance. King and Lijek began giving street directions while the Iranian woman, conversant in English, translated these into Farsi.

As soon as he was satisfied that they were all ready, the Marine led them down a flight of stairs leading to the empty ground floor, where clerks behind glass windows normally received visa applications. Anders couldn't help noticing with amusement that, even in their hurried exit, the evacuees were careful to avoid brushing against the freshly painted walls.

When the first group reached the bottom, the Marine

stopped them. "Hold it. Before we open the door, there's something I gotta do first."

He picked up a large steel bar, walked behind the glass windows, and began smashing what Anders realized were visa plates. The Americans and Iranians, momentarily distracted, watched with unguarded delight. "This will teach those suckers," the Marine said. "No way they'll be able to forge visas."

His job completed, the Marine unlatched the door and backed away to let the others pass. Bob Anders opened the door onto the street, as everyone strained to get a look. The rain was falling in torrents.

At the State Department operations room in Washington, David Newsom emptied his third Styrofoam cup of black coffee and massaged the back of his neck. Speaking alternately with Elizabeth Ann Swift at the embassy and Bruce Laingen at the Iranian foreign ministry — both of whom, in effect, were prisoners — Newsom was beginning to lose hope that the Iranian military police would soon be moving to rout the invaders from American property. Dammit, he thought, the Iranians had on three prior occasions pledged to safeguard the U.S. embassy.

Only three days before, Newsom learned from Laingen, a senior official had interrupted the consul-general during a tennis match to warn him of an impending student march against the embassy. "Have no fear," the official had told Laingen. "We will protect the compound against all incidents." And now the authorities were sitting on their hands, afraid to move against the right-wing fanatics who were despoiling the tradition of diplomacy.

Over the long-distance hookup, Swift had told Newsom that the first of the militants had already penetrated the ground floor of the chancery through a window. "It's only a matter of time now, sir," she told him. But time quickly ran out. Just before dawn in Washington the phone connection between the State Department and the embassy operations centre went dead. Newsom called for the technicians, whose verdict confirmed his worst fears: "Nothing wrong this end, sir. Somebody pulled the plug over there."

Newsom rose from his chair, left the room, and walked down the hall to the office of Secretary of State Cyrus Vance. He entered without knocking.

Charged with the adrenalin of revolution, the students swarmed into the second-storey offices of the chancery expecting a fight, but they were disappointed. With few exceptions, they easily tied up their captives with ropes, blindfolded them, shoved them into the corridors, and ordered them to sit quietly. It was a quick operation; Brother Ali and his followers found the Americans in a passive, despondent mood.

The militants ransacked the offices, leaving only the filing cabinets intact. One student emerged from an office carrying a giant portrait of the Ayatollah Khomeini punctured with dart holes that he had taken down. Within minutes, they located the vault and began banging at it with pieces of wood. Embassy staffers were forced to open the vault and inside the militants found a handful of Marines and embassy officials clustered around a barrel full of shredded documents. Among the confetti-sized fragments were bits of computer memory tape, microfilm, and pounds of paper. An enterprising youth also located a small arsenal of weapons, including an M3 automatic rifle, an automatic shotgun, a .38-calibre handgun, and a high-powered rifle with a telescope mount.

None of the weapons had been fired.

During Washington's early-morning rush hour, as cars were jamming the Key, Memorial, Roosevelt, and 14th Street bridges leading into the city from Virginia, Newsom received a message from Bruce Laingen that gave him a spark of hope — the first in a long, bleak night.

"I've just spoken to Yazdi," Laingen reported over the long-distance line between the foreign ministry in Tehran and the seventh floor at State. "He tells me our people will be freed by tomorrow morning, Tehran time. He is deeply concerned."

I'll bet he is, thought Newsom.

WITHIN HOURS OF THE SEIZURE, the new occupants of the embassy, dubbed the "Followers of the Line of Khomeini" by the Western press, issued their terms to Washington: the hostages in exchange for the Shah, a hundred bodies for one, a straight-up swap. Nothing more and nothing less than total capitulation. The revolution wanted its pound of royal flesh.

But the royal flesh was 7,000 miles away, ailing and not disposed to travel. The exiled monarch, after a painful pilgrimage through Egypt, Morocco, the Bahamas, and Mexico, now lay on his back in a two-room, $900-a-day suite at New York General Hospital – Cornell Medical Centre. The seventeenth-floor suite was not new to the Shah. He had convalesced in these very rooms in 1949, during an earlier visit to the United States. Now, high above the East River, one of the world's richest rulers had only a colour television set, a half-dozen bodyguards, and a clutch of high-priced specialists to keep him company. He had a few visitors besides his next of kin, however: Frank Sinatra stopped by to croon his condolences, as did Tricia Nixon Cox, who might be expected to have sympathy for a ruler who had fallen from his countrymen's favour. And, of course, there was the familiar presence of Henry Kissinger, the Shah's *envoyé extraordinaire* in America, who had appealed to his countrymen not to treat Pahlavi "like a flying Dutchman who cannot find a port of call."

Kissinger, with some help from David Rockefeller of the Chase Manhattan Bank, had secured the Shah his latest haven. Two weeks earlier, a charter jet had left the Mexico City Airport. Anyone who asked was told that the plane bore a "valuable shipment" from the Bank of Mexico bound for New York.

Security along the route was airtight. During a routine customs and immigration check at Fort Lauderdale, Florida, an unwitting official asked if the pilot intended to dump any garbage along the way to New York or whether any plants were on board. When the jet touched down at La Guardia Airport in New York, an official greeting-party was conspicuous by its absence.

The Shah, whisked by limousine to a side entrance of the Manhattan hospital, was not only suffering from a malignancy in the lymph gland — cancer — but he also had gallstones clogging his bile duct, which had brought on jaundice. Illness had taken its toll on the once virile, magnetic ruler: his skin was the colour and texture of old parchment; he was scarecrow thin, with hollowed cheeks and eyes that seemed to be retreating into his skull.

The Shah was well aware that in accepting Carter's offer to come to the United States for treatment, he had become the unwelcome guest of a reluctant host. The president had been forced to accept the Iranian ruler on "humanitarian" grounds, and as a gesture of remembrance of the "friendship" that had existed between the two nations for many years. As soon as he heard of the hostage-takers' demand, Carter was to repent of his generosity. He damned the State Department officials who had lobbied for the Shah's admission to the United States and his Intelligence people who had not anticipated the violent reactions of the fundamentalists in Iran. But it was now too late to withdraw his support from Pahlavi.

In the long hours between treatments for his lymphoma, the Shah had ample time for reflection. To his aides and close family members he broached the idea of returning to Tehran to face his subjects. "Nonsense," they told him. "You are too ill to travel; besides, those fanatics would tear you apart." The ruler, whose titles included "The Shadow of God on Earth", nodded sadly. He passed his time watching television reports of the demonstrations by Iranian students in the streets of New York and shuddered at learning that a black man wearing a white robe and calling himself a Muslim had somehow slipped into the hospital library and threatened three doctors with a samurai sword. The man had been quickly arrested and the Shah's guard increased. Meanwhile, in Tehran, a fanatical cleric, the Ayatollah Khalkhali, urged that zealots break into the Shah's hospital room and dismember him.

Now a virtual prisoner, the Shah pondered the unkind irony of his situation. His thoughts wandered back to his coronation as the second ruler in the Pahlavi "dynasty", in October 1967. In preparation for this cosmic event, he and his wife, the Empress Farah, had watched a film of the coronation of Queen Elizabeth II more than a dozen times, until they had memorized every regal gesture, every ostentatious accoutrement. But the coronation was just a family get-together compared with the ceremonies the Shah staged at Persepolis in 1971, to celebrate the 2500th anniversary of the Persian Empire. In the presence of invited kings, princes, and prime ministers (Washington, to its later embarrassment, sent Spiro Agnew), the Shah had evoked the spirits of Iran's ancient rulers, Cyrus and Darius, in whose image he liked to style himself. The highlight was a multi-million-dollar procession of pomp and ceremony worthy of an Eastern Cecil B. de Mille, but not everyone in the audience was appreciative. As a former member of the Shah's government later commented: "With the parade over, the illustrious guests followed their imperial host into the sumptuous tented village built and decorated by French experts. Millions had been spent on housing and feeding the attending heads of state and other dignitaries. In Iran, outside of the sovereign's immediate entourage and the career sycophants, criticism seethed, but was expressed only by discreet remarks in the privacy of people's homes. Abroad, the press had a field day. How could a developing country dig so deep into its purse to put on some sort of fancy-dress party instead of devoting its money to improving its people's standard of living?"

His dynastic pretensions notwithstanding, the Shah's origins were in fact less than exalted. His father was a onetime camel-driver who had risen high in the military and been made hereditary ruler as the result of a *coup d'état* in 1921. The first Pahlavi went a long way toward modernizing Iran and unifying the many warring tribes that made up what was then a semi-feudal state. He outlawed the veil for women, developed education, fashioned an effective army, and sowed the seeds for Iran's industrialization. His son, the Crown Prince, watched and learned. But Reza Shah eventually became a victim of his policy of playing one superpower off against another. In 1941, with the Second World War raging, the British and the Soviets occupied the country and forced the pro-German Shah to abdicate. He was dispatched aboard ship to Johannesburg, South Africa, where he died three years later.

The Shah's twenty-two-year-old son, Mohammed Reza Pahlavi, ascended the throne of an occupied nation. When Germany invaded Russia, Iran had no choice but to join forces with the Allies to declare war on the Axis nations. In return for its support, Iran was promised territorial integrity under the Tehran Agreement of 1943, which was signed by Britain, the United States, and the U.S.S.R. When the Soviet Union later violated the agreement by fomenting revolution among Iran's obstreperous northern tribes, the Shah turned wholeheartedly to the West for military support. In so doing, Iran assumed the strategic role of anti-Soviet policeman in the Persian Gulf — a role that played no small part in the eventual downfall of Pahlavi.

In the delicate chess game of the Cold War years, Iran was increasingly viewed by the West as a valuable pawn, well-positioned on the red side of the board — not an aggressive piece, but one able to hold Soviet ambitions in check. This view coincided with an upsurge of nationalist feeling in Iran, which was accompanied by a growing resentment of the nation's economic concessions to British and American oil companies.

This postwar nationalist ferment produced one of the most powerful and enigmatic politicians in Iran's modern history: Dr. Mohammad Mossadeq, leader of the National Front. His key aim, as he organized the many elements in Iran opposed to foreign interference in the economy, was to regain control over the nation's oilfields and humble the meddlesome British into the bargain. A succession of feeble prime ministers had been unable, or unwilling, to bring the Anglo-Iranian Oil Company to heel, and the Shah equivo-cated. Finally, in 1951, the Majlis (the Iranian Parliament) voted to nationalize the oil industry and demanded that the Shah appoint Mossadeq, then a hale and still-fire-breathing septuagenarian, as prime minister. To underline the demand, violent demonstrations swept Tehran. The Shah had little choice but to accede to the elevation of the most popular politician in the kingdom.

A sudden British withdrawal from the country knocked the breath out of the Iranian economy, but Mossadeq main-tained his popular support with a series of rousing street speeches about the evils of colonialism. Though not a com-munist, he allowed the communist-backed Tudeh Party to operate unhampered because its followers supported his anti-British stance. Inevitably, the Eisenhower administra-tion in the United States began to worry seriously about the direction Mossadeq was taking. Mossadeq's rapid ascen-dancy, which peaked in 1952 when the Majlis granted him almost absolute control over the government, put the Shah (and, by extension, the British and the Americans) in a peril-ous position. The British saw a valuable source of oil slipping away from their control, and the Americans distrusted Mos-sadeq's tolerance of the "Red Menace". Following the cus-tomary tactics of the Cold War period, Washington dis-patched the CIA to mount a coup. A senior CIA Middle East expert, Kermit Roosevelt, was directed to destroy Mossadeq's power base and to restore to the Shah full control of the government.

Even by the CIA standards of the time, it was an unusual operation. Among other questionable strategies, Roosevelt bought the services of a notorious street tough and extortionist named Shaban Ja'afari, or Shaban the Brainless, to lead a mob of armed pimps, goons, agitators, and professional pickpockets. Shaban's crowd could, on cue, galvanize the Tehran bazaar into demonstrations against Mossadeq.

By rallying the mobs, working in close conjunction with the Shah, and buying off the military, Roosevelt and his minions effected the bloodless coup that toppled Mossadeq and brought back the Shah and his Empress from a four-day exile on the Caspian Sea. For his efforts, the Shah warmly shook Roosevelt's hand and presented him with a solid gold cigarette case.

As details of the coup became known, however, many moderate Iranians were outraged at the cynicism of the American action. Reza Baraheni, an intellectual arrested and tortured by SAVAK, the Shah's security police, in 1973, saw it thus: "Imagine a more tyrannical George III being crowned 6,000 miles away by the very descendants of George Washington and Benjamin Franklin with money raised by the American taxpayer."

Firmly back in control, the Shah wasted no time showing his gratitude to the United States, and Washington was only too eager to use that gratitude. As is so often the case, the chief American currency of friendship became military assistance. The young Shah was not blind to the need for an effective, well-armed military force. After all, his own father had been forced to abdicate when the Iranian army had been unable to defend the country against Soviet-British invasion. Shortly after the succession, the young Shah had invited the United States to send in a military mission to help in the reorganization of his shattered and demoralized forces. With American assistance, a proud and compact military machine, stressing modern weaponry and training, was created, and the officers' corps was purged of left-leaning elements. To build loyalty among the military staff, the Shah initiated a policy of buying the newest and most sophisticated American weapons. The U.S. military advisers stayed on, and their presence had a significant impact on the country's socio-political dynamics. Between 1947 and 1969, the United States poured nearly a billion and a half dollars into Iran for military assistance alone. Iranian officers were trained in the United States, and Washington progressively beefed up its military mission in Iran, which, in time, grew to include 1,400 personnel.

It was only in the seventies, however, as Iran's oil revenues began to mushroom, that Washington decided the time had come to shape its staunch ally into a true mini-superpower. The Nixon doctrine — that to assist local armed forces was preferable to a direct U.S. military presence — led to Iranian arms sales exceeding $10 billion from 1972 to 1976. Sleek jet fighters led the parade of technology, followed by tanks, artillery and missiles, destroyers and submarines, and radar and intelligence-gathering systems. With British troops gone from the Persian Gulf area, Iran became the traffic cop of the Strait of Hormuz, through which sixty percent of the world's oil moves in tankers. And, although the Shah signed the nuclear nonproliferation treaty, he left little doubt that Iran was ready to go nuclear if other middle powers decided to take that route.

Until 1977, coexistence with Washington had been the central tenet of the Shah's foreign policy. But in that year an unusual new man entered the White House, a high-principled Southerner named Jimmy Carter, and the new president's ways puzzled the Shah. Previous presidents — Nixon, Johnson, Eisenhower — had never expressed the slightest interest in how the monarch managed his internal affairs, as long as Iran did not waver from its pro-Western policy. But Carter was different. His comments about human rights in Latin America, in Asia, and, yes, in the Middle East, suggested that Washington was injecting a new ingredient into its foreign relations — Western morality. The Shah, who had his own ways of dealing with political dissent, did not appreciate Washington's poking around in his prisons and listening to the growing allegations of torture and terrorism by the monarch's henchmen.

Furthermore, the timing of Carter's subtle interventions was bad. The Shah was having problems at home with religious fundamentalists and right-wing students. Iran's 180,000 clergy had never been fond of the Shah's land reforms, his enfranchisement of women, and his helter-skelter arms buying. From their network of mosques, they openly criticized the way he was spending Iran's newfound oil fortunes. Perhaps even more important, the mullahs were worried that the Shah's industrialization of Iran would weaken their hold on the people. To the Shah's alarm, the agitation of the mullahs was having an effect in the bazaars and the universities. And always, there was the damnable sermonizing — from his exile in Iraq — of the reactionary fundamentalist, Ayatollah Khomeini. The Ayatollah maintained contact with his right-wing, anti-Shah followers by means of tape cassettes smuggled into Iran in the guise of Oriental music recordings. These tapes had proliferated to the extent that copies were even being sold in the bazaars of the holy city of Qom and in Tehran.

Early in 1978 the Shah struck back at his longtime political foe. His methods were crude but effective. He ordered the publication, in a large Tehran daily, of a slanderous article accusing the Ayatollah of being the homosexual son of a cabaret dancer. The unsigned article made much of Khomeini's rumoured foreign birth in India, and resurrected allegations of his being in the pay of the British. As one former member of the Shah's regime later said, this was "the spark which would touch off the powder keg".

The spark ignited first in Qom, where the faithful took to the streets to protest this outrageous calumny. Army and police opened fire on the crowd, and several were killed. This set off the pattern of action-reaction that would eventually send hundreds of thousands of people into the streets — an escalation of public emotion that the Shah stoked with bullets and truncheons. He would realize his mistake too late.

According to Iranian custom, the dead are publicly mourned on the fortieth day after their burial. Thus, when the crowds staged a procession in the streets of Tabriz on

February 18, 1978, to mourn the victims of Qom, police once again aimed their guns into the masses. Forty days later, the "martyrs" of Tabriz inspired marches in Tehran and Esfahan, and once again blood was spilled. In time, this forty-day cycle of tears, guns, and retribution would convulse the entire country, while the mullahs, safe from the SAVAK bullies in their sacred mosques, whipped the fevered crowds on.

In the blindness of his megalomania, Pahlavi ignored the warning signs of his crumbling regime. "It's nothing," he said in April 1978. "Tabriz? Esfahan? It's the price to be paid for democratization. Nothing dangerous. And then who can oppose me? Khomeini? He doesn't count for much....The mullahs? They are incompetents, and often traitors."

Yet while he shrugged off the mounting demonstrations against his regime, Pahlavi implemented a number of liberalizing measures to cool the tempers of the masses. He took steps to hold down the price of food, and the government issued self-serving "bulletins" about victories against inflation. He dismissed the hated general Nassiri, who headed SAVAK, and replaced him with a more moderate man. And he ordered his security police to abandon their Inquisition-like brutality against political prisoners. He boasted that Iran would become an industrial power on the strength of its oil revenues. "In ten years, we hope to be what Europe is today," he told the American newsmagazine *U.S. News and World Report*. "It will not be easy, but in twenty years we hope to be a fully advanced nation." Word went out that Iran would soon have "one-hundred-per-cent-free elections". A period of calm set in during the summer months of 1978, and the Shah packed his cases for a carefree, lavish holiday on the Caspian Sea with two other monarchs, King Constantine of Greece and King Hussain of Jordan.

While the Shah sunned and snorkeled, Khomeini accelerated his campaign from Iraq and, through a number of trusted confederates, tightened his links with Iran's religious centres. Within Iran, the lay opposition to the Pahlavi throne launched an underground mimeograph campaign, denouncing the policies of the Shah that were designed to thrust Iran into the twentieth century.

The monarch had introduced large-scale agrarian reform, breaking down the influence of the feudal land-owners and the aristocracy by distributing land to the peasants. Steadily, throughout the 1960s, per-capita income had risen as industrial growth provided more and more jobs. By 1977, the average annual income stood at $2,200, more than seven times what it had been in 1965. Two-thirds of Iranians owned the houses they lived in. Attendance in primary schools was at more than ten million, and illiteracy, the scourge of so many underdeveloped countries, had dropped from eighty-five to fifty-five per cent. Along with the burgeoning oil industry, agriculture and manufacturing grew in sophistication. And, in the areas of social welfare and health and communications, Iran was making giant leaps.

The Shah knew full well that Iran's influential clergy were uneasy about the pace of the nation's "progress" and its impact on Islamic traditions, but he truly believed he was winning the race for the affection of the people. "Nobody can overthrow me," he boasted. "I have the support of 700,000 troops, all the workers, and most of the people."

The Shah saw himself as a masterful administrator, but he could not completely cover up the defects of his autocratic regime. The high-level corruption of his court was notorious. Kickbacks on contracts went to his brothers and sisters in the form of commissions for everything from the building of dams to the purchase of aircraft. Even in cases of corruption where a member of the royal family might not have been directly involved, the blame would inevitably fall onto the Shah's shoulders because of his unbridled nepotism. In 1977, for example, he launched a program of free meals for school-children, supervised by the mother of the Empress. In one northern community, the truck drivers delivering the food to the schools simply sold it on the open market and pocketed the money. The funds of the vast Pahlavi Foundation, the depository of the family (and the national) fortune, were often used to line the pockets of the aristocracy. As the influential French newspaper *Le Monde* noted in October 1978, efforts to root out this corruption were "a near-impossible task, bearing in mind that the Emperor himself is not above reproach in this sphere."

As the enormous proceeds of the oil boom began to flow into the country, the mullahs turned their attention more and more to the increasingly lavish excesses of the upper classes. In matters of personal morality, the Koran is unremittingly rigid. For the benefit of the oil sheiks who visited Iran, the Shah had authorized the building of casinos and "pleasure resorts" away from the major cities. The island of Kish, for example, became a Persian Gulf hideaway for oil billionaires, stocked (rumour had it) with Parisian courtesans flown in aboard Air France Concordes. Gossip was rife in Tehran about the gambling losses suffered by the Shah's sister, the Princess Ashraf, in foreign casinos. She was frittering away the national heritage, the stories went, on the fickle turn of the roulette wheel. Even worse, there were rumours that another sister had converted to Roman Catholicism. The mullahs bristled. Their fundamentalist sensibilities were further offended when, obsessed with linking his dynasty to the grandeur that was ancient Persia, the Shah abandoned the Islamic calendar, which dated from the Hegira — Muhammed's flight from Mecca in A.D. 622 — and implemented a calendar that dated from the foundation of the Persian Empire by Cyrus the Great. This was no less than an act of outrageous blasphemy to the mullahs.

In the fall of 1978, a worried sovereign, his health already beginning to fail, announced that free elections, barring only the communists, would be held the following summer. But if he expected a cascading wave of public gratitude, he was disappointed. Khomeini was now firmly in command of the fundamentalist clergy — even from exile. Islamic students slipped across the Iran-Iraq border to sit at his feet. They read his sermons, his exhortations to religious rebellion. "It is the religious leader," he had written, "and no one else who should occupy himself with the affairs of government." His key lieutenants, Ibrahim Yazdi and Sadeq Ghotbzadeh, were widening the range of his contacts, Yazdi with Iranian students in the United States, and Ghotbzadeh with his longtime friends in the leftist groups, notably the Palestine Liberation Organization.

In August 1978, Khomeini delivered another thunderblast from Iraq. "Do not obey orders which require you to kill unjustly," he told soldiers and police. He asked for civil disobedience, and for the first time demanded the installation of an Islamic republic. The words rippled through the crowds in the bazaars, the intellectuals, and the middle classes, all of whom were searching for a rallying point in their growing disillusionment with the Shah.

Pahlavi panicked. He could feel the flames of rebellion licking at his heels. With a flourish, he shuffled his cabinet, closed down the casinos, brought back the Islamic calendar, abolished a special women's ministry — a particularly sore point with Islamic hardliners — and allowed the press to publish photographs of Khomeini. But the mullahs, smelling blood, wanted more — specifically, a return to the Constitution of 1906, which contained a clause giving the Iranian clergy a right of veto over any law seen as contrary to the teachings of Islam. With every concession he made, Pahlavi was backed closer against the wall.

The military grew restless. In the palace, they argued that the population was primed for a full-scale revolution. The generals asked for martial law and, on the morning of September 8, the Shah gave it to them. The early-morning communiqué, declaring a period of martial law for six months, was broadcast over Tehran radio. But it came too late. Already, thousands of Iranians were preparing for a massive march to Jaleh Square, and word of the military clampdown did not reach them in time. Hundreds of marchers were killed when security forces opened fire. It was Tehran's "Black Friday", the Shah's Rubicon. It opened up a chasm between the sovereign and his subjects that could never be bridged.

However, the national shock of the "Black Friday" kill-ings brought a lull in the rash of demonstrations. Popular tactics changed. In the bazaars, merchants put up their shutters and workers laid down their tools. Universities and hospitals closed in a general strike, and workers gave notice that higher wages would not buy peace: they wanted the release of their colleagues from police cells and the liberation of political prisoners.

Meanwhile, the Shah took steps to rid himself of Khomeini. He prevailed upon the Iraqi government to isolate the Ayatollah, and, finally, to expel him from the country. Khomeini packed his few bags, was turned away at the Kuwaiti border, and flew to Paris, where he alighted on October 3, a guest of the French government.

By the late months of 1978, the Shah had virtually withdrawn from the leadership of his country. He had long periods of silence; requests for audiences went unanswered. In November, it was the Empress who conducted the negotiations for forming a new cabinet. The Shadow of God on Earth had become, in the words of one close associate, "a dangling marionette". But the courtiers, ministers, and advisers in the Shah's immediate orbit were still busy; fear propelled them to suggest tough action. Ardeshir Zahedi, the Shah's ambassador to Washington, reportedly put forward a "Chile-style" solution: mass arrests and executions to demonstrate that the Peacock Throne still carried clout. There was talk of purges, scapegoats, anything to appease the mullahs for a week, a month. Perhaps a military government was the solution, with powers going beyond "simple" martial law. But the Shah vacillated.

In early November, the Shah appointed yet another prime minister, and went on national television — a humble and conciliatory king. He pledged to correct the errors of the past and restore civil liberties after martial law was lifted. "Your revolutionary message has been understood," he said. "I know everything about why you have given your lives." In this public confession he stopped short of abdication — the one step that could have stemmed the revolution.

Rather than abdicate, the Shah decided to bend even further with the winds. He restored the civilian government and made plans for an "extended vacation". Washington obliged by dispatching a shadowy military "ambassador", air force general Robert Huyser, to tell the Iranian army to support the new government. Iran's generals were as skittery as cats: some wanted to make overtures to Khomeini, others wanted to roll the tanks into the streets and blast the mobs into submission. Huyser, with orders straight from the White House, instructed them to sit tight — and they did. The crack fighting force of the Middle East was neutralized.

On January 9, 1979, the Shah made his final pitch to his subjects. In a royal decree, he announced that the personal property of the royal family — the company stocks, the banks, the factories, the land, and the other holdings, with a total value of $250 million — would be "given" to the people in the form of a foundation whose proceeds would bankroll social programs. "What more can I do to atone?" he seemed to be saying, as he prepared to liquidate his personal fortune. Yet even this was an act of cynicism, for the Shah and the members of his royal court were busily transferring cash to banks in Switzerland, France, and the United States — a hedge against that rainy day of exile.

Huyser was still in Iran when, on January 16, the Shah filled a small wooden casket with a few ounces of his native soil and issued his final order as king: a blue-and-white Boeing 727, the pride of the royal air force, was to be fuelled and readied at Mehrabad Airport. The foreign press was thrown off the scent by means of a bogus press conference at the palace. Collectively fooled, they missed an airport scene rich in pathos.

As the Shah prepared to mount his jet, members of the Imperial Guard hurled themselves to their knees and begged their monarch to stay. One officer tried to kiss the Shah's boots. "Don't worry," he told them, tears rolling down his cheeks. "I won't be away for long." Then, without looking back, he climbed the steps into the aircraft, handed the casket of Iranian soil to an aide, and strapped himself in behind the controls of the jet. He referred to the flight plan that would take him to Cairo and the welcoming arms of his good friend, President Anwar Sadat, and the Boeing taxied down the runway.

In the north, a powerful earthquake shook several villages just as the Shah was leaving Iranian airspace. It was a fitting omen, a final spasm of the land that had expelled its ruler.

With the Shah gone, to roam the world like a pariah, events in Iran moved at a swift pace. Khomeini returned on February 1, and the Iranian military disintegrated like a dustball in a hurricane. The American embassy was attacked by leftist guerillas on St. Valentine's Day, and they controlled the grounds for five hours before Revolutionary Guards moved in to expel them.

Policymakers in Washington pored over their briefing reports, and the American government decided to once again play the role of suitor. Word went out that the Shah was not welcome in the United States, and the State Department even proposed sending a new ambassador to Tehran — former envoy to Zaïre Walter Cutler. But Iran's revolutionary government, relishing the sight of Washington on its knees, said Cutler was unacceptable. Undaunted, the State Department encouraged American businessmen to go back to Iran, in both their interest and the national interest of the United States.

In the late summer and fall of 1979, the Carter administration decided it was time to further accelerate its peaceful overtures to the new regime in Tehran. In August, President Carter approved the sale of $47 million worth of kerosene and heating oil to Iran as a goodwill gesture. The U.S. Defense Department resumed shipments of spare parts for American-made warplanes, helicopters, ships, and trucks. Much of the material was intended for use in the new Iranian offensive against the autonomy-minded Kurds.

At the time, these gestures were privately justified in Washington as part of the politics of expediency, of pragmatic realism. At the State Department, and in the upper reaches of the White House, it was felt that, by moving judiciously, the United States could accommodate itself to the new Iran. This strategy moved into high throttle in the month of October. Secretary of State Cyrus Vance, his deputy, David Newsom, United Nations ambassador Donald McHenry, and other senior officials from State conferred with Iranian foreign minister Ibrahim Yazdi. Yazdi read the American officials the equivalent of the diplomatic Riot Act. No longer would Iran tolerate a "big-brother" attitude on the part of the United States. "Your acceptance of the revolution must be translated into some tangible action," he said. He inquired about American naval deployments in the Middle East, and was assured that the United States had no hostile intentions against Iran. Newsom told Yazdi that, hereafter, the United States had "absolutely no intention" of interfering in Iran's internal affairs.

The meeting with Yazdi convinced senior American officials that a new bridgehead could be built. The Carter administration became bullish. On October 20, it sent a senior State Department official to Tehran on a low-profile mission to talk to a handful of Iranian leaders. He met with Prime Minister Mehdi Bazargan, Yazdi, and two powerful ayatollahs. Significantly, Khomeini would not see him. These efforts at courtship by the Americans received little attention at home, but they made a powerful impression in Iran, where the great bogey of the revolution was a fear of "foreign influence". As *Washington Post* correspondent William Branigan wrote in a lengthy analysis in June 1980, the United States failed to appreciate to just what degree anti-Americanism had become part and parcel of the revolution. "What the Americans were trying to do was reconstruct their old relationship with new partners," one diplomat in Tehran told Branigan. "They acted as if the revolution never happened," commented another diplomat. "The Americans were all over the place and saw lots of people. These visits caused worry. We couldn't believe they were doing it."

Not only were the Americans raising their collective profile again, but they seemed to be blind to the growing rift between the clergy and the Moslem militants and the secular government. They were talking to political transients like Yazdi and Bazargan — men who, for all practical purposes, had no control over the mobs and the mullahs — and were unconsciously widening the chasm between them and the people. Khomeini, of course, had not the slightest wish to see the Americans. Meanwhile, the cocktail parties resumed at the U.S. embassy, symptomatic of the feeling that the rapprochement was working.

The Moslem militants in Tehran and elsewhere became increasingly alarmed. What were the "Yankee devils" up to? Had they purposely ignored all the anti-American signals? Were they blundering around in the dark or was there a deeper method to their madness? In October the Iranian press was publishing warnings about Iran returning inexorably to "dependence" on the United States and blasting Bazargan for meeting with Brzezinski at a conference in Algiers. Khomeini stepped up his anti-American diatribes. In the universities, the plotting began for a death blow against the resurgent American presence.

On November 2, just two days before the embassy seizure, the Ayatollah Khomeini urged the Moslem militants "to expand with all their might their attacks against the United States." Once they were installed in the chancery building and had secured the premises, Khomeini telephoned to express his support of their action. From that moment on, all the centuries-old, gentlemen's club rules of international diplomacy descended to the level of a bazaar merchant's haggling, while the lives of sixty-six Americans hung in the balance.

4

RICHARD QUEEN and Dick Morefield were first out of the consular building door, and they were immediately drenched by the pounding rain. Then came the others: Bob Anders, the Lijeks, the Staffords — Kathy clutching a black umbrella — Kim King, and an American woman (we will call her Jane; not her real name). Tentatively, the others filed out into the street: the twenty or so Iranian staff workers, and then about two dozen Iranian visa applicants.

They could scarcely believe their luck. Drenched, desperate, they were struck by the ease of their escape. Behind them in the compound they could hear the shouts and confusion of the takeover. Ahead of them lay freedom.

My God, thought Anders, it's early afternoon, and it's as gloomy as the Judgment Day. Already the Iranians in the group were scattering in all directions, anxious to put distance between themselves and the compound walls. They melted into the network of alleyways immediately west of the compound.

But one woman, braver than the rest, offered to stay with the group. She said she would guide them south, along a zigzag route, to the British embassy about eight blocks away. "I live along the way," she said. "I will take you until I get near my home. Then I leave you." It was a small act of courage, and they thanked her warmly.

But almost immediately they confronted trouble. Still in the shadow of the walls, the group came upon four uniformed men. "National police," whispered Queen, a tall, slightly stooped consular attaché with thick, horn-rimmed glasses. The police addressed them in Farsi, and Queen waved to them, smiling. To their collective surprise, the policemen waved back, and the Americans continued walking. Mark Lijek blessed their luck: had those men been Revolutionary Guards, their flight would have been cruelly cut short.

They began to quicken their pace, the Iranian woman leading down what she hoped would be deserted streets. Conversation was kept to a minimum. In minutes, they came within sight of Taleghani, a major boulevard, and the route that the mob of militants had followed from Tehran University to the embassy earlier that day. By now, however, the swarm was concentrated around the perimeter of the U.S. embassy, and the Americans slipped safely across the thoroughfare two by two.

Holding newspapers over their heads, they passed a handful of street vendors and looked the other way. They could still hear the shouts of the militants inside the compound, but with every step they took, the noise receded. They glanced at street signs they passed — Khoshbin, Damghan — and proceeded south. Occasionally they came upon a rain-soaked banner covered with Farsi script that had been abandoned in the open gutters of the streets. Anders toyed with the notion of picking up one of the abandoned placards, to give the group a bit of cover, but he quickly rejected the idea.

They had covered about four blocks when they turned onto a wide street leading to Ferdowsi Square, a rallying point for militant demonstrations over the previous months. They stopped in their tracks. In the distance, they could see a crowd of students standing in the square, listening to a speaker yelling into a megaphone. Anders turned, and the ragtag band of refugees huddled close. "This is where we stop," he said. "We obviously can't risk walking near the square. And the British embassy is just beyond. Anybody have any ideas?"

Richard Queen, breathing hard from the physical and psychological strain of their flight, spoke first. "I think some of us should turn around and head to Richard's house." He was referring to Richard Morefield, the consul general, and the second-ranking American diplomat in Tehran. "We can sit this thing out in comfort, play bridge, and stay away from the windows." Morefield agreed.

Kim King said he had personal business to attend to — securing the next flight back home to the States — and wished the group goodbye.

But Anders said the Morefield house would be risky, since it would be a likely target for a raid by Revolutionary Guards, considering Morefield's status. Besides, he didn't like the idea of backtracking. The Lijeks and Staffords agreed, and the group parted company, shaking hands warmly as the downpour continued to buffet them. "See you back home," Queen said cheerily.

The Anders group, which also included Jane, the American woman, struck off in the direction of Anders' apartment. "Why don't we sit down, dry out, maybe eat something, and think this thing out," Anders said. "Otherwise, we'll be running around like scared rats in this goddam rain until somebody picks us up."

Everyone agreed. The prospect of food and warmth and the safety of four walls and a roof was too good to pass up. And the three women in the group were badly in need of rest. Anders pointed in a direction away from the bustle of Ferdowsi Square and they followed.

They walked with a deepening sense of foreboding. It seemed incredible, they thought, that six Americans should be able to walk the streets for more than a half-hour without being spotted. With each step, they feared that they were overspending their quota of luck. None of them fully understood yet the dimensions of the attack upon the embassy, but they sensed that there would soon be a mopping-up of Americans in the city.

"Slow down," Anders warned them, "or we'll really become conspicuous." They hugged the street-side buildings and alley walls, stopping before every intersection and looking left and right lest they stumble into a patrol. Frequently they stopped to hold to their ears the two-way radios they all carried, but the radio traffic was all in Farsi. "That means the militants are in control of the compound," Anders said. "Otherwise, we would be hearing the voices of some of the Marines. Let's keep moving."

After about fifteen minutes, they came within sight of Anders' apartment building. "Now stay well back," he said. "Look what's across the street." As they craned their necks around the wall, they saw what they knew to be a Revolutionary Guard command post, with its distinctive markings and Khomeini posters. "Now this is the tricky part," Anders said. "The place should be just about empty, but we can't take any chances. We go one by one, casually, eyes straight ahead."

Anders went first, and, after he had slipped into the front lobby of his building, the others followed, knowing they were fully exposed for fifteen seconds but trusting to the luck that had brought them this far. Within five minutes they had all passed the danger zone, and they were safely in Anders' apartment. "Let me find some dry clothes," Anders said, walking into his bedroom. "Then I'll see if I can whip up a meal."

Bundled up in sweaters and flannel shirts, with their wet clothes hung up to dry, they sat down to a hasty meal of curried chicken that Anders had kept frozen in his refrigerator. The portions were necessarily small, but the hot food was bracing. Their host mixed them a round of drinks, and they all stretched happily. Again they switched on their two-way radio units and again all they heard was a babble of Farsi, which they presumed to be communications among the Revolutionary Guards and other militants within the embassy compound. But Anders also picked up a voice he recognized as that of Bruce Laingen, the American chargé d'affaires, who was at the Foreign Ministry. Laingen, Anders was able to determine, was speaking with officials trapped inside the chancery. "Maybe there's still some resistance after all," Anders said. "Damn, when is the government going to send in the troops?"

Anders then went to his private telephone and began dialling the residences of other American staffers who might have escaped via the consular building. There was no reply. He dialled the Morefield home. Nothing. He dialled the British embassy and got through to an official there whom he knew personally. "Have any of our people shown up there?" he asked. The official said no, the only fugitive from the American compound who had found his way to the embassy doors was an Iranian clerk who was too afraid to go to his home. The British had taken him in. Anders thanked him and rang off.

Anders reached into his jacket pocket and pulled out a small notebook filled with telephone numbers. While the Lijeks and the Staffords stretched back in their easy chairs, slowly recharging their psychic batteries with the help of the food and the drinks, Anders rapidly called several numbers from the book.

But it was futile. Could it be that they were the only fugitives? "Maybe they're just not answering their phones," Kathy Stafford said. "It's possible," Anders answered. But privately, he doubted it. A ringing telephone could mean good news, as well as bad, for any American on the run, and human nature dictated that a fugitive would answer the ring.

Jane said she would try to reach her husband, an Iranian. Perhaps he could help. She tried her home, but there was no reply. Then she contacted a family relative whom she felt she could trust. Jane explained where she was and asked that her husband be directed to pick her up there. "I'm with a group of Americans," she told the relative. "And they need help."

Midway through the reply, the telephone line clicked and went dead. Jane held the receiver away from her head and turned to the group in the Anders apartment. "That's strange," she said. Anders put the phone to his ear, and a puzzled expression came over his face.

Cora Lijek jumped to her feet. "God," she said. "The line went dead just after you said 'Americans'." Mark put his arm around her and told her it was a coincidence, nothing more.

Anders poured another round of drinks and they sat in silence, occasionally muttering reassurances to one another. But the words were leaden, without conviction. They began to feel that they were only stealing a few hours from their eventual fate: capture and a forced march back to the compound. After about half an hour, a sharp knock on the door broke the stillness. They pitched out of their seats, all eyes on Anders as he moved to the door and whispered, "Who is it?" The reply calmed them. It was Jane's husband.

The man stepped in quickly and Anders bolted the door again. The newcomer was carrying two paper bags, which he opened with a flourish. "Dinner, my friends," he said, displaying several cardboard cartons full of steaming barbecued lamb. Joe Stafford sniffed the heavily seasoned carry-out food and let out a whoop of joy. After a round of introductions, the group settled in to their second meal in two hours. They ate with gusto, muttering gratitude to their Iranian friend between swallows. Tactfully, they asked him no questions about himself. They knew that even the slightest hint of collusion with the American "devils" could bring death at the hands of the militants, and they did not want to have any information that could endanger their good samaritan. They declined an offer by the man to drive them to his home and, after another round of well-wishing, he and his wife departed.

Later that evening, Anders asked a neighbour — a woman whose discretion he trusted — for the use of her phone, and decided to gamble on a bold stroke. He needed the kind of help that only a half-dozen people in Tehran could provide, and nearly all of them were captives. He dialled the number of the Iranian Foreign Ministry and, fighting to control his nervousness, asked to speak with Victor Tomseth. Tomseth was one of the three American officials who were being "detained" by Iranian authorities, held, they were told, for their own protection.

After several minutes' delay, and a series of excuses from assorted minor officials, Tomseth came on the line. Elated, Anders told Tomseth about his situation and that of his colleagues. "We need help," he concluded. "I've tried everybody I can think of. Nothing. We need mobility. We need a safe hiding place."

Tomseth congratulated Anders on his escape, and then addressed himself to the problem. "I think I know somebody who can help. He's somebody who has worked for a number of U.S. embassy officials, a Thai national named Somchai. A cook. Discreet. Trustworthy. And he has a car. Knows his way around the city. I can reach him and send him to your building tomorrow. What's your address?"

Anders told him.

"Okay," Tomseth said. "Meanwhile, I'll get in touch with somebody at the British embassy who might be able to put you and your group up for a day or two. Now, what number can you be reached at, without delay?" Anders told him the number of the neighbour who would take a message and thanked Tomseth effusively.

"What are the prospects for the embassy, Victor?" he asked.

"I think they're pretty good," Tomseth said. "Yazdi is working on it. But for the time being, you people have to stay on the run. Keep in touch."

"I will, Victor," Anders said. "And thank you."

When Anders brought back the news to the Staffords and the Lijeks, they were delighted. They were not utterly isolated, and the thought that the British might put them up for a while was encouraging.

They prepared for bed and discovered, with some surprise, that they were bone tired. By midnight, the Anders apartment was dark and silent.

Somchai, their mysterious "chauffeur", arrived early the next morning with a few taps on Anders' door. He was cheerful, not at all afraid, and while the fugitives pressed some breakfast on him and packed their few belongings, he told them of his recent life in Iran.

His full name, he told them, was all but unpronounceable by the Western tongue: Somchai Sriweawnetr. He was thirty-nine and, until the revolution, had been a cook in a downtown restaurant. He was able to speak both Farsi and

English fluently. Through a friend he had discovered Victor Tomseth, who spoke Thai himself, and offered his part-time services as a cook and domestic. Tomseth referred him to a number of other U.S. embassy officials who could use some kitchen help, and Somchai soon became a familiar sight in the American diplomatic households.

Within minutes of the seizure of the embassy, Somchai demonstrated that his value went far beyond his ability to whip up an omelette or roast lamb. He rushed to the homes of his employers — now captive in the compound — and collected any documents which he felt might be incriminating. "In three days," he would say later, "I took all the secret papers and burned them." He never specified, however, what secret papers embassy officials might keep in their homes.

But the night before, he told his new American charges, Tomseth had telephoned him and given his most important assignment — the safekeeping of five American fugitives. And here he was, Somchai at their service.

Anders was delighted.

Somchai quickly proved himself indispensable. That very day he drove the Staffords and the Lijeks to their respective apartments where they gathered up clothing, returned to the Anders apartment, and drove the group several dozen blocks north to a British-embassy-owned residence that was made available to them. Tomseth had been as good as his word.

But while the captive Tomseth and sympathetic British diplomats could provide shelter for the Americans, they could not guarantee security. By the evening of November 6, a Tuesday, the fugitives were on the run again, spooked by servants at the residence who eyed them warily.

Somchai, in the two days that followed, drove them to the homes of two American embassy officials who were being held in the embassy. He spoke in Farsi to the servants in the homes, instructing them that they were to care for their new guests and make them feel at home.

Their first stop was the residence of John Graves, the American public affairs officer in Iran. The house was spacious and comfortable, but the fugitives, now in their fourth day on the run, were so sensitive to telltale noises and bumps in the night that they could barely sleep. That evening they slept barely forty-five minutes, tossing and turning on their beds. They heard what they believed were police whistles, and were convinced the house was being surrounded. The squeal of tires, or the sound of boot-heels hitting the pavement, conjured up terrifying images. By morning, they were so edgy that they contacted Somchai and asked that he collect them immediately. They left with such haste that they didn't even take their clothes out of the automatic washing-machine.

The next stop was the home of Kathryn Koob, another cultural official who had been captured by the Iranian militants. The servants were still in the home and greeted the Americans, but treated them with diffidence. On the morning of November 8, one of the fugitives saw two servants whispering conspiratorially. When Anders heard this, he said, "We can't stay here. Not only are we in danger, but we're also a threat to the servants."

He recommended another haven, somewhere where they would surely be safe — for weeks if need be. They talked about his idea, weighed their remaining options, and finally agreed.

"It's settled then?" he asked, looking into their faces. They nodded in turn. Then Anders began dialling a telephone number he knew by heart.

WASHINGTON   *November 5*

Jean Pelletier cupped his hands and breathed into them. A crisp wind was blowing across the Tidal Basin and over the Ellipse, while wispy clouds scudded past the Washington Monument in the background. It was unseasonably cold for the first week of November. The thirty-one-year-old reporter fastened the collar button of his raincoat and surveyed the expanse of grass of the Ellipse — the hub of the nation's capital. It was here that the tourists gathered from April to October, lining up for tours of the White House across the street.

But the Ellipse was empty today, and the mobile chili-dog-and-pizza stands were no longer parked bumper to bumper on adjacent 15th Street. Instead, a few dozen hardy tourists huddled near the South Lawn fence of the White House grounds, their eyes fixed on the familiar columns and arches of the presidential mansion a hundred yards away. A tour guide was droning, "The White House does not have a 'back' and a 'front' door as such, because of protocol. The president could hardly welcome the president of France at the 'back door', could he?" The tourists chuckled on cue.

Pelletier could see that the tourists had little interest today in the minutiae of presidential lore. They hoped instead to witness a small fragment of history-in-the-making — to see Jimmy Carter, deep in thought, striding off to a meeting to discuss the Iranian hostage crisis. A few held copies of the day's newspapers, with such headlines as: "Iranian Militants Seize U.S. Embassy; Demand Return of Shah."

Pelletier continued his circuit of the most famous piece of real estate in Washington. He turned north on 17th Street and, as he passed that monstrous jumble of architecture called the Old Executive Building, he heard the unfamiliar shouts *"Allah Akhbar! Allah Akhbar!"* Turning onto Pennsylvania Avenue, he saw the crowd for the first time, and the banners with giant pictures of the Ayatollah Khomeini and the Farsi script. The Iranian students, most of them wearing paper masks with cutout eye-slits, had gathered in Lafayette Park, across from the north portico of the White House, and their chants split the air. "Send back the Shah. Send back the murderer!" Pelletier pulled out his notebook and waded into the crowd. He stopped the first student he brushed against and asked why he was wearing a mask.

"There are SAVAK agents everywhere. With cameras. We are not afraid, but we have relatives and friends in Iran. And the SAVAK are butchers," the masked figure muttered.

"But SAVAK is no more," Pelletier said. "The revolution has succeeded."

The student shook his head, as if bewildered by this North American's naiveté, and moved away.

National Park police tried to isolate the Iranians from a growing crowd of onlookers, fearing the mood might turn ugly. A group of hardhats from a nearby construction site had wandered over to the perimeter of Lafayette Park, and they were shouting abuse at the Iranians. "Go home, you foreign bastards." "America, love it or leave it." Cars coursing down Pennsylvania Avenue, sometimes called the "Gawkers' Strip" because it afforded the best view of the White House, slowed down and honked their horns.

Pelletier chatted with a number of the students, interviewed a few of the onlookers, and had a word with a police sergeant. He took few notes, committing the quotes to memory and soaking in the "atmospherics". Then, turning his back on the demonstration, he walked the two blocks to the National Press Building. At the ground-floor news kiosk, he bought the latest edition of the *Washington Post* and took the elevator to the tenth floor.

As he squeezed in among the crowd of newsmen, most of whom were headed to the thirteenth-floor bar, Pelletier scoured his memory. Tehran. Was it 1975 that he was there? Or 1976? It was a brief stay, a week at the most, with a press contingent from Quebec City, covering an official visit to Iran by the then Premier of Québec, Robert Bourassa. A dull affair, as Bourassa met for long business sessions with government development officials. With little work to do, Pelletier had converted his dollars into Iranian rials and accompanied his colleagues to the famous Intercontinental Hotel, one of the four deluxe hotels in the city. But he soon tired of the scotch and the bar talk and decided to stroll the city streets, snooping in the bazaars. He vividly recalled the eyes of young Tehranians, probably students, in their threadbare suits, as they watched him cautiously. He had sensed something then — an uneasiness, a suspicion, a wariness. Maybe a coiled energy.

But he had dismissed the sensation, and allowed himself to be distracted by the exoticism of the city in the late afternoon haze.

One evening, he took himself to the campus of Tehran University to hear a speech by Ivan Illich, the radical social philosopher who headed a famous school in Mexico. Illich held the students spellbound. Later that night, Pelletier had the good fortune to meet Illich at the residence of the Canadian ambassador to Iran at the time, Jim George. The philosopher spoke incessantly, and with great fervour, about the political oppression he had found after just a week in the Shah's kingdom.

Pelletier strained to remember Illich's words. "I was told by my hosts at the university," the man had said, "that if I wanted to speak about dictatorship and oppression, I was to do so in the most general terms, and make no direct allusions to Iran. The Shah, of course, has ears everywhere. So I chose my words carefully, but the students understood exactly what I was saying. They knew I was talking to them, about them and their country." Then Illich had leaned forward, and said to Ambassador George, "This country is going to explode." Pelletier remembered that the ambassador had nodded without hesitation. Both men felt the quickening pulse of revolution — even then.

On the last night of the Bourassa visit, Pelletier was granted an interview with the then prime minister, Amir-Abbas Hoveyda, at his residence in the ancient quarter of Tehran. Hoveyda, he recalled, was in terrible humour, and the interview lasted barely twenty minutes. Aides were scurrying around madly, and everything seemed in disarray. For a young reporter in a strange country thousands of miles from home, these things had held little of significance. As far as he knew, the Shah was secure in his oil-rich kingdom, and Illich's "explosion" was nothing more than the cerebral ramblings of a man who saw upheaval everywhere.

But now, five years later, Pelletier knew that he had glimpsed the faint beginnings of a genuine revolution.

The brass sign on the wooden door in the National Press Building read "1041, Jean Pelletier, LA PRESSE". The wooden door was inherited from the previous tenant, and it was a nice touch along a corridor of offices with tacky glass doors and gold lettering. When he had arrived in Washington, Pelletier had wanted a second sign, reading "The largest French-language daily in North America" — the phrase that appeared on the masthead of his newspaper. But his bosses said this sounded a bit immodest, at least for Washington, D.C.

He had had his two-hundred-square-foot office newly carpeted and had installed an old United Press International teleprinter in one corner, specially boxed to absorb the constant clattering of the keys. On the wall he had tacked a map of the United States and one of his favourite bits of memorabilia: a genuine campaign poster from a gubernatorial race in Alaska, bearing the words "Merdes for Governor". He had picked up the poster of the unhappily named (and defeated) candidate during a canoe trip through Alaska.

On his desk he had placed a photograph of his year-old son, Jean-David, right next to his telephone recorder with its cassette carrying a bilingual message: "'Bonjour, Jean Pelletier à l'appareil', 'Hello, this is Jean Pelletier'." A nearby bookshelf sagged under the weight of volumes on American politics, biographies of past presidents, bound congressional committee reports, and stacks of *Time, Newsweek*, and *Penthouse* magazines. A two-foot pile of old *Washington Post*s lay on the floor next to the bookshelf. Nearby sat his telex machine, which he used to file his stories back to head office in Montreal.

On this day, a bleak Monday, November 5, 1979, Pelletier rolled a fresh piece of typing paper into his Olympia, and at the top of the page he typed the words *Washington — Réaction crise Iran*.

As always, the first paragraph, or "lead", came quickly. Pelletier rarely laboured or agonized over his stories; his background as a radio reporter in Ottawa and Quebec City, before he joined *La Presse* as a political writer, gave him a good feel for the nub of a story, the essential "news" that merited first-paragraph mention. In many respects, Pelletier was an old-fashioned journalist, preferring the traditional style of reporting to the modern orthodoxy of the "new journalism" with its upfront biases and first-person posturing. Only rarely did he inject his own strong political views into his dispatches and, even then, not at the expense of the facts.

Midway through his story, Pelletier backed away from his typewriter and gazed out the window that overlooked F Street, with its cluster of shoe stores, electronic-equipment shops, and fast-food outlets. He was heading into his third winter in Washington for *La Presse*, and he was pleased with his ground-breaking work in the American capital.

It had been a novel experiment when, back in the summer of 1977, the 185,000-circulation newspaper decided to pull Pelletier out of Ottawa to open a bureau here. None of Montreal's three French-language dailies had a man in Washington. They placed people in Ottawa and Quebec City and a stringer in Paris, but they chose to rely on wire services for American news. The city's French press had long been accused of insularity, and *La Presse*, a big-budget paper with a solid reputation for following Canadian affairs, was ready to expand its horizons.

After two years in Ottawa's House of Commons, Pelletier was excited by the prospect. He would be opening up virgin territory for his newspaper. He was fascinated by the dynamics of American government, and the Washington beat would put him in direct contact with stories of international import. Besides, he would be a bureau chief and enjoy a freedom of movement that few Canadian newsmen could boast of. *La Presse* had told him there would be few restrictions on his work. His travel budget was virtually unlimited.

It had been a good two years, Pelletier mused, as he stared out the window on that early November day. His circle of contacts was widening, his relations with Canadian embassy staff were solid, and he was making some small but useful inroads into the White House and the State Department. *La Presse* "played" his articles well, and his commentaries on everything from the political prospects of Edward Kennedy to the subtleties of Canada – U.S. fishing agreements were earning him kudos back home.

His job, together with the regular freelance commentaries he did for CBC radio, brought in an annual salary in excess of $30,000. A few months before, he had moved his family out of Washington's inner city and rented a comfortable lakeside home in the experimental "new town" of Reston, Virginia, a lush, airy community that offered the best of suburban living within forty minutes' drive of downtown Washington.

He felt he was holding a temporary mortgage on a piece of the American dream, with a backyard barbecue and a lawn that sloped down to a man-made lake, which he would navigate in his metal canoe, white wine in hand.

What more could he ask for?

Four hundred yards away, behind the gates of 1600 Pennsylvania Avenue, the thirty-ninth president of the United States reread the detailed briefing reports on the Tehran embassy seizure and scanned the list of Americans who were being held captive. Among the documents was a small notation that a handful of embassy staffers had managed to escape and were loose in the city. He also reviewed the latest report on the Shah's medical condition: the monarch was too weak and too ill to move.

Jimmy Carter, thrust into the worst crisis of his troubled administration, probably told himself he should have trusted his hunch about the Shah. Two weeks earlier, when the pressure to admit the exiled monarch had been building, Carter had put the question to his aides: "When the Iranians take our people in Tehran hostage, what will you advise me then?" There is no record of how the men in the immediate presidential circle greeted this prescient comment.

On this day, November 5, Carter had called a special meeting of the National Security Council, the most influential executive body in the government. The NSC was headed by

Zbigniew Brzezinski, the president's national security adviser, and it included the best foreign-policy and intelligence minds in Washington.

To the men sitting around the huge rectangular table, Carter made two succinct points. First, the United States would not undertake military action to free the hostages. Second, it would not expel the Shah from the country.

Carter and his close advisers knew that the first point would not sit well with the clutch of generals at the Pentagon, who were all for putting together a show of American military strength. But the president was determined to establish his "politics of patience" quickly and unequivocally. He was convinced that if the full force of international diplomacy were brought to bear on Iran, its rulers would crack and release their captives.

The second point would be easier to defend. America could not and would not yield to blackmail at the hands of terrorists. As the State Department spokesman would tell newsmen later that day, in words that would echo Carter's sentiment, "No surrender! He's going to stay here for medical treatment until it's completed." This had a nice, gutsy ring to it. Relayed to the American people by Walter Cronkite and the other commentators of the mass media, it would evoke true grit and that fine old tradition of standing by your friends and staring down your enemies.

Carter had one or two other ideas for the NSC members. On the following day, two Americans, Ramsey Clark and William G. Miller, would be dispatched to Tehran to begin negotiating for the release of the hostages. Both men had credentials that should help ease their access to the revolutionary leaders, the NSC was told. Clark, U.S. attorney general in the Lyndon Johnson administration, had visited Iran just before the Shah's departure, and he had returned with the conviction that ninety-nine per cent of Iranians supported Khomeini. On the way home, he paid a courtesy call on the Ayatollah, who was then living in exile outside Paris, told him of his findings in Iran, and emerged to describe the aging cleric as a man of courage who had been the first to speak out against the Shah. Clark's left-leaning liberalism, which put him well outside the orbit of the Washington political establishment, was well known.

Bill Miller, staff director for the Senate Intelligence Committee, was also known to be sympathetic to anti-Shah elements in Iran. A political officer in Tehran for three years in the early sixties, Miller spoke Farsi and had opened lines of communication with Iranian dissidents at a time when the U.S. government was helping hold up the Peacock Throne. Miller made no public comment on his distaste for the Shah, but there was no question where he stood. "As the Shah began to collapse," an associate said of him, "Miller's smile got broader."

The Clark-Miller appointment was, at best, a tentative gesture, a sign that the White House simply did not know how to react to the Tehran crisis. The Carter administration, in those early days, was still hamstrung by an uncertain policy toward Iran — a waffling that dated back years. There were, in reality, two policies forwarded by two rival groups within the administration. One was led by the so-called "old Iran hands" at the State Department and by Brzezinski himself, who had wanted the United States to throw its unequivocal support behind the Shah when he began to totter. The other faction, headed by people like Human Rights Bureau director Pat Darien, and a few other senior officials, was offended by the Shah's disregard for human rights, and wanted the United States to push the Shah into a more liberal stance.

Now that the focus of both these policies — Pahlavi himself — had been eliminated, the administration was utterly at a loss.

When he left the NSC meeting, Carter was not smiling. But he was confident that, by handling the crisis gingerly, without panic, his administration could weather this latest storm.

He made a mental note to request more information on Khomeini, the religious madman who had apparently set this train of events into motion. What was the man's psychology? Where were the pressure points? What were his motivations? Would this black-robed demagogue stand up to the United States of America when the screws were tightened?

Carter knew he had a formidable adversary, and without more data on the man, he would be unequal to the task that would dominate the remainder of his presidency.

5

*J*OHN SHEARDOWN, Canada's chief immigration officer in Tehran, couldn't recall ever having to handle such a volume of work. His desk in the Canadian chancery was like a paper factory, with folders and envelopes and reports precariously balanced on every available square foot of the desk. At times, he felt as if he were stage-managing a mass exodus. Thousands of Iranians were besieging the Canadian embassy with visa applications, anxious to leave behind the revolution and the shortages and the forty-per-cent unemployment rate. It was shirtsleeves work, and Sheardown, a big, round-faced man with a barrel chest and a neatly clipped beard, relished it.

Shortly before noon his desk telephone rang.

"Yes, John Sheardown here."

"John, it's Bob Anders speaking."

"Bob, what the hell. . . . You mean you're not — "

"John, listen. I want to keep this brief. There are five of us, myself and four other staffers, who managed to get away Sunday."

"On your own?" Sheardown said. "Jesus, Bob, why didn't you get in touch with us right away . . . ?"

"It's a long story, but we're fairly secure right now. We've been in touch with Tomseth, at the Foreign Ministry. We're all right for the moment, but we might need a place to camp for a while within the next couple of days. My people are nervous as hell. Can you help us?"

"Hell, yes. Of course." Sheardown brushed the perspiration from his brow. "Anything we can do for you now, Bob, you name it."

"Nothing for the moment, thanks. We're gonna sit tight. I'll be back in touch tomorrow or Saturday. We, er, know this can really put you people on the spot."

"Listen, Bob," Sheardown said. "Count on us. I'll speak to the ambassador right away. You know you can reach me here or at my home. You know the number?"

"Yeah," Anders said. "I'll get back to you. And thanks. I feel better."

Sheardown replaced the receiver. His palms were wet. He picked up the telephone and punched the numbers for Ambassador Taylor's office. "Laverna," he told the secretary. "It's John. I have to see the ambassador right away.... Yes, immediately. Tell him it's urgent. I'll be right up."

"John, what is it? Laverna said you had something urgent." Ken Taylor motioned for him to sit and offered Sheardown a coffee. The big man threw himself into the chair, and took a breath. "I just had a call from Bob. Bob Anders."

Taylor's eyes widened. He knew Anders well, had played some tennis with him. But surely he was a captive in the U.S. embassy. How had he gotten to a phone?

Sheardown recounted the brief telephone conversation. The ambassador asked one or two questions, nodded, and leaned back in his chair. "So they're at Kathryn Koob's. Is it safe?"

Sheardown said the group was getting nervous; the servants were becoming suspicious. "And they've been in touch with Vic Tomseth."

Taylor drummed a pencil on the top of his mahogany desk. "We have a day or so before they call back?" Sheardown nodded. "Okay," Taylor continued. "Where can we hide them?"

It was that quick, the decision. There was no question of turning the Americans away. The only question was: how to effect sanctuary?

For several minutes the two men weighed the options. There was the Canadian chancery, several blocks away from the U.S. compound downtown. Advantages: military guards, clear-cut diplomatic immunity. Disadvantages: downtown was "hot" — anywhere within a mile or two of Embassy Row was a danger zone. Furthermore, there was too much "local" traffic in the chancery.

"I'd say, on balance, the chancery is out," Sheardown said. "Guards or no guards, the security is bad. And where would they live?"

"I agree," Taylor said. "But let's not reject it too quickly. What about my residence? It's got immunity, it's in the outskirts. But — "

"No guards," Sheardown interjected. "And if we transferred Gauthier [Sgt. Claude Gauthier, head of the six-man military-police security force] and a couple of his people out there, it would raise suspicions."

"We could split them up. Two or three with me, the others distributed among the staff residences." Taylor was disturbed. All of the options had risks. "Hell, we're talking about diplomatic immunity. What does that mean in Tehran today? No, we have to keep them away from downtown. They'll be our guests. We'll pass them off as Canadian tourists. Anyway, it'll only be for a week or so. They lie low, we go on with our business like nothing's changed, and we wait."

"Ken," Sheardown said, "I can take two or three of them. Zena and I have the space."

"How would your wife feel about that arrangement?"

"I'm certain she'll understand what we have to do here," the immigration officer replied. "I'll talk to her tonight."

"Okay," Taylor said. "I'll lay this all out for Ottawa. Maybe they'll have some ideas. John, would you stay while I put the cable together?" The ambassador reached for a legal pad and a sharp pencil and began framing the four-hundred-word message to Ottawa.

For twenty minutes or so, he was absorbed in the drafting of the cable, while Sheardown sat quietly. Occasionally,

Taylor would raise his eyes, and the two men would discuss a fine point of phrasing, the best way to frame a suggestion. Sheardown noted the neat handwriting, the attention to syntax, the careful marshalling of the points that led to an inevitable conclusion: we must take the Americans, whatever the risk.

Taylor and Sheardown were not close friends, even though they shared a mutual respect. Indeed, they were a study in physical and intellectual contrasts: Taylor, the trim, extroverted, carefully groomed, Cardin-suited, dry-martini lover, impatient with detail, a man who thought in terms of "operations" rather than policy; and Sheardown, who in contrast seemed rumpled and plodding, much more the solid civil servant, a man at home with filing cabinets and statistics, a linear thinker.

Sheardown marvelled at how easily Taylor seemed to be reacting to the bombshell that had landed in his lap. He knew enough about Taylor's background to realize that the ambassador was not a "crisis man". Dispatched to Iran in August 1977, Taylor was valued more as a kind of super-salesman, with the credentials in commercial affairs to promote the sales of such high-profit items as Canadian-made pulp-and-paper equipment and parts for thermal power plants.

Iran was a valued Canadian trading partner and the relationship was growing: $700 million in goods by 1977, and continued growth as the Shah accelerated the industrialization of his kingdom. Taylor, at the time the director-general of the trade commissioner service in Ottawa, had jumped at the opportunity for his first ambassadorial posting in a nation bursting with business opportunities.

Ken Taylor was, and is, a man of phenomenal energy. Colleagues noted that he could, without trying, charm the secretaries out of their shoes. With his bush of curly, prematurely grey hair, his self-effacing style, and his toothy smile, he carried all the earmarks of a winner. He had voracious appetites: for spy thrillers and Altman films and French cuisine and double-breasted blue blazers and smooth gin — Boodles preferably — with just a drop of vermouth. His penchant for parties and high living made his superiors in Ottawa's stuffy Department of External Affairs more than a bit nervous.

When Taylor had worked in Ottawa his office didn't even have a desk, or a filing cabinet. He preferred to work at a round table. He eschewed all the trappings of the bureaucrat — the in-and-out trays, the desk calendars, the leatherbound appointment book. Once, when a photographer from the Ottawa *Citizen* came to take a picture of him for a feature story on the trade commissioner service, he was dismayed to find Taylor's work environment not at all what he expected.

"Er, is this your office?" the photographer asked, searching desperately for all those familiar accoutrements that marked a mandarin.

"Of course," Taylor said.

"Well, don't you have a desk?"

"No," Taylor said matter-of-factly. "I work at this table."

"Well, why don't you just sit in this easy chair and I'll take a picture of you reading from a file. You *do* have a file folder somewhere?"

"Well, not handy," Taylor said. "But I could ask my secretary to find me one."

"Good, well, why don't you open it up, *make* like you're reading it."

As he was leaving, the photographer remarked, "Well, I'll let you get on with, er, whatever you do."

Taylor laughed at the man's befuddlement. The story made the Ottawa rounds for weeks.

Taylor had joined the foreign service in 1959, after four years at the University of Toronto and a year at Berkeley, California, where he earned a master's degree in business administration. By no means was the young Taylor setting his sights on a beribboned career in crisis diplomacy. On the contrary, his interests were fairly conventional.

"I really wanted a job in the private sector," he would later tell an interviewer, "but in 1959 there were no Canadian companies with international operations."

So he looked to government for a crack at international

commercial work. He enlisted in the trade commissioner service — a division that generally produces colourless civil servants who live by the calculator and the statistic — and in the next six years, he hopscotched from Guatemala to Detroit to Karachi.

In London, where he was posted in 1967 as a counsellor to the Canadian High Commission, Ken Taylor discovered the good life. There was the Savoy, and there was Bond Street, and there was culture. He loved the food and the tailored clothes, and he rewarded himself for those years of toiling in Latin America and Pakistan. He sampled the perks of diplomacy, and he wanted more.

In 1971, he returned to Ottawa, and colleagues noted his new hairstyle and the fashionable cut of his wardrobe. He looked crisp and trendy and he had earned a reputation for good work. Within three years, he was general director of the trade commissioner service, and was moving up.

In mid 1977, when External Affairs went looking for a replacement for Ambassador Jim George in Tehran, Taylor's name found its way onto the short list. George was a serious intellectual, fascinated by social and religious trends in Iran, and his cables were neat monographs of style and erudition, but he was hardly a balance-sheet man. The embassy in Tehran needed a fresh infusion of energy, somebody who could cultivate the Iranian businessmen and commercial bureaucrats, who could tap the hundreds of millions of dollars that the Shah was pouring into his nation's development. They were confident that Taylor, for all his minor eccentricities, could deliver.

Taylor was fascinated by his new assignment. He became an ardent student of the Shah and his government, and showed a facility for political reporting — one of the most crucial tasks of an ambassador. As the fabric of the Shah's regime began to fray (with a subsequent drop in Canada's trade with Iran), Taylor's job took on a new emphasis.

Taylor's stock in the eyes of his superiors back home took a quantum jump in early January 1979, when Iran's political structure was in collapse. The Shah was clearly on his way out, and Iran was becoming too hot for Westerners. Eight hundred and fifty Canadians would have to be pulled out — and fast — before the anticipated bloodshed began. To make matters more difficult, these Canadians were scattered throughout the countryside, working on oil rigs and power projects in the south, on a pulp-and-paper project in the north, and even on an archeological dig close to the Iraqi border.

In a masterful feat of organization, Taylor got out the word that the Canadians should pack their bags and converge without delay on Tehran. There, Hercules transports from the Canadian military base in Lahr, West Germany, would collect them and fly them out.

Working around the clock, Taylor and his aides cleared the Canadians' travel papers through the Iranian Foreign Ministry. The ambassador personally carried scores of passports to the appropriate authorities, secured the necessary stamps and visas, and liaised with an American air force colonel at a military airfield in Tehran to have the Canadians safely evacuated. The operation went through with scarcely a hitch, only days before the Shah fled the country.

Taylor, of course, remained. While he often put in eighteen-hour days, with the kind of high-octane energy that had dazzled his colleagues back in Ottawa, Taylor still found time for his favourite leisure activities: tennis and golf. A story that circulated in the close-knit Tehran diplomatic corps highlights Taylor's mania for the latter sport. The ambassador was engrossed in a game one afternoon in February 1979 when the crack of gunfire and the scream of curfew sirens split the air. It was hardly an unfamiliar sound in Tehran at this time, but the man he was playing with, Danish Ambassador Troels Munk, suggested that they call their game and rush home. Taylor, gazing down the long, sloping fairway of the eighteenth hole, suggested they finish their round. Munk reluctantly agreed — as long as they picked up the pace a little. Along adjacent fairways, they could see other Saturday golfers in full flight. Scorecards were being flung in the air and the caddies were chattering excitedly. Taylor's drive hooked slightly, but his second and third shots were true and he won the hole. Later, the two men learned that while they had been pulling their carts down the last fairway, the Iranian army detachments had made their last stand against Islamic revolutionaries. As Taylor was drawing a bead on the cup in the centre of the green, the last remnants of the exiled Shah's regime were being expunged.

Another popular story that later became part of the Taylor legend concerned a shipment of whiskey destined for the Canadian embassy. The cases were intercepted by Iranian police and stored in a mosque under armed guard while authorities argued over what to do with the forbidden liquor. When Taylor learned of this breach of diplomatic protocol, he picked up the telephone and complained bitterly about the seizure of his booze. After weeks of tireless arm-twisting and cajoling he was successful in having the cases released and delivered to the chancery, and in securing the Iranians' shamefaced apology.

Taylor now stopped writing and passed the legal pad to his immigration officer. Sheardown read the draft of the cable and nodded. "Yes, I'd say that pretty well covers it."

"Good," Taylor said. He buzzed his secretary, and told her he had a communiqué for Ottawa. It should go out before the end of the afternoon, he instructed, so that it would be on the proper desks in Ottawa in the morning.

Before handing the message over for typing and transmission, he pencilled in six groups of letters at the top of the page. The letters referred to five offices at the External Affairs Department in Ottawa and the Canadian embassy in Washington. The cable was top secret, and no one except those designated could read it.

Taylor checked his watch. Two p.m.

By this time tomorrow, he should have a reply.

Canada's two hundred embassies, consulates, and missions around the world communicate with Ottawa via high-speed telex machines patched into small computers. The computers are programmed with a complex code; each foreign mission has its own alphabet code. The code, for all practical purposes, is unbreakable, since it is keyed to a randomly chosen "grid" of words. The "grid" might, for example, be a page of an obscure book known only to a senior embassy staffer, the communicator in the mission, and the decoding computer in Ottawa. The code may be regularly changed by reprogramming the computer. The system, while not foolproof, is felt to be more than adequately secure. Foreign-service communicators are subjected to the most rigorous security checks by a special branch of the Royal Canadian Mounted Police — checks that have been known to take as long as a year. This top-level security gives Canadian communicators, scattered around the globe, a special *esprit de corps*: they are among the most closely watched of civil servants, with unrestricted access to documents vital to their nation's interests.

Virtually every cable that passes among the ambassadors and their superiors throughout the seven floors of the Lester B. Pearson Building, which houses Canada's Department of External Affairs, at some point finds its way to the desk of the chief communicator in Ottawa, an amiable, red-haired, gold-chain-bedecked, nonstop smoker whose name, fittingly, is George A. Happy. From his desk in the centre of the "incoming cables" room, one of four his department occupies deep in the bowels of the Pearson Building, Mr. Happy speaks proudly of his network of communicators — 190 distributed throughout foreign capitals and 110 in Ottawa — much the way a football coach talks about his defensive line: with a fond paternalism and trust. Behind him is the constant and peculiar zipping noise of the jet-ink telex machines that spit out two hundred words a minute.

Visitors to this brightly lit enclave with its orange-and-rust-coloured motif and its thick steel doors are kept well away from the two machines. Most of the communications that come over these machines have already been unscrambled by a computer and are ready for photocopying and delivery. By and large, they are innocuous messages: details of itineraries and accommodations for travelling Canadian cabinet ministers; prosaic situation reports from the Cameroons or Ecuador; sugar-beet price increases in Central America; an analysis of the new junta in El Salvador. But the security rules apply to every syllable.

Mr. Happy is the lord of this demesne. He sees that low-classification cables are slotted in one of the three hundred pigeonholes that cover an entire wall of an adjacent room. Secretaries and clerks from upstairs, all of whom wear identification badges, come here for their daily pickups. If, however, a cable should carry a top-secret designation, Mr. Happy will photocopy it himself, place it in a specially marked envelope, and deliver it in person. When he emerges aboveground, it is a clear sign that a crisis is about to land in some unsuspecting bureaucrat's lap.

On the morning of November 8, 1979, Mr. Happy walked into the anteroom of the communications centre, gave a brisk "good morning" to the security guard already at his desk, and proceeded to his own table. He glanced at his in tray and picked up a cable running about four hundred words. It was still coded, but he immediately spotted the top-secret designation. He noted that the cable was marked for delivery to, among others, the Minister for External Affairs herself. It was from Ambassador Taylor in Tehran. The jumble of capitalized letters meant little to him, but Mr. Happy sensed a message of great import.

He rushed to a nearby cubicle and passed the cable to another man behind a desk. "I'll need this decoded as quickly as possible." The man behind the desk nodded.

Once it was converted to readable English, Mr. Happy photocopied the cable a half-dozen times and slid the copies carefully into the envelopes with the distinctive red-x stripes. He then assumed what he hoped was an inscrutable expression and took a walk upstairs.

6

A S H E E N T E R E D his well-appointed office on the second floor of the Pearson Building, Michael Shenstone, Director General for African and Middle Eastern Affairs, glanced out the window at the tree-covered Gatineau Hills, now a splash of bland winter-white-and-grey across the Ottawa River. He hung his coat up behind the door, ran his fingers through his bushy hair, and adjusted his glasses to inspect the latest batch of cables on his desk. The Taylor telex was on top of the pile. He noticed immediately that it was marked for top-level distribution, including the minister's office. He read the first few sentences and blinked. He raced through the four hundred words which five hours ago had been nothing but a meaningless babble of letters in code, clattering across a telex machine in the communications room.

Shenstone was thunderstruck. This was astonishing. Taylor...five fugitive Americans...in a city that was going to hell in a hurry. The implications were incredible. My God, what do we do? What is the minister, Flora MacDonald, saying at this very moment? Grasping the telex in his hand, he strode into the office of John Fraser, director of the Middle East division.

"John, you've read this?" he asked anxiously.

Fraser, a large, bluff man who affected conservative three-piece brown suits and a Chamberlain-like moustache, brandished his copy of the cable. "Yes," he said. "Quite a way to begin the day, isn't it?" Unlike his immediate superior, Fraser seemed unruffled by the news.

"John," Shenstone said, "we'll have to take the Americans in, of course. Hardly any alternative, is there? But we're going to have to brainstorm this thing quickly. Now, let's see. We must have a reply out by this afternoon, somebody has to discuss this with the minister, and..."

Shenstone's thoughts were racing. Nick Etheridge of the Iran desk — where was he? The cable had also been designated for Klaus Goldschlag, a senior political officer. Where was he? The office of consular affairs, the legal people, the security people, and, of course, Gotlieb, the deputy minister...Jesus, talk about a bureaucratic nightmare!

Taylor's bombshell set off all kinds of bureaucratic alarms, catching a half-dozen senior civil servants in the middle of their morning coffee with a crisis that demanded action and decision. David Elder, administrative assistant to the minister of external affairs, Flora MacDonald, buzzed Shenstone while the latter was pacing in Fraser's office, and told him he was trying to contact Flora, but she was off somewhere taping a television interview.

The next hour was one of frantic meetings in hallways, and hasty telephone calls, with senior bureaucrats rushing from office to office, gathering opinions, information, whatever they needed to make their unprecedented decision. Shenstone had Etheridge of the Iran desk consult the legal people for their opinion about the relative immunity of the chancery and the staff residences in Tehran. He needed some definitive answers: just exactly what did the Vienna Convention and the body of diplomatic tradition say about the sanctity of an ambassador's home and the homes of his staff?

And security? Should Taylor be encouraged to transfer some embassy guards to his residence, or would that be too risky? What about Washington? Someone should contact the Canadian embassy staff there, find out if they had contacted the Americans. And what did the Yanks have to say?

Bit by bit, the answers began to trickle in. The central question, as Shenstone saw it during his frantic pacing between his and Fraser's office, was this: under what circumstances was an embassy entitled to offer asylum? It had long been accepted that an embassy in a foreign country could give haven to anyone in imminent danger, as long as the fugitive was not wanted on purely criminal charges. Yet, in Iran, the Americans were being accused of spying. Would the Iranian government, under international law, have the right to demand that the five be handed over for trial? And if their demand was refused, could they claim any right of forcible entry?

Etheridge came back with the opinion of the department lawyers. "No problem under international law," he told Shenstone. "And there's another important point. There are no warrants out on these people. They are not fugitives in the strict sense. As far as we can determine, the Iranian government—"

"Whoever that is," interrupted Fraser.

"—the Iranian government," Etheridge continued, "is not officially behind the seizure of the embassy. Until they sanction what happened, and admit it to the world, they cannot openly demand that anybody hiding Americans turn them over."

"Of course," Shenstone said, "if we want to be pessimistic, let's say the five are discovered on our premises. We can't physically defend them against a mob. That's obvious. We can't just go on pretending that they're Canadian tourists."

Shenstone walked over to the window in Fraser's office, paused for a moment, and continued. "Sure they're here, we tell them. But nobody asked us. Nobody said we couldn't take them in. Does the government see them as criminals? Are there charges against them? Are there warrants out?" Shenstone was calmer now that a scenario was taking shape.

"It's a tricky game," Goldschlag, the political officer, remarked. "My God, we're appealing to a mob on the grounds of reason and law and justice."

"If it comes to that," Shenstone replied. "It probably won't. Hell, this whole thing could blow over in a week. Remember that. What we're talking about here is the worst case. If our people are exposed, of course we play dumb. We have to. But that means no guards. We can't station a military policeman outside Taylor's house. That would be an admission that we're harbouring somebody we know is hot.''

The discussion went back and forth for more than an hour as more opinions came in from legal, from security, and from consular affairs — the division that deals with an embassy's consular services overseas. By 10 a.m., the implications of Taylor's telegram were fermenting in the minds of perhaps a dozen people in the Pearson Building. No one had to remind them of the sensitivity of the cable. Mentally, they began drafting eyes-only memos, plotting scenarios. Shenstone reminded them that this was to be essentially Taylor's baby. Far removed from the action, ensconced in their comfortable Ottawa offices, the bureaucrats had no choice but to trust the instincts of the man whom fate, aided by the Department of External Affairs, had placed in the eye of the hurricane.

"What about Taylor?" everyone asked. "Can he handle this thing?"

"He can handle it," Shenstone answered confidently, praising Taylor's performance during the evacuation of Canadians in Iran ten months earlier. "I know we can rely on him. And the reply we send this afternoon will make that clear.''

"And our staff over there, what about the risk to them?" an official from the security branch inquired. "Their lives could be on the line.''

"We mustn't get paranoid about this," Shenstone replied. "Remember, we are still dealing with a government over there—some kind of government. It isn't anarchy... yet.''

Flora MacDonald walked into her office in the Centre Block of the Parliament Buildings shortly after ten o'clock with her familiar jaunty step. It had been a gruelling morning. Word had come from Washington that President Carter would not be visiting Ottawa—a long-awaited trip—because of the Iran crisis, and Flora had spent the last two hours in the company of the American ambassador to Ottawa, Ken Curtis, making the rounds of the television studios.

Carter's "rose-garden" strategy — staying close to the Oval Office to manage the Iranian crisis on an hourly basis — had just been instituted, and the Canadian visit was the first casualty. Flora and her boss, Prime Minister Joe Clark, were mortally disappointed. The presidential visit would have made good press for the beleaguered six-month-old Conservative government.

The minister had barely settled behind her desk when David Elder, one of her two administrative assistants, gave a brief staccato knock and hurried into the room. Elder handed her a copy of the Taylor cable. She read it quickly, then a second time more carefully. "Oh, my God," she breathed. "This is, this is — When did this come in?"

"About an hour, an hour and a half ago. You couldn't be reached. On the second floor of the Pearson Building, they've been mulling over this since before nine. Waiting to hear from you."

"Yes, I can imagine," the minister said, somewhat archly. She was on uneasy terms with the people in External. She had heard the whispers, and felt some of the subtle barbs. It was more than the traditional friction between a minister, who rules a department for the duration of a government and then sinks into oblivion, and the career bureaucrats who must implement the minister's policies. The difference was that Flora was a woman, the first in Canada — nay, in the Commonwealth — to sit astride the monolith known as External Affairs. She knew that the jokes and criticism were products of human nature. She hated them, but she lived with them, and she learned to play the game.

"Gignac is waiting for your call," Elder said, interrupting the minister's train of thought.

Jacques Gignac, an assistant under-secretary in External, was indeed waiting for the minister to call. He briefed her carefully, explaining in broad terms the deliberations of Shenstone and his people. "Of course, we feel that Taylor should get the go-ahead," Gignac said. "Certainly," the minister replied. "I have no reservations at all. But of course the prime minister must give his formal approval. I'll be seeing him in a few minutes. We will have a cable to Taylor out by this afternoon. I'll be back in touch as soon as possible."

Walking down the cavernous corridors towards the House of Commons chamber, past the enormous oil portraits of prime ministers and cabinet members and other "great Canadians", Flora MacDonald was trembling with excitement.

The Honourable Member from the constituency of Kingston and the Islands had an unabashed love of her job. After long years of toiling in the vineyards of the Progressive Conservative party, she had been rewarded in May with the plum job in the Joe Clark cabinet. External had a staff of 5,000, and a budget of $300 million, and it carried as much prestige as the finance ministry. Two former prime ministers, Louis St. Laurent and Mike Pearson, had held the External portfolio at one time, and Flora felt herself in good company.

A few degrees shy of handsome, with a distinctive nose and chin and red hair — features that make her an easy target for editorial caricaturists — Flora was by far the brightest light in a generally lacklustre Clark cabinet. She possessed what political strategists call "the identification factor". Letters addressed simply to "Flora, Ottawa" were promptly delivered to her office. Next to Clark's faceless lieutenants, the John Crosbies and the Sinclair Stevenses, she shone. Her very plainness, the heavy purples and dark greens in her wardrobe, and the eagerness with which she applied herself to her job, lent her a distinction that her cabinet colleagues envied.

Flora's most engaging quality is her candour. She shoots from the hip, eschewing rhetorical convolutions. In her maiden speech to the General Assembly of the United Nations only two months earlier, she had delivered a stinging emotional attack on the community of nations for their drift toward bureaucratization and factionalism. She had been applauded, both in the Assembly, where delegates had lined up for fifteen minutes to shake her hand, and at home — except for her criticism of Argentina as a nation "where four thousand people have disappeared" at the hands of a repressive and violent regime. Back in Ottawa, that comment had triggered a great deal of consternation since Argentina was a prospective buyer of a billion-dollar CANDU nuclear reactor, Canada's foremost contribution to atomic energy technology. A few days later, Argentina (which had been far too reluctant, in Flora's mind, to guarantee that the reactor would not be used to produce plutonium, a key ingredient of nuclear weaponry) cancelled the contract. The blame was pinned on Flora's lapel by senior bureaucrats, who grumbled about "that meddlesome woman".

MacDonald belonged to that hybrid class of Conservatives known as the "Red Tories" — a touch too liberal for the party mainstream. She disagreed sharply with party policy to dissolve Petro-Canada, the government's energy-exploration company, and leave the oil industry entirely in the preserve of the private multinationals, as she did on several other important issues. But, a loyalist at heart, she kept her views to herself, or at least to the inner councils of the party. Her fidelity was another quality that enhanced her currency in government. In 1976, Flora had made a determined run for the leadership of the party. When it became apparent that the party was not as "progressive" as it liked to believe, and would not accept leadership by a woman, she looked across the convention floor and fastened her eyes on Joe Clark, widely regarded as everybody's second choice. Then she crossed the floor and, in full view of the delegates and the television cameras, pinned her flower on Clark's jacket. That gesture tipped the scales and, a few ballots later, Clark, the little-known climber from High River, Alberta, had the leadership in his pocket. Clark would falter often as party leader — and as prime minister — but Flora never took advantage of his ineptitude to enhance her own status within the party. Her personal sense of ethics simply would not allow any disloyalty, despite her disappointment and resentment at losing the leadership.

The Clark government, which lasted from May 22 to February 18, 1980, was so pockmarked with blunders and misfires that it will likely be remembered more for the temporary absence of Pierre Trudeau than for the brief ascendency of Joe Clark. Were it not for the contributions of Flora Mac-Donald and one or two other cabinet members, Clark's two hundred days in office would have been an unmitigated disaster. As it was, the minority Conservative government never got off the ground but taxied in circles like an airplane with only one engine working — and that at half-throttle.

Clark had fifteen years in active politics under his belt when he was elected leader of the Conservatives, but he remained tagged with the "Joe who?" label until his defeat. His embarrassments have become part of Canadian political legend: the Richard Nixon victory salute; the time he backed into an official limousine, missed the seat by several inches, and fell ingloriously on his behind; the lost luggage on his world trips; the time he asked an East Indian leader if members of the Hindu faith "go to mass on Sundays"; the "small-business" speech before a group of Calgary oil barons. The Opposition Liberals' attitude to Clark was one of patronizing amusement: "We don't have to push right now. If we just give Clark enough rope, he'll try to shoot himself."

Clark's Middle East policy was a prime example of this prophecy fulfilling itself. His announced intention to recognize Jerusalem as the Israeli capital whipped up an Arabian sandstorm that was staggering in its vehemence. The Arab lobby in Canada called it "a declaration of war on 900 million Moslems". A billion dollars' worth of trade with Middle East nations was jeopardized. The Palestinian Liberation Organization made dark, threatening noises about reprisals. Canadian companies, like Bell Canada, doing business in the Middle East were terrified that their contracts would be invalidated. The Toronto *Star* estimated that as many as 67,500 Canadian jobs would be lost if Arab threats to boycott Canadian goods materialized.

Clark had tugged on the tail of the lion, and it almost bit his head off. On October 29, he sheepishly admitted his mistake and withdrew his Jerusalem policy. During this period, a Gallup Poll showed that only seven per cent of Canadians believed Clark to be the country's most effective leader.

Thus it was not the best of times for Charles Joseph Clark when, shortly after 11 a.m. on Thursday, November 8, Flora MacDonald slid into the vacant seat next to his in the House of Commons. The prime minister was engrossed in the cut and thrust of the daily Question Period, that exercise in free-wheeling democracy in which Opposition members try to pin back the ears of government ministers. The Conservative front bench was being peppered with questions from a senior Liberal member, Marc Lalonde, about the safety of Canadian citizens in Iran and the security of oil deliveries from that country.

Flora MacDonald leaned over and whispered into the prime minister's ear, "Before you leave the chamber, there's something terribly urgent we have to talk about." She was tempted to give him more of a hint, but thought better of it. Clark would be distracted for the remainder of the Question Period and the news could wait an hour. The prime minister, who was to leave Ottawa that afternoon for a number of political appearances, gave her a sidelong glance of curiosity and agreed to meet her in the adjacent members' lobby, behind the heavy curtains along the perimeter of the Commons chamber, at noon.

In the lobby forty minutes later, members of the House of Commons press gallery had already congregated for their daily feeding when Clark and Flora MacDonald pushed aside the curtain and walked out of the members' lobby together. "Excuse me for a moment," Clark said to the press "scrum" and guided his chief minister to a quiet corner. "I'll be right back," he added over his shoulder.

While Flora briefed the prime minister about Taylor's cable, and the prevailing views at External, Clark showed little expression except the characteristic pursing of the lips. It was at such moments that he most resembled his political mentor, John Diefenbaker, the prairie lawyer who had last headed a Conservative government in the 1960s. When Flora had finished, he asked one or two questions for clarification and then promptly gave his sanction to Taylor's "rescue operation".

"Keep me informed," he told his External Affairs minister, before turning to the newsmen and the more mundane affairs of leadership.

With those words, he placed his trust in Flora's ability to oversee the most dangerous diplomatic manoeuvre in Canada's history.

Later that afternoon, Ottawa's chief communicator, Mr. Happy, was handed a cable numbered 212327. It was marked "flash" — for immediate transmission — and was to the Canadian embassy in Tehran. Attention Ken Taylor. It was timed a few minutes short of 3 p.m.

The message was the formal go-ahead for Ambassador Taylor to provide, if necessary, refuge to the five fugitive Americans. Where he put them up was his business, but he should remember, of course, that the security guards in Tehran had a very limited function.

It was an unprecedented mandate, and Ken Taylor, the reluctant bureaucrat who had often been criticized for his unorthodoxy, was to prove the ideal man for the job.

7

*L**IKE EVERY MAJOR CITY*, Tehran has its exclusive residential area, with plush homes and trimmed hedges maintained by gardeners, away from the noise of the inner city and the crush of the bazaars. Tehran's Westmount is called Shemiran. It occupies the heights to the north of the city, rising a thousand feet or more, and is cooled by rippling streams. It is here, in Shemiran, that the kings of the Qajar dynasty had built their summer palaces, and today their tombs are popular tourist attractions. Behind the stone walls that surround the luxurious residences, one can almost forget the open gutters of the streets — Tehran has no sewer system — and the desperate poverty in the stinking alleyways of south Tehran. Shemiran houses the government officials, the well-to-do import-export merchants, the old monied families, and most of the city's senior diplomats.

The house that acts as the official residence of the Canadian ambassador is a white, two-storey masonry structure, set well back behind an eight-foot wall. A covered walkway leads to the street. The rear of the residence, a high colonnaded patio, looks out over an expanse of lawn, a rectangular swimming pool, a small tiled pond, and poplar trees planted in neat rows along the perimeter of the grounds. It is airy and restful. During Taylor's stay there, the only incongruity was a twenty-foot flagpole on which flapped the red maple leaf.

Friday was Pat Taylor's day off from her job as a research microbiologist at the Iran Blood Transfusion Centre. She could sleep in, eat a leisurely breakfast, spend some time with the household staff of eight, and, if it was warm and sunny, relax on the roof of the residence and read a good book. Except for the five-times-daily call to prayers that issued from a nearby mosque, her Fridays were generally quiet and peaceful. Even on this day, just five days after the seizure of the American embassy five miles to the south, she could close her eyes and imagine she was spending an indolent weekend in Rockcliffe, the upscale civil-service suburb of Ottawa.

Shortly after noon, the telephone rang. Ali, the Indian-born head servant, answered it and told the lady of the house that Mr. Taylor was on the line. With some trepidation, Pat Taylor took the receiver and put it to her ear.

"Pat," her husband said, "we're picking them up today. The schedule's been advanced. Bob" — he did not use Anders' full name — "called John Sheardown a few moments ago and said they had to move right away. He sounded terribly nervous. I'd guess you'd better tell the servants we're going to have guests tonight."

"Anything from Ottawa?" Mrs. Taylor asked.

"The cable was here this morning," the ambassador replied. "We can go ahead. It's been cleared through the prime minister and Flora's office. I'll call you in a couple of hours and let you know when we're on our way over."

Pat Taylor put the phone down and walked up the curving staircase to the upper floor. At the head of the stairs were two adjoining rooms — a bedroom and a sitting room — that had already been prepared for the guests. Fresh sheets had been laid down, and extra blankets in case the nights were chilly. Pat Taylor made sure everything was in place, and then returned downstairs to instruct the head servant.

"Ali," she told him, "we will have some guests staying with us tonight. For a few days. They are Canadian friends of the ambassador's, tourists who want to see the city. I'm afraid I don't know them, so I can't tell you more about them. But you might want to tell the rest of the staff. And the cook should know there will be two extra for dinner tonight."

"Yes, madam," the head servant nodded obediently. "We will make them feel welcome."

An hour later, a much-dented American-made car, with an Oriental-looking driver and five passengers, pulled up to the Sheardown residence near Fereshteh Avenue in Shemiran. Bob Anders glanced out the car window and saw John Sheardown in front of the house, a garden hose in his hand. What in God's name, he thought, was the man doing, watering his wretched little patch of grass — and in November, no less?

Then it dawned on him. Of course. This was the signal to the driver. Somchai was to look for a rather large man watering his lawn, in case he got the house address mixed up. "Couldn't he have picked a more innocuous signal?" Anders asked Lijek, grinning widely. "My God, he doesn't even have a garden!"

The Americans piled out of the car, and Sheardown came to meet them. Anders made the introductions. Within seconds, Ken Taylor arrived in his green Volvo. Together the group walked toward the front door.

Inside, Zena Sheardown greeted them effusively. Taylor could see that Sheardown's Guyanese-born wife was trying to mask her nervousness as she led the party to the living room and asked them to sit while she prepared some drinks and sandwiches. She fled to the kitchen.

The Americans settled into the couches and stretched out. For the first time in five days, they relaxed. And they were anxious to talk, to dispel the anxiety that had seized them since their flight from the embassy on Sunday.

"There were others," said Anders, "maybe a half-dozen, who left with us. Dick Queen and five other people from my section. I'm afraid they must have been picked up. I've been in touch with Vic Tomseth and he feels the same way. They're not at the Morefield house; we telephoned and the servants answered, but there's nobody staying there."

Sheardown asked for details about their escape. Why hadn't they made it to the British embassy? Kathy Stafford told of the mobs they'd encountered on the way to the embassy, and how they'd been forced to change their route. "We had to get off the streets, and fast," she said. "We were lucky, I guess. Are they still picking up Americans in the city?''

Taylor noted that, according to his information, the militants at the embassy weren't interested in any more hostages. "In fact, they had to turn some captives away," he said. "The Revolutionary Guards scoured the city, went through the hotels, business offices, everywhere. Picked up every American they could find and took them to the compound. But the militants inside said they didn't want any more Americans. No room at the inn, I guess," Taylor laughed.

"Makes sense," Anders remarked. "I guess they know they've got enough on their hands. But what's the latest from Washington? Jesus, the president must be squirming."

Taylor briefed them on the apparent failure of the Ramsey Clark mission — Clark and Miller were still in Istanbul, unsuccessful in their attempts to secure a personal meeting with Khomeini — and the American decision not to send back the Shah. It was with the mention of the Shah that the usually easygoing Anders began to get hot.

"I'll never understand it. Not as long as I live. Dammit, they had to know this would happen if they allowed the Shah into the country. They had to be blind not to see it. What's his condition, by the way — the Shah, I mean?"

Taylor told the group that some medical complications had come up. Gallstones, jaundice, the advance of the lymph cancer. "While he's getting the deluxe treatment up there on the seventeenth floor, the Iranian students in New York are raising all kinds of hell."

Anders nodded. Ironically, many of those students had probably been processed through his section, the consular department. Mark Lijek broke in. "What's the situation in this area of the city?"

Sheardown explained that the *komitehs* patrolled all the streets, even in Shemiran, but they didn't bother any of the residents. "That's our only security problem. But it's not a serious one. You'll just have to remember to stay out of sight."

Zena Sheardown came in with coffee and a tray of

sandwiches. She was accompanied by a maid, whom she introduced briefly to the "guests". Then she sat down quietly in a chair, hands clasped. John Sheardown looked at his elegantly dressed and coiffed wife solicitously. He could sense her anxiety, but she was putting up a brave front.

"When you're finished eating, I'll show you your rooms," she said. "I think you'll be quite comfortable." She glanced at the suitcases. "Is that all you have?" Cora Lijek smiled and answered, "We didn't have a long time to pack. We even left some things in the washing machine, we were so happy to be leaving. I'm afraid we're going to have to impose on you for some articles."

Taylor explained the arrangements. The Lijeks and Bob Anders would be staying at the Sheardown home. The Staffords would be staying with him and Pat. "It's the best and safest setup," he said. "We have a staff of eight. They're trustworthy, but any more than two guests could lead to problems."

The ambassador explained that he had considered moving some of the Canadian military guards to the residences to provide extra security, but that idea was rejected because it might raise suspicions. "The one thing we don't need is more attention right now."

"Anyway," John Sheardown said, "enjoy the holiday. It won't be a long one. This thing will be over in a few days, and you'll be able to go back to your normal lives."

The guests nodded nervously.

A short while later Joe and Kathy Stafford stood in the entranceway of the Taylor residence and gaped at the opulence. To Pat Taylor, they seemed like a pair of orphans just in from the cold; between them, they had one small suitcase. She greeted them warmly, and Ali, the head servant, took their suitcase and carried it upstairs. His expression was quizzical. Why would tourists who had come all the way from Canada to Iran carry so few belongings?

"They like to travel light," Mrs. Taylor explained to him

later, anticipating his question. "They'll be visiting the north and they just don't want to be loaded down with a lot of baggage." Ali did not ask for elaboration.

Mrs. Taylor took them on a tour of the house, trying to make the young couple feel more at ease. They seemed painfully shy, but when she led them into the "Persian room", with its rich carpets, mosaics, and camel bags, Kathy remarked on the décor. "It's the room we love the most," Mrs. Taylor said. "Where we eat supper most often."

During the brief tour, Joe and Kathy met the maids, the cook, and the gardener, whom they engaged in casual small talk. In each case, Mrs. Taylor introduced them as tourists, and the servants were impressed when Joe spoke a few words in Farsi. "I...er...studied the language back home," he explained. Only the head servant and the cook were conversant in English.

Upstairs, in the privacy of their guest suite, Mrs. Taylor answered all their questions and made a number of suggestions. "It would be best if you remained inside during the day," she said. "I'm afraid even the lawn would not be safe. Neighbours can look over the wall. Especially now that winter's coming and the trees are bare. And don't worry about the servants. They are completely trustworthy."

Later, over dinner, the Taylors explained their daily schedules to their new guests. Six days a week, Friday excepted, they would be leaving the residence between 7 and 7:30 a.m. Mrs. Taylor normally returned in mid afternoon, and the ambassador in the early evening. As for the Staffords, their days would be spent entirely on their own. "And please feel free to use the house. Sleep in late in the mornings, as late as you like. The servants will prepare breakfast and lunch whenever you ask them.

"And of course I don't need to tell you not to answer the telephone or the doorbells. There are plenty of books and there's a radio. I'm afraid we don't have many games in the house, but we'll try to find some for you."

The Staffords ate their first full-course meal in a week with a huge appetite. Ken Taylor cracked open a bottle of good French wine and toasted the Staffords' freedom. Joe and

Kathy raised their glasses to their hosts, and Kathy said, "You can't possibly know how much this all means to us." Pat Taylor saw that she was getting moist-eyed.

After dinner, the ambassador took Joe upstairs and rummaged through his wardrobe. He found a wool sweater, a few shirts, and some underwear. "Here, this will supplement your wardrobe," he said. Joe stammered his thanks and said he and Kathy would probably be turning in early.

In the privacy of their room, they lay down quietly, unable at first to sleep. It was past midnight before they dozed off. For the first time since their flight, they slept soundly, confident that their plight would soon be resolved.

OTTAWA November 10

Allan McKinnon, Canada's avuncular minister of national defence, picked up a scrambler phone in Ottawa and reached Dr. Harold Brown, his counterpart in Washington.

The "secure" conversation was brief and to the point.

"Secretary Brown," McKinnon said after the polite niceties, "my government is concerned about U.S. plans in connection with your hostages in Tehran. We are of course prepared to accept the five" — Brown had already been briefed about the appeal by the six to the Canadians — "but my government is naturally concerned about any military plans you might have in the near future. I don't have to tell you that American military action could complicate things for us over there, especially if we were not forewarned."

Secretary Brown, who a decade earlier had earned himself the nickname Bomber Brown among his Pentagon colleagues for his hawkish propensities, put McKinnon's fears to rest. "The president has no plans to use the military, Mr. Minister. We will explore all peaceful avenues. That is official U.S. policy as the president enunciated it several days ago. We fully understand your concern, and we would certainly not initiate anything that could catch you by surprise."

"I'm happy to hear that," McKinnon said. "As a former military man, I can tell you it is my feeling that you would need at least a battalion to free your hostages, and you could anticipate many casualties, maybe as many as a thousand. This would be no quick-strike Entebbe kind of operation. This would be large-scale."

Secretary Brown thanked him for his assessment, and the two men wished one another well before ringing off. With that, McKinnon instructed his driver to take him to the prime minister's official residence at 24 Sussex Drive for a meeting with Joe Clark and External Affairs Minister Flora MacDonald. This news could not wait.

In Washington the next day, the chairman of the Joint Chiefs of Staff, General David Jones, arranged for a meeting with Major-General James Vaught, a much-decorated para-trooper. Vaught was handed a highly sensitive assignment that originated from within the Oval Office. He was to hand-pick a special operations team, and begin training them for a mission in Iran. No expense was to be spared, and the officers of the team were to be sworn to the strictest secrecy.

The classified nature of the assignment would be exclusive. As far as the American allies were concerned — and this included Canada — no aggressive action was being considered by the U.S. government. The ignorance of America's friends was part of the Carter game plan.

TEHRAN November 10

The first week went by slowly, interminably. The Staffords rose every morning between 9:30 and 10, and as they descended the staircase, Ali would invariably ask what they would like for breakfast and where they wished to eat it.

After eggs and coffee, they sauntered into one of the two ground-floor dens, and Joe would turn on the radio. Every hour, he waited for the Farsi-language newscasts, pen and paper in hand, and he jotted down notes. No item of information was too insignificant — even the propaganda statements he duly noted on his pad.

By studying the Tehran newspapers that the Taylors brought home each day, Joe became something of an expert on Iranian events and personalities. Already fluent in the language, he picked up the subtleties and the idiom quickly. He could identify the members of the Revolutionary Council; he paid careful attention to the almost daily statements issued by the Ayatollah Khomeini, and picked out small nuances he felt were important.

The newscasts carried little detailed information about day-to-day goings-on inside the American embassy, so Joe was riveted to the radio on Monday, November 12, when the militants released thirteen women and blacks and the group held a major press conference in Tehran. The newscasts concentrated on statements by the Americans that were even remotely critical of the United States for having welcomed the Shah. Knowing that the heavily censored Iranian press was selective about what it carried, he suspended judgment on what he heard.

Later that day, as they were sitting down with cocktails, Joe told the Taylors that he was suspicious of the militants' motives in releasing the thirteen. "Khomeini has this crazy idea that American blacks are ready to rise up against their government, with the right kind of provocation," he said. "He's hoping to drive a wedge between them and the Carter administration by letting the blacks go, with a great deal of fanfare. The guy's sadly mistaken."

The Taylors were appreciative sounding-boards for Stafford's theories about Khomeini, the militants, and what would likely happen to the hostages. Often, the ambassador would modify or amplify Stafford's hypotheses with some hard information of his own about events and his gleanings from conversations with diplomatic colleagues and members of the international press corps. All this made for vibrant dinner-table conversation, with all four joining in with great enthusiasm.

It took at least a week for Joe and Kathy to overcome their initial shyness. When Pat Taylor arrived home from work in mid afternoon, they would usually be in the study reading or talking. When she walked in, they would rise quickly, somewhat embarrassed, and make some excuse for going upstairs to their rooms. "Please, stay where you are,"

Mrs. Taylor had to tell them. "This is your home. Don't feel you have to shut yourselves in upstairs."

After a fortnight, the Staffords began to get a little stir-crazy. They had already plundered the Taylor library and read every available magazine. They ate well, slept more than ten hours a night, and were full of energy; but they had no way to expend it. They watched enviously when the ambassador would prepare to leave the house for a tennis match.

Even though the Taylor home was constantly bathed in sunlight — Pat Taylor had chosen not to hang curtains on the large windows, because she wanted the natural light — the Staffords yearned for even a few moments outdoors every day. But even that was too chancy.

Their first diversion came in late November. The Taylors were having some people for dinner — a handful of diplomats and some prominent journalists — and it was obvious that the "houseguests" would have to leave for the evening.

"Shall we stay in our rooms?" they asked Pat Taylor.

"No," she answered. "The servants would ask questions. I spoke to Ken, and he thinks it best that we take you to the Sheardowns for the evening."

Kathy was delighted. It would be a marvellous break from the routine, an opportunity to sit down and relax with three of their colleagues. They would have a party.

Later that afternoon, the cook approached Mrs. Taylor with a puzzled expression on her face. "Madam," she said, "there must be something wrong. I have a menu for ten people, but the Staffords are not included. Will they not be dining with you?"

"No," Pat Taylor answered hastily. "Just by coincidence, some friends of theirs are in town, and they'll be spending the evening with them." She had anticipated the question, and her reply was casual and offhand, but she was uneasy about the deception. There would surely be some suspicious mutterings in the kitchen.

Only the day before, Ali had wondered aloud why the "tourists" slept in so late every morning and never left the house. Mrs. Taylor shrugged off the question by saying that

Joe and Kathy welcomed the chance to relax as much as they could. "They had a very rugged trip, and maybe they're a little nervous about going out into the city."

"Of course, madam," Ali said. But there was little conviction in his voice.

On Wednesday, November 21, Taylor took a call in his office from the Swedish ambassador. Sundberg had an unusual request of his Canadian colleague, and Taylor could not help smiling at his obvious discomfiture. "Mr. Ambassador," the man said, "for the past two weeks, we have been... entertaining a young American embassy staffer, a Mr. Schatz, whose office was actually outside the compound. Mr. Schatz came to us, seeking protection, and we put him up at the home of one of our people.

"Now I would like to ask a very large favour of you. Mr. Schatz could easily pass as a Canadian, and we felt that he might therefore be safer under your care. We realize it would be a tremendous imposition, but we wonder if... well... if you would mind taking him in with you. It would be greatly appreciated by myself and my government."

Taylor leaned back in his chair and fought to keep the laughter out of his voice. "But of course, Mr. Ambassador. We would be happy to. After all, we are already taking care of five other Americans. We could easily make room for one more."

"*Five others?*" the Swedish ambassador sputtered. "You mean — why, this is a great shock. I had no idea — "

"Of course not," Taylor said. "They've been with us since early this month. Look, I'll have one of my people — John Sheardown, he's head of our immigration office — come by tomorrow to collect him. Could you or someone on your staff accompany Mr. Sheardown when he goes to pick him up?"

"Certainly," the Swedish ambassador said. "I'll arrange it immediately. Why, this is... you've taken me completely by shock...."

The next day, a large black Mercedes pulled up at the door of a Swedish diplomatic residence and two men stepped out. John Sheardown and a Swedish official walked up to the front door and the official asked the servant to bring Mr. Schatz to them.

"Please don't tell him who I am. I'd like to keep this a surprise, at least for a while," Sheardown told the official. The Swede nodded in agreement.

When Lee approached, Sheardown said in an abrupt voice, "Mr. Schatz, you will gather your things and come with me, please. I'm taking you somewhere where you'll be safer."

Schatz stared at the large man, his alarm only slightly tempered by the North American accent. Who was this curt and stern-looking individual? He glanced over Sheardown's shoulder at the shiny black Mercedes, and the letters "CIA" flashed into his mind. "Jesus," Schatz told himself, "I've been rescued by the CIA!"

"Who are you?" he demanded of Sheardown, and then turned to the familiar face of the Swede. Surely he wouldn't have been betrayed by the people who had put him up for seventeen days and nights? No, it couldn't be.

"Never mind," Sheardown said. "Please follow me." Schatz said he would have to go inside to fetch his belongings — a couple of shirts, a tie, some underwear, an extra pair of socks, and a telescoping umbrella. The clothing all went into a red knapsack, which he hoisted over his shoulder. "Okay, I'm ready," he said, striding out the door behind Sheardown, who led him to the rear door of the Mercedes limo. Schatz glanced down the street and noticed two Western-looking men sitting in a small car, watching him. "It *is* the CIA!" he told himself. "Son of a bitch. I've been rescued by the Company."

All in all, he was pleased. After spending more than two weeks with his Swedish hosts, mainly cooped up in the residence by himself, sleeping with a large Swedish flag as a blanket, Schatz was ready for a change of scenery.

Beside him in the car, Sheardown was keeping his secret, staring ahead stonily and enjoying his impersonation.

Schatz kept glancing out the rear window. The small car was still there, following them doggedly.

The car pulled into Fereshteh Avenue, and stopped in front of the Sheardown home. Sheardown turned to his new guest, and said, "Okay, I guess I owe you an explanation. . . ." As he spoke, Schatz began grinning, and complimented Sheardown on the success of his prank. "All right," Schatz said, "now introduce me to the others. I'm looking forward to some American company and conversation."

Schatz's optimism could easily have changed to terror, had he been aware of the activities of an eager reporter 8,000 miles away, in Schatz's hometown of Coeur d'Alene, Idaho. Bob Clark, an enterprising young newsman with the local paper, had learned by a propitious accident that the local Schatz family had a son who was part of the American diplomatic corps in Tehran. Aware that he was onto a scoop, Clark located the parents, who confirmed that their son Lee was indeed in Iran, but that he had managed to elude capture on the day of the embassy takeover. Clark's eyes widened. "Where is he staying?" he asked, trying to sound casual. "He's with the Swedes, at their embassy there. The State Department says he's fine, and in no danger," Mrs. Schatz answered blithely.

Clark couldn't believe his good fortune. "Would you happen to have a recent photograph of your son?" he asked, pushing his luck. "Yes, I think so," the mother said. She found a candid shot of Lee in a scrapbook and gave it to the reporter, who promised to send it back the next day.

A jubilant Clark rushed back to his newspaper desk and wrote the story, leaving out the identity of the embassy that was sheltering the fugitive. But as he prepared to leave the office, the Schatzes called him, frantic that they'd made a terrible mistake. They should never have told Clark about their son, and would he please withhold publication of his story. Clark then received a call from a senior State Department official in Washington, pleading that under no circumstances should the Swedes be mentioned. "It's a matter of the greatest security," the official said.

Unaccustomed to such high-level attention from the nation's capital, Clark said he had left the Swedes out of his story, but that he intended to publish the rest nonetheless. The next day, the Schatz story, complete with photograph, appeared on the front page of the newspaper. Astoundingly, whether by design or by oversight, the story of the young American in hiding didn't get a line of national exposure.

Schatz was overcome by his welcome at the Sheardown home. Bob Anders pumped his hand, and the Lijeks buzzed around him with questions about how he had escaped, and how he had spent the past two weeks with the Swedes. To the three virtual prisoners, Schatz was a breath of fresh air — cheery, ebullient, and wry.

He was given a tour of the Sheardown home, a roomy, multi-levelled house in which the four guests could easily coexist without falling all over each other or their hosts. He dropped his bag in his bedroom and the group sat around in the living room. "This whole thing was supposed to be over by now," Schatz said. "What's happening? What's slowing things down?"

Anders explained that their sources of information were severely limited. They could pick up the BBC and the Voice of America shortwave broadcasts on the Sheardown radio, and they devotedly read the English-language Tehran *Times*, the *International Herald Tribune*, and *Time* and *Newsweek*. John Sheardown and Ken Taylor filled in some of the gaps in the information but, by and large, they still felt cut off from what was really going on only a few miles away.

"Hell, nobody knows what's going on," Schatz said. "Least of all Carter. This is the great screw-up of all time. So tell me, how are you spending your days in captivity?"

"Welcome to the Scrabble Hall of Fame," Mark Lijek joked. "We play three hours a day, at least. We're wearing the letters off the tiles. And if you're any good at gin rummy, Bob will take your shirt."

Schatz laughed loudly. "This shirt happens to be my most valuable possession."

He asked about the Staffords. "We don't see much of them. They've been over a couple of times, and they're having about as much fun as we're having. But you'll meet them in a few days. We're planning a Thanksgiving dinner here."

Cora said they'd had the opportunity to write one or two letters home to their parents and relatives, which were sent through the Canadian diplomatic pouch. "We'd write every day if we could, but we've been rationed to about once every two weeks. Security and all that."

"But the big problem is exercise," she added. "God, what I'd give for the chance to jog around the block for a half-hour every day. But as it is, I have to satisfy myself by running up and down the stairs every day."

"You're kidding!" Schatz said.

"No, I'm not. It's boring, but it keeps the muscles toned. You should try it."

Anders filled him in on their daily schedule. "Imagine you're in a holiday villa, and there's a constant blizzard outside. So you're stuck inside, and you make the best of it."

Within only a couple of days, the novelty of his new surroundings wore off for Schatz and he drifted into a dreary torpor in which one long day melted into another, changeless and without meaning. He tried to keep a diary on his role in the politically and socially crumbling society, but soon abandoned the project. He lost any concept of time and the relation between the calendar and what was happening at the American compound and in Washington. Only the five-times-daily prayer chants from a nearby mosque brought him out of his reverie, and Iran would become real and threatening again. For hours, the four guests in the Sheardown house would slide Scrabble letters into slots on a board, staging elaborate competitions and giving small prizes.

The best time was dinner. This was the occasion for both physical and intellectual refreshment. They would argue at great length — about the Shah, about Khomeini, about Ramsey Clark, and, most of all, about the man in the White House and how he was handling his greatest crisis. It was on Carter that Lee Schatz took the extreme line. It had been the greatest folly, bordering on the criminal, to admit Shah Pahlavi into the United States, he argued. The others countered with the view that the attack on the American presence in Iran had been inevitable, whatever the Shah's movements might have been.

They argued about the security precautions at the embassy and about the passive role played by the Marines during the attack. "Surely, after the brief occupation of the embassy in February, they should have increased security tenfold," Mark Lijek said.

Bob Anders explained patiently that an embassy *had* to look to the host government for protection. No way could U.S. Marines shoot to kill even the most determined invaders. The whole delicate structure of world diplomacy would be threatened if foreign embassies were turned into fortresses.

Schatz tended to agree. On his second posting overseas, he had arrived in Iran as part of a new generation of foreign-service officers, more open to change, more sympathetic to the forces that opposed autocratic regimes such as that of the Shah. He had some major reservations — the revolution had, for one thing, swept away many of the U.S.-initiated projects throughout the country, and the bureaucracy had become hopelessly paralysed throughout the summer months of 1979 — but deep down he was beginning to appreciate the rage in so many Iranian hearts.

Schatz admitted there were inconsistencies in his philosophy. For example, he viewed with some disgust the way many young Iranians lusted after American education scholarships and travel papers, even while they mouthed the rabid slogans of the Ayatollah Khomeini. To him, this was the most blatant hypocrisy.

The guests often worried aloud about the safety of their Canadian hosts, and the perilous position their presence had placed them in. "Us, they could only drag downtown [to the embassy]," Schatz said on one occasion. "But the Canadians, they have stretched their necks out on the block as far as they can go." They itemized all the possible "flukes" that could possibly expose them, and vowed to do everything to reduce the chances of their occurring. They worried about what would happen if one of them were taken seriously ill — could they be safely taken to a Tehran hospital?

Over the weeks the Americans watched Zena Sheardown, who rarely left the house, become increasingly jumpy. She lived constantly in terror of the banging on the front door that would signal the arrival of the Revolutionary Guards. When she shopped, she worried that the shopkeepers would become suspicious of the amounts of food she purchased. She worried about the servants, about the landlord of the house they were occupying. (Not long before the Sheardowns returned to Canada, the landlord brought prospective purchasers to see the house, and the guests had to be evacuated.) The guests were aware that Zena lacked the protection of diplomatic immunity because she was not a Canadian citizen.

Nevertheless, when the long-awaited Thanksgiving dinner party occurred on November 27, spirits were high around the Sheardown table. A number of ironic toasts were drunk to the Ayatollah, the mullahs, the hothead students, the Revolutionary Guards. There was some debate about the wisdom of Idaho Congressman George Hansen's visit two days earlier with twenty of the hostages, part of a "mission of mercy" paid for out of personal funds. There was bitter laughter about how the U.S. Congress, still solidly behind President Carter's handling of the crisis, had jumped all over Hansen and his trip. House Speaker Thomas O'Neill called him "out of bounds" since he was known to favour a congressional investigation of the Shah's activities. The mood dampened considerably when Mark Lijek told the group that, in a statement earlier that day, the student militants announced they had surrounded the U.S. embassy with explosives and had planted mines in the compound to ward off any attack by U.S. "mercenaries".

"Jesus," Schatz exclaimed. "These guys aren't fooling!"

The group around the Sheardown table was not eager to talk about the possibility of a military rescue. Too much havoc, too much confusion, they agreed. At evening's end, fortified by wine and after-dinner drinks, they reached a general consensus that as much as they enjoyed one another's company, they hoped they would not be sitting at the same table together for Christmas dinner, a month away.

While his American charges settled into the routine of their captivity, Ken Taylor turned his mind to security matters at the Canadian embassy. By comparison, the U.S. embassy had been a fortress, yet it had been a pushover for a determined mob. Taylor knew that the Canadian embassy, at 57 Darya-e-Noor Street in downtown Tehran, could be easily seized by a handful of armed men. They could penetrate the "secure area" on the third floor within minutes, break into the cipher room within a half-hour, and control the premises by the time the final "urgent" cable had been transmitted to Ottawa. All that was needed was the incentive. And as Ambassador Taylor arrived at his office on the morning of Monday, November 12, he knew only too well that by providing sanctuary to the Americans he had given Tehran's fundamentalist revolutionaries more than enough incentive. It was a sobering thought.

His chauffeur dropped him off in the basement parking area, and Taylor stepped out, briefcase in hand. A security guard buzzed him through a reinforced steel door, and he walked up three steps into the main building. Ahead were two elevators flanking a stairway. On this morning, Taylor took the stairs to the main floor and stepped out into the lobby. In an adjacent reception area, Iranian citizens, most of them in their early twenties, were already beginning to gather, waiting for their appointments with immigration clerks. Revolution or no revolution, Taylor mused, the consular bureaucracy grinds on. The ambassador stopped for a moment at John Sheardown's office, but the immigration chief had not yet arrived. He strolled to the elevator and punched the button for the third floor, where his office was located.

Visitors who stepped out of the elevator at the third level knew immediately that they were in the embassy's "inner sanctum". Or almost. In fact, as they stepped over the elevator threshold, they were in what was called the "tomb" — an enclosure five feet by thirty feet that separated them from the vital innards of the embassy. Directly ahead was an impregnable door, swinging inwards, that could be opened only by pressing the correct series of numbers on a wall-mounted panel that contained ten numbered push buttons.

Despite this elaborate setup, Taylor felt uneasy as he went through the ritual of pressing the numbers that opened the door leading out of the tomb. He was aware that this area would be the focus of any resistance to an attempted embassy seizure. Guards could lob tear-gas cannisters into the tomb and give the invaders a few anxious moments, but a sustained attack would quickly penetrate the door. It was simply a matter, he told himself, of applied force. With a hostage or two, a terrorist could break through the tomb without firing a shot.

But what bothered Taylor even more was the fact that the embassy did not even have an adequate emergency exit. One could, in case of attack, dash down to the garage, but from there the only way out was into the arms of a mob on the street. There was a fire escape in the rear and a supply of knotted ropes on every floor that could be thrown out of windows. But the prospect of scrambling down ropes in case of attack was laughable. No, Taylor reflected, if it came to that he would greet the attackers in his office, leaning back in his chair with his feet on the desk.

Besides the ambassador's office, the third floor also contained the cipher vault, a hermetically sealed eighty-square-foot room that housed the embassy's communications equipment. A few steps away, also encased within four-inch steel walls, was the registry room, where documents were stored. The registry room had one window with metal grilles. This area, Taylor knew, would be the immediate target of attack, along with his own office on the other side of the building on the same floor. Taylor had no illusions about the security of the cipher vault or the registry. At the U.S. embassy, these had been opened within two or three hours, and the militants had found enough unshredded documents to keep them busy reading for days.

In his office, Taylor called for his head of security, Sgt. Claude Gauthier. "We have to start shredding," the ambassador told the burly native of St. Eustache, Quebec. "Anything that is not of the highest priority. It's going to be a helluva job, so we'd better start right away. If the worst happens, we don't want to be stuck with a ton of paper on our hands and no time to destroy it. Lesson One from the Americans. I'll get someone to prepare a list of what has to go and what must be kept."

According to the book, embassies must be able to shred, burn, and generally eradicate within fifteen to twenty minutes all the cables and classified and semi-classified documents they are storing at any given time. That is the theory. In practice, embassies are overflowing with paper that would take hours or even days to reduce to confetti. For the next week, Gauthier mounted a meticulous search-and-destroy operation, winnowing through files and carrying bundles of paper to the shredder. On at least three occasions, the machine gave up the ghost, blowing out the electrical fuses under the workload. But by late November, the job was done. The files had been reduced to a manageable volume. The boxes of confetti, Taylor mused, could have served for a decent ticker-tape parade.

If we ever have anything to celebrate, he thought ruefully.

8

RICHARD QUEEN AND DICK MOREFIELD had tasted an hour of careless freedom "lollygagging", as they called it, through the stinking narrow alleyways of Tehran known as *kouches*, after leaving Anders and his group on that rainy afternoon of November 4. But the odds had been stacked against them and their companions as they followed their circuitous route in the direction of the Morefield home.

It was Queen who first heard the sounds of pursuit. He turned and saw a handful of khaki-clad militiamen, waving their submachine guns, yelling, and chasing them. "Stop!" one of the pursuers screamed. "CIA! Stop." Then there was a babble of Farsi, and one of the guards fired his rifle into the air.

"Keep walking," Morefield whispered. "Don't run. Keep your eyes straight ahead. Don't give them a reason to shoot *at* us rather than over our heads."

"Well, it was a pretty good idea at the time," Queen said wistfully. "Now I guess we'll never get to play cards and sip gin at your house."

The militiamen — Queen recognized one of them as having been among the group he'd encountered just outside the consular door — surrounded the Americans. Queen, tall, pale-faced, so transparently Western with his thick-framed glasses, knew he couldn't possibly bluff his way out of this. The guards aimed their weapons at the Americans' chests and tied their hands. Resistance would have been futile.

The guards hustled their new captives toward the embassy grounds, whose walls were now decorated with the trappings of the revolution. Placards condemning Carter and all Americans were being plastered to the brick. Queen noticed the Iranians leaving floral wreaths at the gates — tributes to the militants inside. Some of the occupiers had already thrown down prayer rugs in the courtyard, where they would kneel several times a day, facing Mecca, and chant their prayers. The guards went to the gates and spoke through the bars, gesturing at the Americans. There was a brief discussion, and then the gates were unlocked. Queen and his colleagues were marched inside. He heard the gate slam behind him and the chain being secured. He was suddenly struck with a terrible sense of gloom.

Queen spent the first hours in a small room in the ambassador's residence, bound and sightless and terrified. In the evening, the blindfold was removed and he was escorted downstairs to the kitchen. There a number of young women in revolutionary garb were trying to plumb the mysteries of North American refrigeration. They had managed to open a giant meat-freezer, and were piling mounds of frozen beefsteak on a counter.

They were arguing among themselves, as Queen and a half-dozen other Americans watched, bemused. One of the women threw a frozen steak onto a frying pan atop the stove and turned up the heat. The meat sizzled and quickly turned black.

She picked it up with a fork and threw it on a plate, placing it in front of Queen. "Eat," she said. Queen's guard untied his hands — the thin nylon cord was cutting into his wrists — and he picked up the steak and began chewing. "No point asking for a knife and fork," Queen told himself. But, as they bit into the beef, Queen and the other Americans realized it was still frozen solid inside. They gnawed for a few minutes at the superficially cooked meat, and finally gave up. The "cooks" watched them curiously, and Queen had to force back a smile.

The next day, a male guard took him out of the ambassadorial residence and escorted him to a building at the rear of the embassy compound. He thought it was a warehouse. "Where are you taking me?" he asked. "Quiet," someone barked into his left ear. "You will not speak."

He was led down a stairway, and the blindfold was removed. What he saw sent a chill through his body. Two or three dozen Americans, all men, were kneeling or sitting in a hallway, hands secured behind them, and most were wearing white blindfolds. One or two had been tied down in chairs, and they were facing a wall. Queen gasped, and a strangled cry came from his throat. "Silence," one of the guards screamed.

Queen would never forget this first glimpse of his home for the next hundred days: a badly lit and poorly ventilated basement area that would become known as the "Mushroom Inn". He stared at the faces of his fellow captives; on those that were unmasked, he saw terror and despair, and he smelt death — the death of hope.

The capture of the American embassy in Tehran by right-wing Islamic fundamentalists had hastened the end of the last semblance of representative government in Tehran. Two days later, on November 6, the country's prime minister, Mehdi Bazargan, a moderate, resigned his office. Bazargan was a small, balding engineer with a white goatee and a callused knob on his forehead — the mark of a devout Moslem who crouched in prayer five times a day. He had been the titular head of the Iranian government since the Ayatollah's return from Paris in February, but real power lay in the hands of the fifteen-member Revolutionary Council, a group hand-picked by Khomeini from among the country's clergy and his lay lieutenants. The council, taking its cue from the Ayatollah, controlled the Islamic tribunals which had ordered the execution of 630 "enemies of the state", and it oversaw the Islamic Guard, a militia set up to protect the country's more powerful mullahs. Bazargan had protested in vain the firing squads and the jury-rigged tribunals. Twice before, he had submitted his resignation to Khomeini, but it had been refused. Now, with the U.S. embassy in the hands of religious fanatics, he saw his position as intolerable. To make it worse, the militants described him as a "traitor" for having met with the Americans in Algiers two weeks before. "A traitor?" he cried. "I, who spent years in prison for my opposition to Pahlavi?" On resigning, he described his government as "a knife with no blade" and handed the symbolic reins of power to the emerging theocrats waiting in the wings.

With Bazargan gone, Khomeini felt the time right to set his political plans into motion. The Revolutionary Council became the official government of the transitional period, acting, as always, at the whim of the *taqih*, or supreme religious leader, Khomeini. An Assembly of Experts was created to draft a new constitution that would formally establish Iran as a theocratic state. The constitution said that henceforth the nation would be ruled by a "just, brave, and popularly accepted theologian who is abreast of the times." This theologian would have the power to dissolve Parliament, dismiss the president, and veto any legislation that was deemed contrary to Islamic law.

It was the dawn of Khomeini's long-awaited Islamic state. Moderate Iranians grumbled quietly that "the tyranny of the throne has been replaced by the tyranny of the turban."

And on Tehran's Embassy Row, a European diplomat caused some furtive chuckles at a reception when he quipped: "What do you do when faced with a mad geriatric case?"

Seven thousand miles away, President Carter grappled with the same question, and none of the answers were satisfactory. The Clark–Miller mission had gone aground in Istanbul. It was an awful embarrassment. Relying on some assurances from moderate Iranians close to the sources of power in Tehran, the Carter administration had sent the two men jetting toward Iran, only to have Khomeini announce that he would not see them. Ramsey Clark spent a few desultory days in the Turkish capital, seeking out contacts within the Palestine Liberation Organization, but nothing much came of this venture.

Midway through the first week of the hostage crisis, PLO leader Yassir Arafat appeared in Tehran, wearing the robes of an international peacemaker. Arafat let it be known that he was ready to intercede on behalf of the Americans, to negotiate for their release. Although there were suspicions in Washington about Arafat's motives, the president was ready to try anything: there were few enough counters on the checkerboard, and none could be easily dismissed. Besides, the PLO had helped several hundred Americans escape from Beirut when civil war erupted in Lebanon in 1976. It was apparent that Arafat was out to make some public-relations points for his organization, but Washington was not about to foreclose on any options. So the PLO's intervention was quietly encouraged by the White House and the State Department.

Israeli intelligence was greatly interested in the PLO action. And worried. They smelled an elaborate con-job. Israeli agents in Tehran were convinced that the PLO was busily working both sides of the fence to gain maximum advantage from the hostage crisis. The Mossad (the Israeli intelligence organization) made careful note of their observations, and forwarded them to Washington. For example, just before Arafat had flown to Tehran, he was quoted as having told a Paris-based Arab newspaper: "We dismantled the biggest spy centre of the United States in Iran." Was this an empty boast, or had the PLO indeed played a crucial role in the embassy takeover? The evidence suggested the latter.

Israeli intelligence also noted that the PLO and certain elements of the "Iranian underground" had clasped hands during the 1960s. Terrorist camps in Lebanon, Iraq, and South Yemen, under the aegis of PLO splinter groups, had opened their doors to Iranian militants, and the curriculum included such items as psychological warfare and the use of hostages as bargaining chips. In 1974, the Israelis maintained, the PLO's military arm, Al Fatah, began training members of Iran's Muhajadin movement, hard-line right-wing Muslims who are widely believed to have engineered the November 4 embassy takeover.

Did Washington want names? Tel Aviv had an interesting file on Sadeq Ghotbzadeh, a close Khomeini lieutenant, who had been educated in the United States and Canada, had been asked to leave the former for his political activities, and, in 1970, had undergone training at a PLO-linked terrorist school. Khomeini had elevated Ghotbzadeh to minister in charge of Iranian radio and television, and he was marked for even higher things.

Arafat himself was no stranger in Iran. Just after the Shah had departed early in 1979, Arafat had appeared in Tehran and begun sending down roots into the country's political jungle. In February, he had appeared at ceremonies marking the opening of the PLO mission in the capital city — not coincidentally, the organization took over the building recently vacated by the Israeli mission. Nor was it much of a secret that Arafat had offered his services to Khomeini as a consultant in setting up an Iranian internal security service, SAVAMI. He had also offered medical assistance from the so-called "Palestinian Red Crescent", and stood ready to dispatch Palestinian engineers and other technicians to the troubled Iranian oilfields. The PLO tendrils slowly spread throughout the country.

The Mossad believed that PLO activities in Iran may have gone deeper, perhaps extending as far as the embassy takeover itself. Here the evidence was more sketchy, but no less provocative. There had been reports that Palestinians wearing *kafiyas*, the Palestinian headdress, and speaking Arabic were among the six hundred who swarmed over the American compound walls on November 4. The Italian weekly *Il Settimanale* carried a sensational report some months later that Arafat was paid $10 million for his help in organizing the attack on the embassy. Furthermore, there were reports that Arafat had taken a hand in the training of the Revolutionary Guards.

The U.S. State Department studied this information with

great interest — and took no action. With its silence, it tacitly encouraged Arafat to do what he could. Such was the scope of American desperation in that first week of November.

From Tehran there was some bad news, and some good. The militants happily released a letter, purportedly signed by thirty-three of the American captives, in which the Carter administration was urged to expel the Shah from the United States. The president was heard to utter to an aide, "These last two days have been the worst I've had."

At the end of the first week following the seizure came word that Khomeini had ordered the release of thirteen women and blacks.

At a press conference in Tehran soon after their release, the thirteen gave details of their captivity to an audience of more than two hundred correspondents. The listeners were told that men and women prisoners had been carefully segregated within the walls. Most of the men were kept in the "Mushroom Inn", and the women, guarded by Iranian girls wearing *chadors* and carrying guns, were herded into two bungalows on the grounds. The typical day for both groups began at 6:30 a.m. The ropes were removed from the captives' wrists, and they were escorted to the bathrooms. Conversation was strictly forbidden. Breakfast, to everyone's surprise, was plentiful, even though the fare was bland. Bread, butter, and cheese were available in quantity. After the meal, smokers were permitted one of their three cigarettes per day. Non-smokers had their hands tied again. Some of the non-smokers, jealous of those few extra minutes of freedom accorded to the smokers, asked for cigarettes. As one of the freed captives told newsmen, "They coughed and everything, and finally it got to be better to be tied up than to try to smoke."

Treatment of the captives varied, depending on the personalities of the guards. Some of the students kept their clusters of prisoners blindfolded all day. Some captives were forced to sit motionless on chairs for up to sixteen hours, and for those used to regular exercise, this became a torture. One

Marine, Kevin Hermening, fell ill after three days of this treatment, and begged the guards to allow him some exercise time. They relented, and most of the hostages were allowed two brief exercise periods a day in a heavily guarded outdoor enclosure.

One practice never varied, however: the psychological pressure. Hostages were awakened from their pallets during the night and subjected to noisy anti-American harangues. "Your countrymen have forgotten about you," the guards taunted. "They would like you dead." There were endless interrogations about alleged American spying in Iran. James Hughes, a thirty-year-old hostage, was blindfolded and made to sit on a table while questions were fired at him from all sides.

The general strategy for treating the hostages involved disorientation and submission. They were ordered not to speak to one another, and had to ask permission of their captors for the most minor things, such as the right to drink a glass of water. They even had to seek permission to go to sleep. "They were our mothers and fathers," one of the hostages said. Out of this grew a humiliating dependency.

Rumours had circulated among the Americans that executions might soon begin. Some of the hostages overheard whispered conversations about "shootings". The militants were worried about an American rescue attempt, and they discussed how they would retaliate against their captives. But a number of the Americans, familiar with the writings of the Koran, reassured the rest by telling them the Islamic scripture expressly forbade the killing of hostages.

In those early days, before the Americans were granted a little more leeway by their captors, they took heart from another discovery: a handful of their colleagues had indeed escaped. "We managed to take an accurate nose count, and there were some not accounted for," one of the hostages said later. A half-dozen or so had managed to get away. That had to be the explanation. The other possibility — that they had been killed during the "invasion" — was not even considered.

In the long and boring hours of confinement, the hostages, with nothing better to do, took stock of their captors. There were the ones to avoid at all costs, like the guard nicknamed Hamid the Liar, a chronic bully who delighted in telling his charges that the CIA had forbidden their relatives in the United States to write to them, indeed had told parents and siblings that the hostages would never be freed. Surprisingly, the bullies were a small minority. Most of the guards, as time wore on, began to treat the Americans civilly. At the same time, they grew sloppy. Richard Queen, for one, noticed that they were careless in tying his hands before sleep. During the night, he could easily free himself and sleep comfortably, but he always remembered to tie the ropes around his own wrists when he awoke the next morning.

Queen also noticed that the captors seemed untrained in the use of their firearms. Often the weapons were fired accidentally, and two of the guards actually injured themselves in this way. The Americans also got a great laugh from the embarrassment of their captors when they were accidentally confronted by women while escorting their charges to the bathrooms. Whenever this occurred, they quickly hustled the male prisoners away, shouting angrily at the female guards.

The average age of the militants, who numbered about four hundred, was twenty-two, and despite scepticism in the West, most were indeed students. Most, too, had majored in the hard sciences — mathematics, chemistry, engineering, and medicine. A few were theological students. About a quarter of them were women, who wore either the dark-blue head-scarves or the full *chador*. The men favoured U.S. khaki army jackets, and they sported light beards or thick moustaches.

It quickly became evident that their seizure of the American embassy and its occupants was no spontaneous and random act of revolution. The militants were well organized. At the top of the hierarchy was an eight-member central council, which met on alternate days. They were guided by the social and religious philosophies of two men: Khomeini, whose "man" on the council was a forty-one-year-old colleague named Muhammad Kho'ini; and Ali Shari'ati, an Islamic radical and thinker who had been killed under mysterious circumstances in England.

The militants were further organized into committees: operations, documentation, security, logistics, guard duty, and public relations. The latter committee was most visible, preparing propaganda broadcasts for Western consumption and selecting journalists who were sympathetic to their cause, while banning those whose reports were "unfavourable". One of the best-known of the propagandists was "Mary", as she was called in her television appearances. In real life Mary was Nilofar Ebtekar, a twenty-one-year-old chemistry student who had lived for several years in Pennsylvania, where she had presumably learned about the power of the mass media.

But for all their revolutionary zeal, the militants knew little about the dynamics of international politics or about the workings of embassies. As they plundered the embassy files which had not been destroyed, they seized on anything that could be construed as evidence of American malfeasance. Many of their deductions were farfetched: a State Department report on the insurrection of the Kurds, for example, was touted as "proof" that the United States was secretly backing the Kurdish movement for autonomy. The evidence did not stand up well under international scrutiny.

The militants also came upon a huge cache of counterfeit American dollars, German deutschmarks, and Iranian rials in an embassy vault. Here, they cried, was evidence that the Americans had intended to undermine the local economy by polluting it with phoney money. But Washington's explanation was more believable: the counterfeit bills had been brought to the embassy by an Iranian, and the embassy was seeking to track down the counterfeiters. Again, the lurid evidence evaporated.

But these were minor setbacks, of little consolation to Washington. The important psychological victories were all made by the militants and their spiritual leader. Late in November, Khomeini taunted President Carter in a speech by saying that the president did not "have the guts to engage in a military operation" against Iran. The president, according to his aides, went into an "ice-cold rage". He paced the floor of the Oval Office, furious that Khomeini would interpret the American policy of patient international diplomacy as a sign of weakness and lack of resolve.

Out of this rage came Carter's decision to order the 80,000-ton carrier *Kitty Hawk* and five warships into the Persian Gulf to join the carrier *Midway* and twelve other ships already there. Aboard the carriers were approximately 125 jet bombers and fighters. At a news conference, the president hinted darkly of "other measures" available to the Americans if diplomacy did not work. And as the sabres were rattled, the Pentagon was ordered to push ahead with its ultra-secret, long-range plans for a contingency rescue operation.

9

*I*T STARTED WITH THE NUMBERS. They weren't right. They didn't compute, fit together. Ninety. Sixty-five. Forty-three. Thirteen. Fifty. So many soldiers out of step.

Pelletier had the time, the luxury, to think about the numbers. Initially, it was more like a mental game than a journalistic endeavour. Where did the trail begin? they would ask him later. Where did you first sniff out the "error" in the public record? But he wouldn't remember. It was like that. Maybe it was the fortuitous meeting of a lot of stray doubts, little bits of inconsistencies and evasions, hints. Hopes, maybe. There's a story here, if you ferret enough. A newsman's instinct — and imagination.

He would be in his car, crossing the Roosevelt Bridge to Virginia in the evening rush hour, the radio tuned to an all-news station. In the middle of a report on the hostage crisis, a number. "Sixty-five American hostages are in their third week of captivity, and officials here..." In the last three days, three different numbers.

Maybe it was even boredom. Pelletier was familiar with Washington pack journalism. It came with the job. A thousand newsmen writing a thousand pieces that were interchangeable, day in and day out. Shift a verb here and an adjective there, trim a quote, reverse a paragraph or two, and you were in the mainstream.

Jonestown, his last big story, had been different. Pelletier had flown down to the site of the mass suicide in Guyana, the People's Temple camp created by religious fanatic Jim Jones. He had seen the bodies, face down in the vegetation and the dirt — men, women, and children. It was all dread and horror, and he had written about it, without searching for angles or innovative leads. He had seen and smelled a mass graveyard. The story wrote itself. Pelletier could not even bear to reread what he had written.

But the hostage story was becoming drudge work, after fourteen days of covering the dreary State Department briefings and the White House briefings and the Pentagon briefings and the briefings on Capitol Hill, and the background briefings on upcoming briefings. So maybe Pelletier was looking for a loose thread, something he could call his own. Maybe his motives were all wrong, if motives count for anything in the news business.

By mid November he had found a thread and when he began tugging at it, it took on a life of its own. And it bothered the hell out of him. To clear his head, he had begun taking long walks through Washington, but nothing could stop the incessant mental arithmetic that now obsessed him.

As he stepped off the curb at 15th and Pennsylvania, a block from the White House, an oncoming car missed him by inches. "Asshole," the driver screamed, pointing at the red light. Pelletier swore back in colourful French. He knew he was becoming irritable and distracted, that he would remain so until he had untied the Gordian knot of numbers.

He recalled a snippet from a State Department press briefing on November 6. Hodding Carter, III, the deputy Undersecretary of State who normally handled these daily briefings, was being unusually circumspect even by his rigid standards.

QUESTION: "Why are you still uncertain about the number of Americans [in the embassy] — sixty to sixty-five?"

CARTER: "Because we haven't sent anybody in to count them."

QUESTION: "No, I understand that. But theoretically, you

would start off with the total number that you had, those who are outside might be accounted for, and those who are not would be assumed to be inside."

CARTER: "This might be if you had people roaming the streets counting, but we have some difficulties right in through there."

QUESTION: "All right."

But it wasn't "all right", Pelletier thought, not by any stretch of the most ingenuous imagination. Surely it would not be beyond the resources of the United States of America to determine exactly how many of its nationals were being held prisoner in one of its embassy compounds. My God, there were next of kin to notify, there was paperwork to prepare in the rabbit warrens of the State Department. Confusion about the number of people involved might be understandable if there were a total breakdown of communications between Washington and Tehran. But that wasn't the case. State was in constant touch with its chargé d'affaires over there, Bruce Laingen. They were talking to Iranian officials. And the Western embassies in Tehran were surely sending volumes of information on to Washington.

Striding by the spiked fence that marked the White House perimeter, Pelletier recalled another exchange during a recent State briefing, at which Hodding Carter quoted from the Freedom of Information Act to justify the government's refusal to issue a list of the hostages' names. "Our legal authorities," Carter had said somewhat disdainfully in reply to a question, "say we have the legal discretion to determine that to release the names and other information would constitute a clear and unwarranted invasion of the hostages' privacy."

Pelletier forced back a sardonic chuckle. It was so bizarre. Here were several dozen Americans, blindfolded, bound hand and foot, threatened with show trials, presumably ill-fed, prodded by guns in the hands of terrorists, and their government was talking about "invasion of privacy".

Pelletier passed a newsstand opposite the Old Executive Office building and glanced at the headline of the capital edition of the *Washington Post*. The menacing eyes of the Ayatollah Khomeini jumped off the front pages. Pelletier recalled the news photos of mass murderer Charles Manson, that malevolent glare of a madman who would entertain no doubts about the morality of his mission. Pelletier was fascinated by Khomeini. His favourite pastime was to draw doodles of the turbaned figure. His felt-tip caricatures filled entire notebooks: Khomeini riding atop a guided missile, waving sticks of dynamite with the fuse lit, or pulling the feathers from the rump of the American eagle. He supposed it was a way of combating the dread that the man engendered in people. Doodle him into lunacy. Render him harmless with a few strokes of the pen, with captions lifted from the *Little Green Book* — the outrageous sayings of the Ayatollah Ruhollah Khomeini.

The reporter turned into the building at 1750 Pennsylvania Avenue. The elevator took him to the tenth floor, where the United States Information Agency library is located. The library, restricted by law to Agency staff and the city's 1,400 foreign correspondents (U.S. newsmen are barred), is a mine of information — clippings and reference material and government reports. He identified himself as Jean Pelletier, Washington correspondent for the Montreal French-language daily *La Presse*, and the girl chatted with him briefly in broken high-school French. Pelletier complimented her on her syntax. She directed him to the appropriate clipping files, filled with thick folders of newsprint that had not yet been microfilmed. Pelletier gathered up five pounds of clippings, dating back to November 5, and carried them into the reading room.

"This is where it begins," Pelletier told himself, and tried to push the crazy dance of numbers from his mind. Before digging into the stack of clippings, he put his wild hunch under the intellectual microscope. What did he know?: (A) State was being unusually coy about how many of its people were being held hostage, which suggested strongly that (B) it felt this information to be dangerous because (C) some of the Americans in Tehran were "on the loose" and no one wished to tip off the Iranians. (Pelletier admitted to himself there might be one or two fanciful leaps of logic here, but he trusted his instincts and pressed on.)

It was logical to assume that some diplomats in Tehran had escaped the net thrown over the embassy on the morning of November 4. The awful confusion in the city would lend itself to this possibility. Someone might have called in sick that morning, or been on a tour of a provincial city, or even taken the morning off to play a game of tennis. During the storming of the compound, was it inconceivable that a small group might have escaped in the pandemonium? Not at all, he told himself. In fact, it was highly likely.

There was another possibility, suggested to him by the *La Presse* correspondent in the Middle East, Robert Pouliot. There were rumours that a number of Americans had already been taken from the embassy and placed in prisons in preparation for show trials. This could explain why the handful of neutral and Third World visitors allowed to visit the besieged compound were never permitted to see the entire complement of hostages.

Pelletier also knew that the Canadian embassy in Tehran was supplying Washington, via Ottawa, with a daily flow of information about political, economic, and social conditions in Iran. Canada was showing itself to be the most useful American ally in the crisis. Gilles Mathieu, the first minister at the Canadian embassy in Washington, had told him that much over lunch at the Foreign Service Club on K Street. Mathieu was something of a braggart about his contacts in Washington. This always made Pelletier uncomfortable, since he was familiar with the man's background: a French Canadian who had advanced in the department largely because of his elegant manners, his discretion, and his determination to prove that he was appointed for his competence rather than to fulfil the diplomatic service's French-Canadian quota. Mathieu was unhappy in the American capital; he wasn't overly fond of his boss, Ambassador Peter Towe, and he did not enjoy the careless manner of the American senators and congressmen whom he had to lobby regularly. He was so

happy to sit down with a fellow countryman — even a journalist — that he sometimes tended to talk too much.

"We really are helping the Americans in Iran," he had
told Pelletier. "Ambassador Taylor's cables are read here
avidly. He's doing a tremendous job."

Now, as he stared at the mound of *New York Times*
clippings, scenarios projected themselves in Pelletier's mind.
In seven years of journalism, he'd been down dozens of
dead-end streets, propelled by hunches that fizzled and tips
that came to nothing. A sudden collision with a brick wall of
reality is hardly uncommon in this profession, he told himself. The best thing you can do is decrease the risk of embarrassment by not sticking your neck out too far. After all, he
was in Washington, where more than two thousand journalists live and breathe for the story that would launch their
careers. Surely, if there was anything to his speculations,
someone else would have sniffed them out already, someone
with access to the inner councils of the State Department or
the Oval Office?

But what the hell, he finally told himself. The hook and
line are in the water, and it's a quiet day. So enjoy the fishing.

For two hours, Pelletier flipped through yards of
newsprint, searching for the elusive thread, the common
denominator. He neatly jotted down numbers in his
notebook. Beginning with the clippings of November 5, the
day after the embassy seizure in Tehran, he scanned the *Times*
dispatches and tracked down the numbers. The banner story
from Tehran on that day was a dispatch from the Reuters
news agency. The first paragraph noted that Muslim students
had seized "about ninety Americans".

In the report on the next day, in a Washington-datelined
story, the *Times* referred quite specifically to sixty Americans.
Paragraph seven contained an interesting tidbit. "The State
Department," correspondent Bernard Gwertzman wrote,
"said there were believed to be 65 American officials and
dependents in Iran, and about 60 in the embassy at the time
of the takeover."

Pelletier noted the discrepancy, and also that chargé

d'affaires Bruce Laingen and two of his colleagues were at the Foreign Ministry when the embassy was overwhelmed. But that still left some dangling numbers. It was highly unusual for the *Times* to remain so vague, he told himself.

By midweek, the *Times* had its own man in Tehran — John Kifner — and he was referring to "60 or so American hostages...". And on November 7, the Associated Press carried a fascinating item, quoting State Department spokesman David Passage. In addition to being uncertain about identities, the department was unwilling to release a list of the hostages' names because the "publication of names might instigate a search by Iranian students for people who are not listed."

By mid afternoon, the numbers were buzzing in his head like flies and he knew he was getting nowhere. "*Un maudit mélange,*" he told himself. "A goddam mess." He'd already missed the daily State Department briefing and the White House briefing, and all he had to show for his work was a fool's trail of numbers. He threw on his overcoat and walked out, despondent.

10

J UST AS THE GREAT DEPRESSION forced many economists to junk their articles of faith, and Watergate forever changed the way Americans view the mechanics of executive government, so did the events of 1979 and early 1980 in Iran compel diplomacy to take a rigorous look at itself. For some ambassadors, like Canada's Ken Taylor, diplomacy was dealt a mortal blow in the streets of Tehran, and much of the injury was self-inflicted.

For the most part, the diplomatic code of "extraterritoriality" — the special immunity granted to envoys, their families, their premises, and even their menial servants in foreign lands as part of centuries-old tradition — has been rarely breached. (Before November 4, 1979, on only one occasion has a U.S. diplomat been held against his will by a foreign government. That was in 1948, when Chinese Communists detained Consul-General Angus Ward and his staff and held them incommunicado for a year.) Even in wartime, this sanctity has been respected.

Occasionally, this lofty regard for diplomatic privilege has been carried to the absurd. When a fire broke out at the Soviet embassy in Ottawa in 1956, the Russians would not allow firemen into the building until all files had been emptied and the documents carried away by the staff. A hundred Ottawa firefighters stood by helplessly. By the time the Soviets had "sanitized" the building, it had been thoroughly gutted by the flames.

Through fire and abuse, totalitarianism and mobs, diplomatic privilege had survived the test of time since the Italians of the sixteenth century first established permanent ambassadorial missions — an event that coincided with the advent of permanent armies and statesmanship. Diplomats, who were categorized by the Congress of Vienna in 1815, decided they could not function if they were subjected to the whims of sheriffs, bailiffs, process-servers, and the mob. It was unthinkable that an envoy of a foreign prince, engaged in the delicate chore of trying to keep two nations from one another's throats, should be clapped in irons for some minor offence. So the diplomat was placed beyond the reach of civil and criminal law. An embassy became sacrosanct ground, off limits to the authorities (and the rowdy population) of the host nation. The diplomat's home truly became his castle; no one could cross the threshold without the risk of causing an international incident. Indeed, the host government was expected to protect the grounds of the embassy through the force of arms, if necessary. Little of this was ever codified in legal paragraphs, but it carried the force of tradition. The Islamic nations and Oriental rulers, for example, refused to sign the Congress of Vienna, but under strong pressure from the West, they agreed to honour the privileged status of the diplomatic corps. The Vienna Convention of 1961 converted the tradition into a written international agreement, and it was this convention which the United States quoted when it asked the World Court in The Hague for a ruling against Iran.

Thus the Iranian embassy seizure sent shock waves to the very core of the diplomatic tradition. Never before had a large-scale takeover of an embassy compound, and the psychological brutalizing of its occupants for many months, received the sanction of a host government. "For the first time," said Dr. Jules Davids, professor of diplomatic history at Washington's Georgetown University, "we have a government that couldn't care less about diplomatic immunity or international law." Behind the angry taunts and threats of the embassy occupiers was the acquiescence of a government that sat in the United Nations, that produced a significant share of the world's oil, and that occupied a strategic geographical position in the Middle East.

At the U.N., the reaction was predictable. Men of all colours, creeds, and ideologies angrily shuffled their papers, waved their fists, and made the appropriate noises. Even the dictatorships and the Iron Curtain countries (the U.S.S.R. excepted) expressed measured shock. Gaddafi of Libya, the patron of several world terrorist movements, offered any help he could give to free the American hostages, and the White House, through the unlikely intermediary of presidential brother Billy Carter, sampled the offering. Pakistan announced that the Iranian action was a violation of Islamic doctrine. East Germany swung away from the Soviet line and declared that diplomats should be inviolate "under all circumstances", even, presumably, if they were found to be engaging in espionage.

But on Embassy Row in Tehran, silence reigned. As distraught as the ambassadors may have been at the turn of events, most remained publicly mute. Their private anger shrivelled when they were called upon to denounce the Iranian government's inability — or refusal — to put an end to the hostage-holding. For Ken Taylor, in his first ambassadorial post, the collective arthritis of the diplomatic corps was infuriating and disappointing.

Taylor and a handful of other Western ambassadors — Troels Munk of Denmark, Chris Beebe of New Zealand, and Sir John Graham of Great Britain — were straining at the bit to organize a concerted diplomatic protest, which they believed the Iranian authorities could not ignore. Taylor, of course, had his own private reasons for wanting to bring the full force of diplomatic pressure down on the Khomeini regime — he was becoming increasingly nervous about his six guests. Munk, Beebe, and Sir John knew of his double role, sympathized with his delicate position, and shared his frustration over the ostrich-like attitude of the diplomatic corps.

In the last week of November, this informal group managed to bring fifty-nine ambassadors and chiefs of missions together for a strategy session at the Turkish embassy.

(Twelve Soviet-bloc ambassadors and the Chinese envoy were invited but declined to attend. Included in the no-shows was the Czech ambassador, the dean of the diplomatic corps in Tehran, who, according to age-old practice, is the defender of the privileges and immunities of the diplomatic body from injuries and encroachments of the host government.)

Taylor and his colleagues were hoping that the group could agree on a stern message to the Iranian Foreign Ministry. After all, they argued, the continued holding of the American hostages undermined all that they stood for. The flouting of their collective immunity threatened them one and all. But they were too frightened to act. Taylor listened with dismay as the diplomats agonized over the proposed text of the message. It was obvious that Khomeini's unpredictability had emasculated them. "A harsh letter would only make the Iranians more intractable," one of them said. "We must move carefully; after all, we are skating on perilously thin ice here," ran another argument. "There are such complexities here that my government will have to study carefully," said a third. For more than an hour, the ambassadors rationalized an orderly retreat, on the pretext that the takeover of the U.S. embassy was a temporary and isolated aberration.

As they filed back into their official cars, whispering in small groups, Taylor was struck by a depressing thought: the diplomatic corps would thereafter be a lame duck in the crisis. The cop-out was complete. The Canadian ambassador was increasingly aware that he would have to act alone.

A few days later, the rout of the ambassadors was made complete, at the hands of a Western-educated Iranian who sensed their disarray. Abolhassan Bani-Sadr, the acting foreign minister who also held the finance portfolio, invited the entire diplomatic corps, eighty strong, to the Foreign Ministry for a briefing. Dutifully, the envoys postponed their other appointments and trooped over to the meeting. They recognized that Bani-Sadr, in almost daily communication with the Ayatollah Khomeini, would surely be handing them a message from the imam. The message would likely have to do with the unfolding of events at the United Nations, where the

While it appears to be a casual photo of a get-together in a suburban North American home, this shot was in fact taken by John Sheardown in his Tehran living room during the three months in which he and his wife, Zena, hid four of the six American fugitives. From left to right: Mark Lijek, Cora Lijek, Bob Anders, Zena Sheardown, Canadian embassy counsellor Roger Lucy, Lee Schatz.

The façade of the residence of the Canadian ambassador to Tehran, where Ken Taylor hid two of the American fugitives, Joe and Kathy Stafford.

John Sheardown was chief immigration officer at the Canadian embassy in Tehran when he and his wife, Zena, hid four of the six fugitive Americans in their home for three months. Sheardown received the Order of Canada, but he threatened to return it a year later because his wife and Pat Taylor had not also been honoured.

Rejected by his countrymen and in ill health, the Shah and his wife, Empress Farah, left Iran forever in January 1979. In an emotional farewell, one of the ruler's still-loyal troops bent to kiss the feet of The Shadow of God on Earth.

Members of Iran's all-powerful Islamic Revolutionary Council visited the embassy compound on the ninth day of the seizure. Controversy still surrounds the extent to which the Ayatollah's government actively supported the actions of the militants.

Kim King was a tourist in Tehran and present in the consular building during the embassy takeover. He successfully escaped from the embassy with Anders and his group, and left Iran by airplane that day.

During the early days of their captivity, the American hostages were blindfolded and exhibited by their captors to the street mobs in front of the embassy.

Seen here through the padlocked gates of the American embassy, the militants holding the fifty-three hostages kneel in prayer.

Pat Taylor, wife of Canadian ambassador Ken Taylor, who worked as a research microbiologist in Tehran during the time she played hostess to two of the American fugitives.

Jean Pelletier in his office in Washington's National Press Building.

The Ayatollah Khomeini waves to a crowd of his followers from the balcony of his Tehran residence. The most serious error the Americans made at the time of the Islamic revolution was to underestimate the virulence of Khomeini's anti-Americanism and the popularity of his policies among the Iranian masses.

On January 30, 1980, Iranian
Foreign Minister Sadeq
Ghotbzadeh told a Tehran news
conference that ''Canada will pay''
for having smuggled out the six
Americans. A onetime student at
the University of British Columbia,
Ghotbzadeh was later forced to
leave the United States in 1967 for
his anti-Shah activities.

Abolhassan Bani-Sadr was the
Ayatollah's acting foreign
minister at the time of the
embassy seizure. Although he is
one of the Ayatollah's most
faithful lieutenants, his more
moderate, diplomatic approach
to the hostage issue conflicted
with Khomeini's revolutionary
fanaticism; this forced the
Western-educated Bani-Sadr to
resign. Today Bani-Sadr is
President of the Islamic Republic
of Iran.

United States was still hopeful of a complete airing of the crisis that would include Iranian delegates. This meeting, they sensed, would be part of the background manoeuvring prior to the U.N. session. It was unthinkable that any of them should miss the meeting.

Bani-Sadr, always the cordial host, welcomed every one of them personally, with a handshake and a personal greeting. Taylor noted how easily Bani-Sadr, the ascendant revolutionary, mixed with the diplomats. He could be casual and chatty, the very model of tact and manner. While Sadeq Ghotbzadeh, the head of Iranian television and radio and the other high-ranking layman in the new government, would rant and rave and run roughshod over the toes of Western diplomats, Bani-Sadr could spread the balm with all the ease of a courtier.

Alternating between Farsi and French, Bani-Sadr opened his remarks in a conciliatory tone. He spoke with a softly modulated voice. He thanked the diplomats for attending in force. He assured them that Iran was striving to bring stability back to its dealings with the international community.

But as some of the older envoys, who had heard all this before, began to nod off in their chairs, the young minister jarred them awake by coming to the brutal point: "I would like you to prevail upon your governments to persuade the United States of its wrongdoing in Iran, and to recognize before all the nations of the world that the United States has systematically interfered in our affairs." Implicit in these words was the warning that the future of the hostages was inexorably linked to an apology from the President of the United States.

The diplomats were aghast. Erik Lang, the Swiss ambassador to Tehran, rose to his feet and told Bani-Sadr that any kind of compromise would be impractical as long as the Iranian government continued to support a patently illegal act such as the holding of the American embassy. Surely he could see that the United States would hardly apologize under such conditions.

Bani-Sadr glowered. In French, he snapped back, "Mr. Ambassador, I did not invite you here for a lecture on international law. I am telling you what our position is, and I would like your governments to be aware of that position." With the atmosphere of *politesse* shattered, the meeting quickly ended. The eighty men in the room had been given an object lesson: Bani-Sadr, the only "moderate" hopeful in the entire apparatus of the Iranian government, had shown his true colours. Behind his easy manner, Bani-Sadr was as committed to the humiliation of the American government as the most radical of mullahs.

Obviously, the reluctance of the ambassadors to rise in collective anger reflected the mood of their governments. The threatened disruption of Iran's oil imports to major industrial powers like West Germany and Japan was a critical factor. In addition, President Carter's order to freeze Iran's official assets in U.S. banks and in foreign branches of U.S. banks — assets calculated at the time to be in excess of $8 billion — worried foreign governments and bankers. They were afraid that other oil-producing nations might attempt to withdraw their own deposits from the United States in fear that these deposits would be frozen in a crisis. (OPEC held $45 billion in U.S. accounts.) West Germany expressed concern that Iran might shift to a currency other than the U.S. dollar in its oil dealings once the freeze was lifted. On November 23, Bani-Sadr threw a scare into world bankers by announcing that Iran intended to welsh on debts incurred abroad amounting to between $10 and $15 billion, a statement later repudiated by Iran's central bank.

Two days later, Iran's oil minister, Ali Akbar Moinfar, said an oil boycott would be imposed on countries hostile to Iran. This was widely taken to refer to any countries which allowed U.S. banks to freeze Iranian assets in their foreign branches. Meanwhile, the country would increase its daily oil production. The carrot-and-stick approach had its desired effect: governments in Europe and Japan wavered in their public support for the American position in the crisis.

Meanwhile, the varied estimates of the amount of

money that the exiled Shah, through the Pahlavi Foundation, had funnelled out of Iran for the use of himself and his family helped foster among American allies a growing cynicism about Washington's support of the monarch. How could an administration that placed such stock on morality, justice, and human rights throw its mantle over a man who had so enriched himself from Iran's resources? What kind of foolishness had impelled Washington to accept the Shah, and as a consequence trigger what President Carter himself called the gravest international crisis since the Second World War?

It was a question on which only history could make a judgment.

OTTAWA *Late November*

As Taylor's deep personal disappointment at the failure of diplomacy drove him to consider less orthodox solutions to the predicament of the houseguests, it was fortunate that he was not receiving detailed and dispassionate reports on how the "secret" was being guarded in Ottawa. Considering the broad hints, hairline leaks, and gossipy speculations that were rampant around Parliament Hill in the months of November and December, it is a marvel that the story was not blown in the early weeks of the crisis.

At first, of course, the lid was down tight. Both Joe Clark and Flora MacDonald were manic about the need for secrecy. The "need-to-know" principle was in effect — no matter how senior the official, in whatever department, he would not be informed of the presence of the houseguests unless such knowledge was crucial to the performance of his or her job. The most striking example of this policy was Defence Minister McKinnon's decision to keep the secret even from his senior Canadian Defence group, including the chief of staff himself, Admiral R. H. Falls. This was quite a feat, considering that McKinnon had initially been briefed on the houseguests by a senior intelligence official who worked directly under the admiral!

Ironically, it was Joe Clark and Flora MacDonald themselves — the very people who were most obsessed with confidentiality — who nearly let the secret slip out on the floor of
the House of Commons, the most public forum in all of
Canada. Luckily the press gallery had its mind on other things
during the emotional exchanges across the floor, which were
triggered by tough and nasty Liberal Party questioning. This is
the kinder assessment. Harsher critics might say the gallery
was shockingly inept in not picking up the provocative clues.

Minister MacDonald has described the three critical
months of the Tehran operation as akin to "living under the
gallows". In this analogy, she saw the Liberal Opposition,
notably Pierre Elliott Trudeau, among the ranks of the execu-
tioners. On an almost daily basis, and for reasons of their own,
Trudeau and Allan MacEachen, the Liberal critic for external
affairs, kept up a relentless attack on the Conservative government for its supposed "non-policy" on Iran.

This criticism reached a high point on November 26,
when Trudeau fired a blunt query at Prime Minister Clark:
"Has the prime minister considered, and has he in effect
gotten on the phone to talk to Helmut Schmidt, Margaret
Thatcher, Japanese Prime Minister Ohira, or the prime minister of Italy, because once harm is done to these hostages, there
is no guarantee that the United States will not say: 'Well,
nobody is willing to help us in this and we must act alone.'"

Across the aisle, Clark felt he could no longer keep the
information from the Opposition leader. The best way to
defuse this constant harrying from the other side of the
Commons floor, he reasoned, was to take Trudeau into his
confidence. Surely he would understand the need for discretion and non-partisanship in this crisis.

So, in the midst of the questioning, with the television
cameras following him, Clark crossed the floor and sat down
beside his political foe. He whispered, "Mr. Trudeau, there is
something important I have to tell you in connection with the
Iranian matter. Are you free later today?" Trudeau said he
had a meeting in Montreal but could, of course, cancel it. Still,
he would prefer not to. "Then let me give you the gist of it,"

Clark said. "We have given sanctuary to six Americans in Tehran. They are members of the diplomatic staff and they would otherwise be hostages, but they managed to get away and make contact with us."

Clark, sensitive to the niceties of the parliamentary process, made it clear that he was not asking Trudeau to cease all questioning. "I would just like to have your questions conditioned by this information," the prime minister said. Trudeau barely flinched. As Clark would recount later: "He thanked me, and that was it. That was his only reaction."

In the days following this disclosure, Trudeau indeed behaved as if nothing had changed. The very next day, again during Question Period, the Liberal leader said his party would "soon be condemning this government if it continues to take such standoffish attitudes" in the Iranian crisis.

Flora MacDonald was stunned. She glanced at Joe Clark and rose to her feet. The Speaker of the House acknowledged her. The few dozen reporters in the press gallery yawned, some making a note of the question but most showing little interest when Ms. MacDonald said that the prime minister had been a "staunch" supporter of the United States during the preceding twenty-four days "through actions, many of which cannot be publicly conveyed, and of which the honourable member [Trudeau] should be aware are taking place in everything we do."

Referring to the Liberal leader, she continued: "This is no time for grandstanding by him or anyone else. The question is much too serious because it involves not just the breaking of the Vienna Convention, but it involves the lives of human beings."

At this point, Hansard, the official record of Parliament, notes that Liberal M.P. Allan MacEachen made a petulant interruption: "It is about time you understood that——"

Ms. MacDonald continued, dismissing the interruption. "It involves the lives of American human beings who are hostages in Iran," she said. *"It involves as well the lives of Canadians who are in Iran—and that is something we must never forget."* In her barely controlled rage and astonishment at

Trudeau's persistent criticism, the minister (who had kept even her private secretary of eight years, Margaret Herman, in the dark about the houseguests) almost blurted out the secret in front of a national audience. But the members of the Ottawa press gallery missed the implication altogether. "They never even asked me about it later, thank God," MacDonald recounted months later. "I have never been able to lie without my face going all scarlet. It would have shown the truth."

The parliamentary reporters got another opportunity to peek under the lid of secrecy a week later as Pierre Trudeau, seeming to enjoy this game of cat and mouse, slammed the government for not making enough effort to whip up international indignation against Iran. "A month will have elapsed tomorrow since the taking of the hostages," he said. "We have not been effective."

This time it was Clark himself who took the floor. His comment was a circuitous one, but it should not have escaped the notice of veteran Commons reporters. "I repeat to the right honourable leader of the Opposition, who of all members in this House should understand the delicacy of the situation, that this is not a matter where the desire for domestic publicity should be allowed to interfere with the effectiveness of international action."

11

AS HE RUSHED through the massive foyer of the United Nations building in New York, *La Presse* correspondent Jean Pelletier reflected ironically that there was something about the vast tapestried hallways of the U.N., something about the hubbub of a hundred different nationalities, something about the earnest faces of the men and women who worked there, that cast a brief spell over even the most cynical. Surely, he thought, this institution, erected amid the chaos of the post-Second World War world, can bring some order and decorum to the relations between governments. Making his way to the National Security Council press lounge, he wished he could forget the U.N.'s sorry record in periods of crisis, the huge chasms between the platitudes and the performance.

In late November, the United States government had turned to the U.N. for a solution to the three-week hostage crisis in Iran. The fifteen-member Security Council, under American pressure, had already called for the immediate release of the hostages and, on November 23, the Carter administration had submitted a five-point proposal to Iran's representative, Ahmed Salamatian. The U.S. timetable included a Security Council meeting on the twenty-seventh, the simultaneous release of the hostages, and the creation of a U.N.-sponsored commission to investigate violations of human rights under the regime of the Shah. The Carter administration made a further concession: Iran could use American courts to lay its claim on the billions that the Shah had salted away in U.S. banks. The United States was also prepared to re-establish friendly relations with Iran, in accordance with the United Nations Charter.

Privately, President Carter did not expect Iranian authorities to embrace this package with gratitude. It was simply another step to bring Iran to some kind of bargaining position. Thus, when the revolutionary government came through with a counterproposal, through Ramsey Clark, optimism began to bubble. The counter-offer wasn't much really — an investigation of the Shah's regime coupled with the pledge to begin the process of evacuating the U.S. embassy — but it was a significant step beyond Iran's former intransigence. The Americans based their hopes on the fact that Iranian Foreign Minister Abolhassan Bani-Sadr, widely perceived as a moderate who viewed the hostages as a kind of albatross around the neck of his nation's economy and, indeed, its security, was expected to appear at the U.N. on December 1. Surely the Western-educated minister could be made to see the folly of the Iranian position.

These hopes were shared by the dozens of journalists who were waiting with Pelletier as the Security Council members met in a private session. When the delegates filed out to stretch their legs during the ten-hour meeting, they were besieged by TV cameramen and representatives of the written press. As the hours passed, Pelletier could sense his colleagues' growing anticipation. U.S. Secretary of State Cyrus Vance would surely be coming to meet with Bani-Sadr. The community of nations was preparing to tell Iran: "Enough. The hostages must be released."

On and on the delegates deliberated and the press corps kibitzed. Some seasoned U.N.-watchers, men and women who clung like good soldiers to the belief that rationality and civilized dealing among world leaders could solve any problem, predicted a breakthrough. Younger reporters nursed their rum and Cokes and plastic glasses full of beer and worried about deadlines. In his chair nearest the door, Pelletier glanced at his watch. Two more hours before filing time for the next day's first edition. He distractedly flipped through his ragged copy of that day's *New York Times*. "Why doesn't

Thomson come out?" he wondered aloud. (Bill Thomson was the Canadian U.N. delegate sitting as an observer in the meeting room; Canada was not a voting member of the fifteen-man Council in 1979.)

Finally, late in the afternoon, the doors swung open and the delegates began to file out. Donald McHenry, the United States ambassador, attracted the first press "scrum". Then came Waldheim, and pandemonium broke out among the newsmen pushing and stumbling and jostling for position. Pelletier collared Thomson and drew him off to a corner. All the delegates had roughly the same message: the Security Council would agree to postpone for three days a debate on a resolution condemning Iran to await the appearance of Bani-Sadr. The Iranian foreign minister had assured Waldheim that the American hostages would not be harmed in the interval. The Americans, once again, had compromised, agreeing to adopt a wait-and-see stance.

The day's only press conference was held by the Iranian delegate, Dr. Mansour Fahrang, accompanied by two young countrymen recently arrived in New York to prepare for the Bani-Sadr visit. The three men headed straight for the briefing room, reporters scurrying ahead to grab the best seats. Fahrang, who had once lectured at a California university, opened the proceedings by announcing that one of his associates would be reading a brief communiqué from the Iranian government. Then questions would be taken.

The communiqué was predictable in tone and content: a quick review of the Shah's crimes and the need for the Security Council to acknowledge the criminal collusion between the U.S. government and the Pahlavi regime. The hostages got scarcely a mention, except that the foreign minister would of course be raising the subject on Saturday in front of the Security Council. In the first row of seats, an American TV reporter had his hand up. "Mr. Fahrang," he said, "is it not true, yes or no, that the American hostages, who have now been held more than three weeks, are being brainwashed and subjected to other psychological pressures? Please just answer yes or no."

Fahrang sighed and shook his head. "This is so typical of

the American press," he replied, with professorial impatience. "You do not ask about the thousands of people killed, and the millions who suffered under the Shah. You just want to know about a few dozen Americans—"

"Mr. Fahrang," the reporter broke in, "are the hostages being brainwashed, yes or no?"

Another shake of the head. "Sir, obviously their circumstances are not entirely pleasant, but they are not being ill treated, certainly not nearly as badly as the American-supported Shah treated so many million Iranians before he fled the country. Now can we please have questions on other subjects."

For nearly an hour, the press conference continued in a similar tone, point and counterpoint, with a clear undercurrent of hostility. Fahrang kept repeating that the world must surely see the connection between the hostages and the American meddling in Iran prior to January 1979. Surely these two subjects could not be dissociated. Would America never understand? Finally, Fahrang and his colleagues gathered up their papers and stalked out of the room, brushing off further questions.

Skimming through his notes later, Pelletier would reflect on the terrible irony of what he had just witnessed: America being rapped on the knuckles, on its own soil, by agents of the very government that had kidnapped its nationals. And the kidnappers were impatient because the United States was not reacting in a "rational" way. What kind of ethical and moral surrealism is this, he wondered. When he put the question to a longtime United Nations observer, the man replied without hesitation: "Why, it's diplomacy, of course. Welcome to the real world."

The hopes of the Americans and their allies for a speedy resolution to the painful Iranian crisis were soon to be frustrated by the actions of one of the world's most eccentric and little-understood rulers, Ruhollah al-Musawi ibn Mustafa ibn Mustafa ibn Ahmad al-Musawi al-Khomeini. The Ayatollah's ancestors had been Indians from Kashmir who moved to the central Iranian town of Khomein, where Khomeini, the youngest of seven children, was born in 1900. His was a family steeped in the Islamic faith: his grandfather, his father (who was killed on a pilgrimage to Iraq when Khomeini was but nine months old), and his eldest brothers were all ayatollahs. When he was sixteen, he began his religious studies, and he later travelled to Qom, which some have described as the Oxford and Harvard of Shiism in Iran.

Some of his strongest recollections as a young man were those of Russian troops of occupation, milling through the town square during the First World War. And in the Second World War, American, British, and Russian troops seemed to be everywhere. As he would later remark, weak nations like Iran "are subjected to invasion and bullying in peacetime and in time of war." With no first-hand exposure to Western thought, Khomeini became a strict isolationist, and he never apologized for it. "Let them erect a wall around Iran and confine us inside this wall," he proclaimed. "We prefer this to the doors being open and plunderers pouring into our country."

Though they were the most bitter of antagonists, Khomeini and the Shah were in many respects alike. Both were obdurate and vindictive. They both had a simplistic view of the world — and of Iran's place in it. Neither would be contradicted, and they were both undisputed and ruthless leaders, because each felt he was guided by the Almighty. (The Shah: "Without God's support I would be a man like all the rest." Khomeini: "When I saw the scale of the [Islamic] revolution, I saw God in it. This cannot be the work of man.") Likewise, they were intolerant. Khomeini saw Marxists as ignorant "children"; the Shah said they were adults who "acted in a childish way". Both freely censored the press in the name of "popular feeling". Like the Shah's SAVAK, Khomeini's internal shock troops, the *komitehs*, made arbitrary arrests, issued summary verdicts, and indulged in public executions.

Khomeini's soft, almost diffident, voice belied the extent

of his authority over at least thirty-two million Muslims. Photographed in his customary cross-legged pose on the bare floor, the seventy-eight-year-old cleric would have appeared a benign, grandfatherly figure were it not for his hooded eyes, arching brows, and wide forehead. He was a kind of modern Abraham, who would, he freely admitted, plunge a dagger into his son's heart for the crime of adultery. His unmitigated ruthlessness was appalling to Western observers. "God willing," he said once, "reports of the Shah's affliction with cancer are true."

Khomeini was — and is — in every sense a zealot: ascetic, intensely spiritual, and cunningly political. This political involvement by "a man of the cloth", although puzzling to many Westerners, makes perfect sense to anyone familiar with the tenets of Shiism, the Muslim sect that makes up Iran's religious majority. Shiism is a splinter sect that grew out of a seventh-century schismatic dispute over who was the proper successor to Mohammed, the original prophet of Islam. (In most other Islamic countries, the more moderate Sunni sect predominates.) A key feature of Shiism is the central role of the *imams*, or high priests, who are regarded not only as the only true followers of the Prophet, but also as the rightful political rulers of Iran who have had their power usurped by the corrupt secular regime. Thus, as the foremost holy man of Iran, the Ayatollah Khomeini believes he has a God-given right to govern his country according to the fundamentalist tenets of his faith.

Although the priests had been meddlesome in the past, the Shah and his father had respected the "freedom of the pulpit", and the mosques where the mullahs increasingly preached their discontent were still regarded as inviolate. But in the early sixties, Khomeini became something more than an irritant. Elevated by the death of a noted ayatollah (a word meaning, roughly, "sign of God") to prominence in the religious hierarchy, Khomeini now used his position to launch a campaign of relentless opposition to government policy. In widely distributed public statements, he denounced the Shah's plans to give the vote to women, describing this as a blatant violation of Islam. He was arrested in 1962 for a number of violent speeches against an election bill.

But it was a year later, in 1963, that Khomeini achieved national prominence. This time the target of his outrage was a series of land reforms that the Shah hoped to incorporate into his famous Six-Point White Revolution. Khomeini became an energetic pamphleteer, issuing tracts in which he argued that the Koran held sacred the concept of sanctity of private property. His rabble-rousing inflamed theological students at Qom, whose demonstrations in turn led to a crackdown by SAVAK, the Shah's security police. The police arrested student leaders, and occupied mosques, shrines, and religious schools.

That year, during the early-summer holy days of Moharram, Khomeini's picture was splashed across the bazaars of Iran as a symbol of opposition to illegitimate authority. The names of Hossein and Hassan, martyred sons of Ali and the most venerated personages in the Shiite faith, were evoked in a campaign that crystallized around Khomeini. The Shah was forced to move against this threat to his authority. When the holy days ended, police went to the Khomeini residence before dawn on June 4 and arrested him. The word of his apprehension spread quickly. Within two hours, mobs had gathered in the Tehran bazaars, and the Shah's troops opened fire. Further rioting erupted in four other cities, and when the disruptions were finally quelled, thousands lay dead in the streets.

What followed was the most curious chapter in Khomeini's rapid ascendency. He was detained by SAVAK until early August, and then was released to house arrest! Rather than eliminate the man whose name was now on the lips of millions and thus risk creating a martyr, the Shah sought to alienate him from his followers. SAVAK issued a statement saying that Khomeini had reached an "understanding" with authorities to cease interfering in political matters. In return for mere detention in his private residence, Khomeini "agreed" to stop meddling in the "interests and law and order of the State".

But if the Shah believed that he had removed the

Ayatollah's sting, he miscalculated badly. On the eve of elections for a new parliament in October 1963, Khomeini claimed that the government was interfering in the balloting and ordered his followers not to vote. Once again, the doughty demagogue was removed from his home and thrown into jail. He was held for eight months, and then freed under the terms of a second "understanding" reached with authorities.

Yet no sooner was he liberated than Khomeini repudiated the understanding. By no means did his devout followers view this as a cop-out, an act of cowardice. On the contrary, Khomeini was behaving in accordance with the beliefs of Shiism, which sanctions the use of *taqiyah* (the Muslim equivalent of making a promise with one's fingers crossed) to conceal true feelings. Nevertheless, Khomeini kept a low profile for five months, restricting his activities to making tape-recorded sermons and dispatching copies quietly to key religious centres.

Khomeini was marshalling his thunder for the big blow-out. This finally came in October, when the Iranian parliament passed a bill to confer diplomatic immunity on American military personnel in Iran. A few days later, the Majlis passed another bill, accepting a $200-million loan from the United States for the purchase of military equipment. This was too much for Khomeini to swallow. It smacked of the capitulations to foreign powers that Iranian leaders had indulged in during earlier generations. Khomeini struck back, in the form of a pamphlet whose anti-American language would be recalled sixteen years later. He called the government action "disgraceful"; it would surely lead to the "bondage" of the Iranian people by the Americans. "...America is the land of the dollar," he roared, "and...the Iranian government needs dollars."

Wise to the ways of the throne, Khomeini must have realized that the Shah could not sit still in the face of such rhetoric and, when Iranian police once again swooped down on his residence, he could not have been overly surprised. They hustled him aboard a military plane and flew him to

Turkey, where he was kept under house arrest with the co-operation of Turkish authorities.

SAVAK issued the following statement:

"Since according to reliable information and sufficient evidence, Mr. Khomeini's attitude and provocations have been considered contrary to the interests of the people and to the security, independence, and territorial integrity of the state, he has been exiled from Iran effective November 4, 1964."

During his years in exile, Khomeini was both a proselytizer and a student of the ways of international diplomacy, especially as it had affected his native country. Thus, when the United Nations became the main forum of discussion on the matter of the hostages in the final days of November 1979, Khomeini paid close attention. And when Iran's acting foreign minister, Abolhassan Bani-Sadr, announced his intention to fly to New York and address the world community, the Ayatollah felt it was time to move. On either November 28 or 29, he called a meeting at his modest bungalow in Qom, a detailed summary of which was later reported in the pages of the Paris newspaper *Le Monde*.

Gathered with Khomeini were members of the Revolutionary Council, the clergy-dominated executive body through which the Ayatollah wielded power. After the conventional formalities, the young foreign minister began by explaining his planned course of action before the Security Council, how his appeal for justice for Iran could not possibly be ignored before this world audience. The Ayatollah interrupted. There was silence in the room as he spoke.

"What we forget is that the Security Council is dominated by the United States. We must accept that as fact." He was speaking slowly, measuring his words as if in prayer. But there was a force behind the words that was not at all prayer-like. "Carter has been able to inflame the international community against Iran through false propaganda. Iran will be condemned by the Security Council. I therefore cannot allow my representative, the representative of the new Iranian government, to be manipulated in this forum. It would be humiliating. Only by boycotting this meeting can we avoid humiliation. We will not attend."

The majority of the council members, who had opposed Bani-Sadr's initiative from the start, nodded their approval. The imam was echoing their sentiments exactly. And his words had the force of an imperial decision. But the foreign minister could not quit that easily. He knew full well how critical his appearance in New York would be — and not only in a symbolic way.

"It was I who asked the U.S. Secretary-General, Mr. Waldheim, for such a meeting," Bani-Sadr said, "and it is the best place to examine the many charges we wish to lay at the feet of the United States. I must ask you, Imam, and the members of this revered council to consider this point."

Bani-Sadr continued, but as he surveyed the eyes of his listeners, his initial optimism began to drain away. Not a particularly forceful speaker, he felt further handicapped by his Western-styled clothes in a gathering of those in traditional clerical garb. "In light of the fact that Mr. Waldheim has agreed to call an extraordinary session at which our grievances can be aired, how can we refuse to attend now without giving the impression that the Iranian government has fallen into total incoherence?"

More sensitive than his council colleagues to the weight of world opinion (despite his occasional anti-U.S. harangues), Bani-Sadr was convinced that whatever position his nation took, it must be ready to debate that position in an international forum. "It is wrong to assume that we will be capitulating by standing up in the Security Council," he continued. "Of course, the seizure of the embassy and of the Americans will be criticized, even condemned, by the Western nations, but we have enough support to get a resolution also deploring what the U.S. has done in Iran."

From there, he argued, the next logical step was a Security Council discussion of the Shah's legal responsibilities for the excesses of his regime. "The United Nations could be turned into a tribunal against the Americans, and I am ready to go on a speaking tour of the United States to argue Iran's case."

The foreign minister was confident that a special task-force of civil servants he had appointed could compile an impressive dossier on the Shah's "crimes" and U.S. complicity. A search through old government filing cabinets was already unearthing valuable data. There was evidence of slush funds to buy off American businessmen, reporters, and military officers. There were records of secret, and potentially sensational, dealings between the Shah and Henry Kissinger on certain U.S.–Iranian arms deals. Bani-Sadr was convinced that a dossier on American malfeasance could be put together which would jolt the U.S. Congress and the American public and put the Carter administration on the defensive. And it was absurd to suggest that President Carter could manipulate him, Bani-Sadr concluded. "I myself have allowed this crisis to reach this stage, so as to better expose the American government and force the president to capitulate."

Brave words, but they did not budge the Ayatollah. Khomeini was ready to risk Iran's economic and political isolation, if that was to be the price for continuing to stonewall the Americans and to feed that hungry leviathan called the revolution. And Khomeini, who was nothing if not a brilliant judge of the national mood, was beginning to sense a unanimity of feeling against the American "Satan".

No, he would not venture into the enemy camp to explain what his nation was doing, and why, and he would certainly not send his foreign minister to New York City to speak on his behalf. The question was closed. There was no formal vote, no show of hands, no further lengthy discussion.

Thus, the United Nations initiative was blown out of the water, and with it went the first, best hope for the resolution of the hostage crisis.

Bani-Sadr had few options left to him. Returning to Tehran, he wrote out his resignation as foreign minister and recommended that Sadeq Ghotbzadeh, head of Iran's state television-and-radio complex, assume his portfolio. The Revolutionary Council accepted the resignation, and promoted Ghotbzadeh, a demagogic and hard-line anti-American with little of his predecessor's mitigating diplomacy. The shuffle was duly announced in a communiqué issued by the official Pars news agency.

The young, ambitious Bani-Sadr was by no means abandoning his political hopes. On the contrary, he would continue as economics and finance minister, and begin to lay the groundwork for his successful run at the Iranian presidency several months later. The historic meeting at Qom, so devastating to American hopes, was merely a fork in the road for this enigmatic man.

In a nationally televised press conference in Washington, President Carter, obviously depressed by the setback at the United Nations, warned that Iran faced "grave consequences" if the hostages were harmed. The United States, he said ominously, "has other options available to it...but it would not be well-advised for me to speak of those specifically tonight." It has since become clear that Iran's decision to turn its back on the United Nations was the single greatest impetus for the Carter administration to construct, on paper and on a desert training-ground, the April commando raid to free the hostages by force.

The day after Carter's press conference, the United States filed suit in the International Court of Justice in The Hague, asking for reparations and demanding that those who seized the American embassy be brought to trial on criminal charges. Of course, the court had no authority to enforce any such rulings. While waving its right hand in moral indignation, the United States was shaping its left into a fist behind its back.

TWENTY-TWO-OH-ONE C Street Northwest ranks second only to the White House in the list of Washington's important addresses. At one time the property was a fetid swamp, a source of noxious gases that would settle over the nation's capital in the dog days of summer and make the business of government unbearable. Today, it is the site of the United States State Department, repository of some of the best minds in the nation, minds plucked from the better schools to wrestle with the mechanics of American foreign policy. It is here that the cosmeticians and therapists of the American image abroad do their noble work. It is a hopelessly crowded building, with miles of corridors housing a staff of 6,200. The brains of this mammoth organization are located on the upper six floors. Yet, in the course of time, the distillation of most of this energy filters down to a room on the second floor, adjacent to banks of teletypes and cubicles used by the State Department press.

This is the briefing room, one of the world's most famous news pits. Here, the beribboned diplomatic correspondents — the Marvin Kalbs, the Ted Koppels, the Dan Oberdorfers — keep a careful watch on the map of the world: the movements of armies, mass immigrations, coups d'état in Africa and Latin America, the rise and fall of despots, elections in Asia, and nuclear-arms talks with the Russians. Only slightly less glamorous than the White House press corps, and lacking the frenetic pace of the news galleries at the Senate and the House of Representatives, State is nonetheless the stamping ground for the most seasoned and self-important newsmen in Washington. There is no pettiness here. This is where history marches with heavy feet and is recorded in elegant longhand by the best-dressed men and women in the communications industry.

The briefing room itself is of somewhat spartan design. A series of curving tables with banks of microphones faces a podium and a wall-sized relief map of the world. Every day, generally at noon, a senior State Department official, followed by aides and secretaries, enters the room with a stack of "briefing notes" under his arm. He then comments briefly on the state of the world and takes questions. This briefing is piped lived to a number of sites in Washington, including the Foreign Press Centre at the National Press Building on 14th Street. Briefing rules are strict. No one is permitted to leave the room until the question-and-answer period ends. On days of momentous occasion, this prevents a disorderly rush to file stories.

It was in this venerated chamber, early in December, that Jean Pelletier picked up the thread that tied a neat knot around his theory. The top item of the day was an attack by mobs on the American embassy in Tripoli, Libya. It was the latest in a series of outrages against U.S. missions around the world. Washington had barely recovered from the attack on the embassy in Islamabad two weeks earlier, in which a Marine guard was shot and killed. The Middle East, in the eyes of U.S. policymakers, was going to hell.

For Pelletier, still absorbed in unravelling his numerical speculations, this would be a Page Five story in *La Presse*. He listened to spokesman Hodding Carter, III, with only half an ear. But then something jolted him out of his reverie. Carter was relating how the dependants of U.S. diplomats in Tripoli had been given refuge in the embassies of France and Great Britain during the mob attack. This, of course, was standard procedure. In times of crisis, friendly embassies regularly open their doors to beleaguered citizens of other nations.

To your average veteran Washington scribe, this would have been about as exciting as last year's state-of-the-union message. But to Pelletier, it was a bell-ringer. If embassies in Tripoli and Islamabad opened their doors to endangered Americans, might this not also be the case in Tehran? It was apparent that some Americans in the Iranian capital were unaccounted for. Was it not possible that they had flown almost instinctively into the arms of foreign ambassadors?

A quick skim through the press room "black books" — the transcripts of previous State Department briefings — unearthed another nugget. Pelletier jotted the exchange down in his notepad. It had come two weeks before, on November 14. Pelletier could not understand how he had missed it.

QUESTION (*to Hodding Carter*): "Hodding, have you had a chance to talk to this chap Kim King who told the story of his escape from the embassy after it was seized and his reference to eight Americans who escaped?"

CARTER: "...Well..."

QUESTION: "...including two Marines, if I'm right..."

CARTER: "Let me deal with that one just by saying this. If there were any Americans who are at large in Tehran or elsewhere, who belong to the official party, the most irresponsible thing I could do would be to confirm it. I'm simply not going to deal with the question under any of these guises."

Sharp bastard, muttered Pelletier under his breath. Not only had he evaded a monster of a question, but he had thrown it back with an adjective that was freighted with threat: "irresponsible".

Pelletier's adventuresome theory was taking shape. Since he wasn't a card-carrying member of the State Department press "network" — with its elaborate set of unwritten rules — he felt free to follow his speculations wherever they might lead him, and damn the niceties. He knew, however, that he was still days, and perhaps weeks, away from the point where he could begin pounding his portable Olympia. The next stage, the most critical one, was getting confirmation. This would be the dog's work of the profession, the bloodhounding, when a reporter must stop congratulating himself on his deductive brilliance and start gathering the hard evidence.

He reached for his contact book, a small black diary, tattered and dog-eared, filled with names and phone numbers that he had accumulated over the course of thirty months in Washington. In a sense, the contact book was an index of every important story he had written during his posting. He never went anywhere without it. But on this day it offered no magic key, no talisman that would unlock the important doors. Pelletier decided to follow the classic routine: he dialled the press officer on duty at the State Department.

After identifying himself and his newspaper, he came straight to the point. "Do you have anything to add to the theory that some of the American diplomats in Tehran may have escaped or been away from the embassy grounds during the attack on November 4?"

"I wish it were true," the press spokesman said, "but unfortunately, the only ones now out of the embassy are the thirteen women and blacks released by the militants in mid November."

"Any clearer idea of how many captives there are?" Pelletier continued, trying to make it sound like an afterthought. "Nope," the press man said. "That has been a hard-and-fast rule since the beginning. No names or exact numbers. I think the reasons were made clear by Hodding Carter in the noon press briefings."

The voice, Pelletier determined, was neutral and matter-of-fact. The guy wasn't trying to hide anything. Attach him to a polygraph and the squiggles on the paper would have been constant and steady.

Pelletier rang a contact at the U.S. Commerce Department, Bill Desrochers, a man who had been useful in the past on a U.S.–Canada trade story. It was the longest of long shots, but maybe Desrochers knew somebody who knew somebody at State who knew something about the Iran crisis. "Jean, it's been a while," he said. "You're calling about the auto pact, aren't you?"

"No, not this time," Pelletier said. "We're all working like dogs on the hostage story. What do you hear over at your shop?"

"Me?" Desrochers said, laughing. "I just read the newspapers. Commerce doesn't pick up a whole lot of scuttlebutt from the Middle East."

"Bill, listen," Pelletier said. "I just wondered if you might have heard anything at all about the possibility of some of the Americans in Tehran being away from the embassy when it was taken over."

"No, Jean, but I have been wondering about that. I would have expected that some of them would have been out of town, or at least away from the compound at the time. It's a natural possibility. Hey, give the crisis centre at State a shot. They might be able to give you an educated guess, if nothing else."

"They don't even give out the time of day," Pelletier said.

"Try them anyway," Desrochers urged. "You might get a nibble."

This was getting him nowhere, Pelletier thought, as he cradled the receiver. What he needed was access to somebody deep in the White House, or somebody on the seventh floor at State who shuffled papers and knew a little more than he should and wouldn't mind helping a foreign correspondent put two and two together. But he knew he was whistling in the wind. Those guys exist, of course, but they are choice property. They don't advertise; they don't buy space in the *Washington Post*: "Young foreign-service officer who knows too much, contact P.O. Box __."

But Pelletier was still nagged by a blizzard of questions: Why was everybody so coy about the numbers? Why did visitors to the compound report seeing twenty-nine to forty-three hostages — totals that never jibed with the State Department estimates? Where was the damn list of embassy staff that should have been released on the first day, the brief biographies on every single man and woman being held prisoner?

Pelletier's imagination began to race. He placed himself in the inner councils of the White House or State, the meeting rooms with guards at the doors. He mentally sketched the scenario: senior officials around a circular desk, aware of exactly who is "missing" from the embassy, who is being harboured by the British, the Swedes, the New Zealanders, hell, why not the Canadians...and all of them as skittery as cats, worrying about the search parties of Revolutionary Guards carrying photocopied lists of the Americans who had escaped the net. He placed a clean sheet of paper into his typewriter and tapped out four sentences. One. The law of probability alone suggests that some of the embassy staff in Tehran are on the loose. Two. By simple reflex, they seek help from a Western embassy they know won't reject them. Three. They are still somewhere in Tehran (a supposition: if they have already fled, the story would have leaked). Four. I will not publish the story until they are out of the country.

The telephone rang. It was his immediate superior at *La Presse*, editor Claude Saint-Laurent, with whom he spoke virtually every day. Saint-Laurent was putting together his foreign news lineup for the next day's editions.

"Jean. Saint-Laurent here. Anything special for tomorrow?"

"Nothing overwhelming. The Americans are taking their case to the International Court in The Hague. Depressed about the lack of movement in the United Nations. That kind of thing."

"Anything more on Pouliot's tip about a transfer of a half-dozen hostages from the compound to Evin Prison?" (Robert Pouliot, *La Presse*'s stringer in the Middle East, believed that the militants were moving hostages in preparation for show trials, but he hadn't been able to nail the story down conclusively.)

"Zero from State and the White House on that one. No confirmation or clear denial. There may well be something to Pouliot's theory, but there's little chance I can pry any confirmation out of Washington."

"Okay. What are you working on?"

"Well, Claude, I have something that may develop" —
Pelletier glanced at the four sentences he had typed just
before Saint-Laurent called — "but it's all very preliminary.
I'll need a lot more time."

"Oh yeah. What is it?"

Pelletier shifted in his chair. I knew it would come to
this, he told himself. It was a mistake even to hint at a story of
this magnitude. Saint-Laurent was known for leaning on his
people hard once they had even a whiff of a story. He was
an editor of the give-us-everything-you've-got school, all
hush-hush and encouraging and supportive, but persistent to
a fault. He didn't appreciate any of his staff nursing a story on
the sly without his knowing all there was to know about it,
secret sources and all.

"*Écoute*, Claude," Pelletier said, "I'd prefer to get back to
you later on this one. It's just too...er...vague at the
moment. Too many wrinkles, too many question marks...."

"C'mon, Jean. Is it about the hostages? Hell, you can tell
me that much on the telephone."

"Hey, give me a break, Claude. Look, I have to run. I'll be
back to you soon."

"This afternoon. I'll be waiting."

Pelletier hung up. He swore. The guy was like a lion at
feeding time. He wondered what he would slip into Saint-
Laurent's cage that afternoon.

Pelletier had one more call to make before lunch. It was a
name that had been sitting in the corner of his mind for days,
the name of a State Department official he had met a week
earlier at a cocktail party. The man had hinted at information
about Iran that was far too nebulous to use in a story. He had
maintained a careful distance under closer questioning; he
made it very clear that he preferred to talk in generalities. But
Pelletier had extracted the man's job title and his telephone
number. He dialled the number and told the secretary a
casual fib in order to get the official on the line.

"Jean, how are you?" the official said when he came to
the line. "Anything I can do for you?"

"I'd like to discuss something with you, but not on the

telephone. Maybe we could set up a lunch."

A brief but significant silence. "Give me a rough breakdown," the voice said. Pelletier began to speak. He outlined his theory in a few sentences, stripped of all elaboration. As he spoke, his words sounded transparent and a bit ridiculous. The hunch now seemed hopelessly porous. "What I am looking for," he concluded, "is not so much a confirmation as to find out what State intends to do about this situation. I am confident about my...er...facts."

Pelletier held his breath, his heart pounding, while he awaited the man's response. He expected anger or laughter. At best a gentle ribbing, a patronizing evasion; at worst a scathing putdown. Instead the man answered calmly, even casually: "You've really been working away on this one. Is this your own baby, or is it the prevailing gossip over the Press Club bar?"

Exhaling silently, Pelletier insisted that his thesis was strictly a personal one. By no means was it the subject of beery debates, and nothing had been set down on paper for publication. "I know perfectly well what is at stake here," the reporter said.

"Sure, sure," the man said quickly. "Listen, are we on background here? I mean deep background. No quotes. No reliable sources. This is for your private use only."

"Of course," Pelletier said. "That is understood."

"No, it's not understood. I want it spelled out. Nothing that could conceivably get back to me. You will understand why in a minute."

His pulses racing, Pelletier pledged that he would honour the ground rules. The man proceeded:

"What I am about to tell you is *not* firsthand information. My job doesn't put me in direct contact with the hostage crisis. But if you write what you have just told me, it could really create havoc in Tehran. You know that the militants have been combing the city looking for all kinds of people: anybody who might have had any links with SAVAK, with the CIA, with the embassy itself. It's a real witch-hunt. Your story would only aggravate that——"

"Listen," Pelletier said, letting some impatience seep into his voice. "I've already explained that I am prepared to sit on this story. I know the risks, the issues. You have to understand that.... Can we meet for lunch tomorrow? I hate discussing this on the phone."

Pelletier knew this was the most critical point in the whole enterprise. If the man begged off because of other business, if he insisted he had nothing more to say, the story would have to go on the shelf. The newsman needed some kind of solid assurance now that he was on the right track, even if it was on the deepest, most inaccessible background. The story hung on this moment.

"Okay for lunch," the voice said. "I can give you an hour or so, at 12:30."

They agreed on a restaurant and rang off. Pelletier got up from his chair, stretched in deep satisfaction, and let out a small whoop of joy. He was so close to the story now he could taste it.

The next day Pelletier met the State Department official (he would later refer to him cryptically as MS) at the entrance to Flaps Rickenbacker, a trendy restaurant-cum-singles-bar near the intersection of 19th and M streets in downtown Washington. The spot was popular with the midtown crowd of lawyers, middle-echelon government people, and secretaries. Pelletier had chosen it for its noisy ambiance, its carefully cultivated atmosphere of casualness. The two men were taken to a wall table that could barely fit four elbows, two steins of beer, and a salad bowl. As soon as a waitress in a tight T-shirt had taken their orders, MS broached the topic, looking the reporter straight in the eye, taking stock of his trustworthiness.

"Okay, tell me more about this story of yours," he said.

"Obviously," Pelletier began, "I am most interested in the role that the Canadian embassy in Tehran is playing in all this." Recalling his conversation with Gilles Mathieu, Canada's number two man in Washington, he noted that the

Canadian embassy in Tehran was a natural sanctuary for any Americans on the run in that city. Canada had been one of Washington's staunchest allies in the hostage crisis so far, and its ambassador in Tehran, Ken Taylor, was known to be resourceful and highly sympathetic to the Americans. Yet, at the same time, Canada had maintained a relatively low profile in Iran since November 4.

Pelletier completed his exposition without asking a question. MS looked at him, his face devoid of expression. "First of all," he said, "as far as you are concerned, we never had this lunch. Now I won't go into specifics. You will have to build this story on your own. But we are not going to pull any of our people out until it is clearly safe to do so."

Pelletier pushed aside his half-eaten baconburger. "How the hell do you go about 'pulling them out'?" he asked.

"There are a number of contingencies being discussed," MS said. "But, remember, I am not attached to the Iran desk. This is not my turf. From what I understand, the risk of their being discovered is minimal as long as nobody blows the story here."

Pelletier made a few more tentative probes about the numbers of fugitives and the conditions of their sanctuary, but he could sense MS retreating. They chatted desultorily about matters of domestic and foreign politics, and about Hamilton Jordan's problems with the charge that he had snorted cocaine at New York's Studio 54.

Then the lunch ended quickly. The bill paid, they stood outside in the winter sunlight, and MS shook Pelletier's hand. "So we agree," he said. "You will sit on your story as long as you can. I can't overemphasize the importance of discretion at this time." For the fifth time, Pelletier gave his assurance.

"Okay, don't hesitate to call," MS said, preparing to signal a cab. He turned around one more time. "And good luck," he said in parting.

Pelletier began the eight-block walk back to his office, but in front of the Mayflower Hotel he hurriedly hailed a cab to the National Press Building. He raced up to his office, sat down behind his desk, and began writing, in furious longhand, everything he could remember of his conversation with MS. He filled three letter-sized sheets of paper with quotes and his own evaluation of what had been said.

From his filing cabinet he removed a red folder labelled "Fisheries". He placed the three sheets inside, locked the cabinet, and left his office.

December 7

Pelletier had spent the last couple of days reviewing what he knew and trying to decide on a course of action. Now he was ready to move on what would become the biggest story of his career.

He removed the "Fisheries" file from his filing cabinet and opened it on his desk. He took a deep breath and quickly scanned the handwritten notes. It was time to take the critical step—the Canadian embassy would have to be confronted. And Pelletier knew just the man to approach.

He dialled the number from memory. "The office of Tom Boehm," he told the switchboard operator. It took several seconds for the connection to go through. In the interval, Pelletier nervously lit a cigarillo and considered hanging up quickly, postponing this moment for another day or two.

"Tom Boehm here. Hello," the voice said.

"Tom, it's Jean Pelletier. *La Presse*. There's something you may be able to help me with." He paused. "It has to do with Iran."

"Yes?" Boehm answered.

"I've stumbled on something over the past few days. Is it true that the Canadians are taking care of a group of Americans in Tehran?"

"Jesus," Boehm said, "that's a tough one."

It was the reply that Pelletier had expected. Nevertheless, he was stunned. He had pressed the right button, he knew it now for certain.

"Listen, Jean. I'll have to get back to you on this," Boehm answered. "Stay near a phone."

The two men had never met, but over the past weeks they had developed what is known as a telephone relationship. Speaking on other subjects that touched on American and Canadian diplomatic and trade relations, they felt that they knew one another well enough to proceed on a first-name basis. But at this moment Pelletier fervently wished he could see the expression on the man's face.

Boehm was in charge of the Iran portfolio at the embassy, a fact ignored by most of the Canadian newsmen in Washington. For all they knew, Canada was doing little more than keeping a "watching brief" on what was happening in Tehran — the way any country keeps itself informed on an international crisis. What could a middle-level Canadian diplomat possibly add to the news story of the decade?

Boehm was the resident expert on U.S.–Canada fishing treaties and maritime boundary questions. Most of the calls that he took from newspapermen dealt with fish. Thirty-seven years old, with a ragged beard, an even more ragged sense of humour, and an informal personality that immediately put reporters at ease, Boehm could engage newsmen with long monologues on scallops stocks off the coast of Maine and the significance of the two-hundred-mile offshore limit. Hardly the stuff of drama and intrigue.

But on this day, Pelletier did not have scallops or salmon on his mind. He was on a fishing expedition of an entirely different kind, and his hook had caught.

"I'll be waiting," Pelletier said.

"By the way," Boehm asked, "how solid do you feel your information really is?"

"I have it from a reliable source," Pelletier answered, measuring his words carefully, "that a group of American diplomats, I'm not exactly sure how many, are hiding outside their embassy, and one of their hiding places is with the Canadians. That's it in a nutshell."

"That's enough," Boehm said. "Get back to you."

Boehm replaced the telephone, and was on his feet. He strode down the hallway of the embassy's third floor, and walked into the office of his immediate superior, Gilles

Mathieu. "Mr. Mathieu," he said softly, "we have a problem." As he spoke, Mathieu's eyes widened. He fidgeted with a fountain pen, and then threw it down on the desk.

Mathieu made two quick calls, and minutes later, four men were together in Ambassador Peter Towe's office directly below — the ambassador himself, Mathieu, Boehm, and Mannfred von Nostitz, the embassy's first secretary for political affairs, in charge of Far Eastern affairs. There was one simple matter on the agenda: the embassy had to come up with an approach to this alarming development. They could all imagine how Flora MacDonald would react to this news, but, equally important, they recognized that the Washington embassy was in a terrible spot. If Pelletier wrote his story, the embassy would be tagged as the source of the leak, and the security division at External Affairs in Ottawa would be breathing down their collective necks.

While the conversation swirled around him, Towe sat back quietly in his chair, puffing on an Old Port cigar and listening to the ricocheting arguments. Mathieu was adamant that they should stonewall Pelletier entirely. "Don't tell him anything, not a word," he said, his eyes on Towe. "We can't be a party to this." Boehm respectfully disagreed. He said he believed he knew Pelletier well enough to know that the reporter would not easily be put off. He had to be trusted, to be taken into their confidence, and made to understand that for *La Presse* to publish the story about the "houseguests" would have disastrous consequences. As he spoke, he noticed a hardening of Mathieu's expression. His boss was getting angry. But Boehm pressed on: "I think we will have to trust Pelletier's sense of professional ethics."

The ambassador broke his silence, and Boehm felt a load lift from his shoulders. "I tend to agree, Tom," Towe said. "If he publishes his story, it won't help us to come out with an official denial. I'll talk to him."

While the top Canadian embassy staff in Washington gathered to discuss "the Pelletier problem", the journalist was on the line to his boss, Claude Saint-Laurent, telling him for the first time the story of the six houseguests. Predictably, Saint-Laurent was astonished, and, even more predictably, he wanted to move with the story. "Can we go with it by the end of next week?" he asked.

Pelletier was alarmed. "Certainly not," he shot back. "You can imagine what the consequences would be for the Canadians in Tehran, not to mention the houseguests. I wouldn't put my by-line on this story now. No way."

While Pelletier appreciated that Saint-Laurent was reacting the way most editors would when first presented with a hot international story, he also knew that the correspondent's best credential in Washington, far more valuable than his White House pass and his Congressional tag, was his personal integrity. If that were damaged — and Pelletier was certain that rushing into print on this story, with all its ramifications, could be a fatal blow to his reputation — the correspondent would be left with no resources. No, the management of *La Presse* would have to be reined in, with an implied threat of resignation if necessary. Pelletier was ready to go that extra step, and he made sure his bosses knew it. Saint-Laurent reluctantly agreed that it would be best to hold off for the moment. They would talk later.

After returning from lunch, Pelletier checked his telephone-message recording reel. There was only one item, and it brought an adrenal rush. Ambassador Towe's secretary had called to let him know that the ambassador was trying to reach him. Could Mr. Pelletier be in his office at about 4:30? The ambassador had called earlier, but Mr. Pelletier had not been in his office. Might he try again?

The revelation to Boehm had done the trick, lighting the fuse that reached all the way into Towe's office. Now I'll get some answers, Pelletier thought.

A tall, ruddy-faced man whose lean good looks and wavy grey hair turned the heads of Washington matrons, Towe was a paragon of punctiliousness. His luncheon talks to congressmen and foreign-service people on Canada–U.S. relations were brisk, uncontroversial, and direct. If he was lacking in dynamism and originality, well, Towe was simply following in the tradition of the succession of Canadian envoys who had come before him. Ottawa didn't send firebrands or tub-thumpers to Washington. They would not fit in with the kind of relationship the two countries shared: easy, low-keyed, and always gracious, at least on the surface. Towe could be sufficiently forceful when lobbying a Senate committee on a matter that affected Canada, but he would always show a great prudence. The ambassador was on close terms with several top-rank VIPs in Washington — people like presidential adviser Robert Strauss, Intelligence Director Stansfield Turner, and, above all, Vice-President Walter Mondale.

As he awaited the ambassador's call, Pelletier also reflected on another of Towe's distinctive traits: he was uncomfortable with reporters. Once a year, he might submit himself to a briefing for a dozen Canadian correspondents, but he rarely agreed to private interviews. He felt most journalists were too simplistic, demanding facile answers to complex questions. Most of the Canadian press corps had tales of frustrations about trying to pin Towe down for a one-on-one talk. Pelletier had spoken with the ambassador once or twice in the past, but the words they had exchanged were little more than inconsequential small-talk.

The phone rang promptly at 4:30. Towe's tone was friendly, and even a touch intimate. He addressed Pelletier by his first name, as if they had known each other for months, but the reporter detected an undercurrent of anxiety in the easy charm. "You have some very sensitive information, Jean," he said. "I'm sure your good judgment would lead you to agree that publication could be very damaging to some people."

Pelletier said he appreciated very well how sensitive his information was. The ambassador continued: "Tom told us this morning that you intended to hold this story, and we commend you for it."

After they had rung off, Pelletier reflected on how well he had been "soaped". It had been a masterful performance by the ambassador. There were no hysterics, emotional appeals to patriotism or ethics, veiled threats, or attempted deceptions — just a friendly chat with your local ambassador, who had taken time out from a heavy schedule to scatter a few commendations and thank you's around. Pelletier knew the routine well, but, like even his most hardened colleagues, he was susceptible to it. One of his job's rare and golden perks was the occasional pat on the head from a VIP; the cynics might sneer over the Press Club bar about the "greasings" they had been subjected to in the practice of their trade, but they secretly relished the attention.

Pelletier was not blind to the true significance of the ambassador's call, however. The Canadians were deeply involved in some kind of sanctuary set-up in Tehran, and they were as skittery as barnyard cattle before an earthquake. He was clearly on the right track. Yet somehow the elation that he had expected to feel was missing.

Towe followed up his conversation with Pelletier with a hasty cable to Ottawa, outlining the problem and the beginnings of a stop-gap solution. The reporter could be expected to keep mum, he cabled. But between the lines, Towe left the inference that the "houseguest" matter had reached a new level of seriousness. If one newspaperman had ferreted out the story, it was likely that others would soon be scratching at the ground. Eventually, someone else would discover the bone. And run with it. Operation Houseguests was getting hot.

13

*T*HE WINE WAS COARSE, and left an unpleasant aftertaste, but the proprietor insisted it was imported French Burgundy. If the bouquet wasn't convincing, the price was: sixty U.S. dollars per teapot. He pocketed the bills quickly, and left Ken Taylor and his drinking companions to their conversation at the small table in a corner of the dimly lit restaurant.

Taylor poured the wine into the cups, then lifted his and tasted. He screwed up his face, and one of his companions made a crude joke about a camel. The men around the table laughed, and somebody proffered a toast to Khomeini.

Officially, Tehran was a dry city, and had been since February when the Ayatollah had returned from Paris to create his fundamentalist Islamic state. Prohibition of alcohol was but one of the official dictates — along with the segregation of men and women on public beaches and the banning of Western music. Dutifully, the mobs had sought to eradicate the last trace of bottled alcohol in the country. They had even stormed the wine cellar of the famed Intercontinental Hotel, and smashed bottles of the finest imported wines in the city's open gutters.

But a Westerner with a thirst could still find a drink if he knew his way around Tehran's alleyways after dark. Ken Taylor was familiar with a number of downtown locations, away from the main streets, where you could grease a palm or two, and have the proprietor bring booze to your table. Next to the roast lamb and rice he would place wine in nondescript teapots. If tastes ran to stronger drink, he would offer 7-Up bottles filled with homemade vodka, or Coke bottles filled with Scotch. The price was high, and only Westerners with an ample supply of U.S. dollars or some other reliable currency found the restaurant-owners forthcoming.

The men sitting around the table with Taylor were American network correspondents, men whose faces were seen daily on North American TV screens. All were on a first-name basis with the ambassador, who met them informally several times a week at the Intercontinental for a mutually beneficial exchange of information.

Tonight, Taylor could see they were edgy, nervously handling their cups. A week earlier, the American embassy in Islamabad, Pakistan, had been besieged in a violent firefight that left two Marine guards dead.

"It was Khomeini's doing, of course," one of the newsmen said. "Look what he did after the attack on the Grand Mosque in Mecca. Blamed the goddam attack on Washington."

Taylor too had been shocked by the incident. A large group of Saudi Arabian extremists had stormed Islam's holiest shrine, barricaded themselves inside, and been finally routed by Saudi troops with great bloodshed. The act had galvanized the entire Muslim world, from North Africa to Indonesia. And Khomeini had blamed it all on an American–Zionist plot in an inflammatory statement: "It is not unlikely that U.S. imperialism did this....It is an attempt to infiltrate the solid ranks of Islam. Muslims...should expect this dirty act by American imperialism and international Zionism." In Taylor's mind, this accusation had been vicious and obscene; there was not the slightest shred of evidence linking the United States with the attack on the Grand Mosque. But the lie had served Khomeini's purposes well. In Islamabad, and later in Tripoli, mobs had attacked American installations, with the Ayatollah's accusation on their lips.

"We are surprised by how far Khomeini will go, but we shouldn't be," Taylor told his companions. "Anyway, you guys know you are welcome with us if it hits the fan here again."

Since early November, Taylor had distributed sixty-five maps to correspondents in Tehran, to guide them to his residence if the Tehran mobs again turned their violence on Westerners. Before the revolution, these maps — expertly drawn in India ink on high-quality parchment — had been sent along with invitations to Canadian-embassy social functions; now, they had a more humanitarian purpose. As Geoff Lewis, an NBC reporter, said later: "The press corps knew that it was to Taylor and the Canadians that you ran if you were in trouble. We all knew him, and we all knew he'd help."

Ken and Pat Taylor had discussed at length what would happen to their lives and safety in Tehran if circumstances drove the American press corps to take the ambassador up on his offer. The Taylor residence would be transformed into an emergency barracks for Americans on the run, with bodies sleeping on every available surface. It would be chaos, and highly dangerous, but the Taylors agreed they would have to take the risk. In a way, the prospect even excited them.

"Hey, what about this Ghotbzadeh?" one of the newsmen said. "How does he rate as the new foreign minister? Does he have any background?"

Taylor sat up in his chair. Sadeq Ghotbzadeh, the man who had replaced Bani-Sadr in the vital portfolio, was on the move, a rising star in the Iranian hierarchy. After years of faithful service to Khomeini while the Ayatollah was in exile, he had finally been handed a plum job, and he was enjoying it to the hilt. The ambassador had been providing Ottawa with as much data on the man as he could muster: bits and pieces culled from his scrutiny of the Iranian press, from conversations with other Western diplomats, and from his chats with newsmen in Tehran. Washington and Ottawa were keenly interested in Ghotbzadeh. Would he be more sympathetic than Bani-Sadr to Western arguments, or less? And just how influential was he in Khomeini's inner circle? What kind of clout, if any, did he have with the Iranian clergy?

"I heard he's in thick with the PLO," one of the correspondents said. "After he was deported from Canada, they gave him a Syrian passport, and he spent some time in their training camps. He's a crafty bastard. Imagine that.

Georgetown University, then up to British Columbia, spending money like he was printing it himself, organizing anti-Shah rallies, then finally getting thrown out of North America, and ending up at the feet of Khomeini in Paris after a spell in a PLO commando camp. This guy gets around."

Taylor had been putting together his own private profile on Ghotbzadeh and, if nothing else, he found the Iranian a fascinating enigma. He was a firebrand in Paris-tailored, three-piece suits, with a taste for fashionable women and ritzy parties that lasted well into the night — a curious mix of coarseness and brilliance. It was Ghotbzadeh who had devised the exiled Khomeini's "cassette strategy", recording his sermons and calls to revolution on sixty-minute tapes and having them smuggled into Iran for wide distribution. Fittingly, Khomeini had made him director of Iran's state-run radio and television in the new Islamic state.

Once installed in office, Ghotbzadeh had made an easy transition from ideologue to pragmatic politician. He left the ideals of the Paris boulevards far behind him, becoming a one-man censor board, determining what the national media could and could not carry. He even censored the music that radio stations were permitted to play. As foreign minister, one of his first official acts was an edict that only he could authorize the granting of visas to foreigners wishing to enter Iran. Then he called for a list of all Iranian diplomats abroad and ordered a major shuffle of posts. The most important went to his trusted confederates.

"Sounds like someone the State Department could work with, no sweat," one of the American correspondents said, drawing a laugh. "Likes the good life, money and prestige. And he's lived in the States. On balance, he sounds like a guy who'll follow the prevailing winds."

"I wouldn't be so sure," Taylor said. "Don't forget his first press conference. He didn't sound like a man ready to steer a middle course." Ghotbzadeh had sought to curry favour with the militants in the U.S. compound by branding Bruce Laingen, the captured American chargé d'affaires, as a spy. "And," the ambassador added, "he said the hostages should be tried, not by Islamic courts, but by the militants themselves."

"Smoke and mirrors," one of the newsmen said. "The man is looking for the main chance. But the clergy will eat him up. Just watch."

The talk went on for another hour or so, as a second and third teapot were brought to the table. Taylor glanced at his watch. It was nearly 9 p.m., almost time to be moving on. The wine was leaving his mouth dry, and he'd have a thundering headache tomorrow if he wasn't careful. But the conversation had shifted to a familiar theme: what would the Carter administration do if the president's policy of patience did not bear fruit? It seemed like Washington's allies in Europe and Japan were not about to jump onto the sanctions bandwagon —at least not without a mighty push.

And what options did that leave? "A military operation," one of the men whispered. "Bet on it. The five-star cowboys in the Pentagon are cooking something up. And you think Entebbe was fireworks! Just wait and see what *they* deliver."

Taylor jumped in. Some kind of "hot" action was inevitable if this thing dragged on much longer. His colleagues on Embassy Row were in general agreement that the Americans were putting together a military contingency plan, just in case. But nobody had any hard information, or even soft for that matter. It was just conjecture. Taylor asked the newsman, as casually as he could, if he had any solid information.

"No, of course not," the man said. "But it's a feeling. There's some sting in Carter yet, and the primary season starts next month. The president doesn't want to go into his re-election campaign with his ass uncovered. The fight's gonna be tough enough, even without the problem of the hostages. No sir. Something is cooking."

Taylor nodded. "Listen, fellas," he said to the circle of familiar faces, "I've gotta run. Anybody need a ride?" The correspondents decided they'd stay for a while longer, and wished Taylor good-night. His Volvo was parked a block or two away, and as he strolled through the night, his mind toyed with a worrying thought: if the Americans did launch an attack to clear out the embassy, what in God's name would he do with the houseguests?

The question continued to nag at him as he eased his car northward, towards home. He had some work to do. But first he needed some answers. And he had an idea where he could find them.

Officially, the only Americans remaining in Iran in early December were those held by the militants in the compound, the three senior officials under a form of arrest in the Iranian Foreign Ministry, and, of course, the houseguests with the Canadians. Businessmen and tourists, like Kim King, had scrambled to leave shortly after the embassy was seized on November 4.

But unofficially, the U.S. government still had a number of agents-in-place inside Iran, Americans who, by birth, deceit, or simple cosmetics, were able to melt into the local scene. Most of them posed as European businessmen, and they were furnished with the credentials to play this role. Their "covers" were strictly non-official ones: men in the import-export business, engineers attached to European-financed projects, experts in the petroleum industry. Their function was to maintain communication with hundreds of Iranian nationals who remained friendly with the United States, and who were privately appalled by the directions that the so-called Islamic state was taking. The agents also kept a close watch, directly or indirectly, on developments in and around the captured American compound, and on the public mood in Tehran's bazaars and universities. The interest they showed in Iranian affairs could, if, necessary, be easily explained: foreign companies were naturally eager to keep up with prevailing social and political matters.

These agents passed on much of their information to their superiors in Washington through a few Western embassies in Tehran, under the strictest security arrangements. Cable traffic was kept to an absolute minimum and was, of

course, in code. One of the embassies that occasionally transmitted their cables was the Canadian mission, and thus,
Ambassador Taylor had come to meet a few of the shadowy
men who worked for the Central Intelligence Agency in
Langley, Virginia.

It was one of these "European businessmen" who met
with Ambassador Taylor in the early days of December. The
agent knew that Taylor was harbouring the six Americans,
and the two men chatted briefly about how they were faring.
The ambassador could see that while some polite concern was
expressed for the "houseguests", the agent had other things
on his mind.

"How is Laingen faring?" the man asked. Taylor, who
had access to the chargé being held at the Foreign Ministry,
said that Laingen was well, as were the two other officials
with him. "The meetings are arranged through the protocol
officer," the ambassador said. "I bring the three men socks
and underclothes and books, and we have time to talk quietly
on more sensitive areas."

Taylor was anxious to return the conversation to the
houseguests. He emphasized that, while they appeared to be
safe, he was worried about how they would fit into American
"plans" for the hostages in the compound. Taylor made it
clear he was talking about "extraordinary" action — namely,
military moves. "If the hostages are freed in some way," he
said, "we are left in a rather awkward position. Do we make
them public, and politely ask the Iranians to give them exit
visas?" There was an edge of sarcasm in his voice, and the
agent's face darkened. Taylor continued: "Or do we try and
link up with whatever steps are taken to get the hostages
out?"

The ambassador left the third option unspoken: should
the Canadians proceed with their own plans to evacuate the
houseguests, with only minimal American involvement?
Taylor knew that the agent was not in a position to make any
such high-level decisions, or to commit the American government to any action. But he welcomed the chance to tell
someone, face to face, about his concerns regarding his

guests. He was confident that those concerns were duly registered by the taciturn man sitting across from him.

The talk then turned to a more specific subject: was Taylor disposed to do a little clandestine work for the Americans? The word "spying" was not used, but the two men understood one another. Taylor replied cautiously. Of course he was prepared to help the American government with any information that might ease their situation. It would be a strictly informal relationship, between Washington and a well-placed Western diplomat who had "access' in Tehran. As always, the information would be forwarded through normal channels: the Canadian diplomatic pouch and the embassy's communications setup.

"How secure are your communications?" the man asked.

Taylor had anticipated the question. "That's no problem. It's as close to airtight as it can be. But I need some guidance about precisely the kind of information Washington is interested in. This would be useful, so that we don't duplicate your efforts."

Subtly and obliquely, Taylor was trying to draw the man out, to lift the veil even slightly on what the American government had in mind should diplomatic efforts to free their people be frustrated. But the agent was not forthcoming. "Anything would be useful," he said, "especially on the routine in the compound, security around the perimeter, that kind of thing. And anything on internal politics. The political setup here is so byzantine I'd be surprised if anybody can really get a handle on it. But of course, diplomats have access to info about that kind of thing."

The two men parted with a handshake and a loose understanding that they would meet again if circumstances warranted. "Good luck," the man told the ambassador. "What you're doing for the American government here is greatly appreciated. You know that. Whatever should happen, you won't be left in the cold. That may sound vague, but it's the best I can do at the moment."

Taylor thanked him with half-hearted gratitude.

For the moment, the Americans continued to deal with Taylor at arm's length, unwilling to take him fully into their confidence. But the ambassador was prepared to co-operate, in whatever capacity he might be most useful.

Khomeini's invidious charge that the U.S. government was involved in the attack on the Grand Mosque in Mecca had had a powerful effect on Taylor. To his mind, the Ayatollah had put himself beyond the pale of negotiation with this incredible slander. He had made his intentions clear: to embarrass and humiliate and jeopardize the United States wherever and however it was in his power to do so. Khomeini's blind hatred for the West in general, and the United States in particular, precluded any early settlement to the hostage crisis. That much was clear to Taylor. The political eclipse of Abolhassan Bani-Sadr, the one Khomeini lieutenant with any real moderate tendencies, reinforced this view.

Taylor reflected on how Sadeq Ghotbzadeh, his successor, dealt with Western diplomats. He would occasionally rant and rail, hurl slogans across a room, and generally practise the crude art of intimidation on anyone who might disagree with him. A bully in sheep's clothing. No, Washington stood to gain little from Ghotbzadeh.

A third factor that increased Taylor's sympathies for the Americans, and softened him to the idea of some kind of aggressive acton, was the abdication of responsibility by the diplomatic corps in Tehran. The ambassador was appalled by the attitude of his colleagues who, with some exceptions such as the Danes, Swedes, New Zealanders, and British, stood mute in the face of the Iranian outrage against diplomacy.

Taylor discussed his frustration with his closest staff members, and with one or two other ambassadors. "The Americans are running out of options," he said.

It was in this frame of mind that, on December 10, a Monday, Ken Taylor received an urgent cable from Ottawa: "The secret is out." A reporter in Washington, Jean Pelletier (whose name meant nothing to Taylor), knew about the houseguests.

Time was running out.

14

CRUISING AT 30,000 FEET above the Atlantic in a government jet bound for Paris, Canada's minister of external affairs was trying to concentrate on the thick dossiers and briefing books that had been prepared for her European visit. The first stop was Paris, to accept an invitation from the French foreign minister, and then on to Brussels for a meeting of NATO foreign ministers.

Fortunately for her own peace of mind Flora MacDonald was not yet aware of Pelletier's discovery. Still, she felt as if she were speeding down a narrowing tunnel. On the one hand was the lingering problem of the houseguests, her obsession of the moment. On the other was the state of the Progressive Conservative government under Prime Minister Joe Clark. Clark's finance minister, John Crosbie, was on the verge of introducing a national budget in Parliament. The budget was the kind sometimes described as a "ballbreaker" — one certain to raise a howl from Opposition members across the floor. Flora was not sure when the budget would be unveiled, but she was familiar with the broad outline. For one thing, it called for an immediate eighteen-cents-a-gallon increase in the price of gasoline at the pumps, as part of Clark's program to bring Canadian oil and gas prices closer to existing world levels.

Clark headed a minority government, but he was confident of the support of a handful of Social Credit party members in the House in the event of an important non-confidence vote. This support would, ideally, give Clark slightly more than half of the 264 votes in the House of Commons — enough to survive a challenge from the Liberals and the New Democrats, who would certainly vote to defeat the government.

Normally, when a government member, especially a cabinet minister, leaves the country, he or she takes advantage of a parliamentary practice known as "pairing". Since the member's departure leaves the government with one less body in the event of a Commons vote, that member enters into an agreement with an Opposition member. The Opposition member, as a courtesy, agrees to abstain from any important vote as long as the government member is away, so that the equilibrium of power is not changed during his or her absence. But in Flora MacDonald's case, the Liberal Opposition had refused to co-operate, and would not agree to a "pairing". Nevertheless, she ignored the writing on the wall, and did not even consider cancelling her trip. She was assured by the prime minister and other top cabinet members that the Liberals would not make a serious run at overturning the government.

Besides, she was distracted during those early winter days by the problem in Tehran. The houseguests had become a fixation with her. Prime Minister Clark could spare little time from his government's domestic problems, so the Iran file had landed squarely on her desk. She was fascinated by the political and social dynamics in Tehran; she would watch the Canadian and American television newscasts and then pepper Taylor with questions about crowds, food supplies, political infighting, the influence of the mullahs, and how foreigners were being treated in Tehran. Since early November, she had issued instructions to her aides that she be kept informed of any new developments in Tehran, no matter how trivial they might appear.

Sitting behind her desk, legs tucked beneath her, she would engage her staff in casual bull-sessions, discussing everything from the acumen of Iranian immigration officials to the American attitudes on the crisis as reported from the Canadian embassy in Washington. She pestered the Middle

East experts at External Affairs with her thoughts and fears. Before long, the safekeeping of the six became a kind of higher calling, a divine mission. Critical questions from the Liberal benches in the house about Canada'a Iran policy incensed her. On weekends, she would return to the house in Kingston which she shared with a widowed friend and try with little success to distract herself with constituency business.

Now the nervousness of her senior External Affairs staff, especially Michael Shenstone, was becoming infectious. Shenstone was all for jarring the Americans into action, making them appreciate the terrible danger that Canada had taken on itself by harbouring the six Americans. Dammit, Shenstone would fume, the Americans seem to feel we will happily feed and house them indefinitely. All they think about is the hostages, squeezing resolutions out of the United Nations, organizing trade sanctions, and issuing veiled threats of military action.

Flora had already been exposed once or twice to Shenstone's sputtering anger, and she had to admit that she was beginning to share his impatience. "Ah, well," she told one of her administrative assistants aboard the government jet, "we'll be seeing Cyrus Vance in Brussels. Time enough to thrash this out."

In Paris, between official functions, she huddled with her aides, David Elder and Hugh Hanson, and gave voice to her mounting concern. The meeting came at the end of a hectic day, and her nerves were frazzled. "Everybody seems to be dragging their feet on this thing," she told them, waving a copy of *Le Monde* with its latest headlines on the hostage crisis. "Dammit, our embassies in Washington and Tehran are working on this, so is the U.S. State Department, and so is External Affairs in Ottawa. When are we all going to get our act together?"

Elder, a soft-spoken and even-mannered man who was an ideal foil for the minister's occasional outbursts, replied quickly: "It's obvious the Americans are not prepared to waste a lot of nervous energy worrying about the six house-guests. Look at it from Washington's point of view. The six are happily buried away from the danger area. As far as the State Department is concerned, there are bigger fish to fry."

The rationale didn't ease Flora's disquiet. "Then Washington has to be told, and in pretty clear terms, just what kind of risks Ken Taylor is taking. No, this just can't go on much longer."

She had a few novel scenarios to suggest to Vance when they met in Brussels. For example, might the houseguests not make a dash to the Turkish border in the north. On her detailed maps, the route seemed fairly direct. "Look," she had proposed to her aides, a pencil dancing over the map, "a short car trip to Tabriz here, then across the border under cover of night. What's the situation like at the border, anyway? Can we find out?"

Her aides had cautioned that an automobile with at least six passengers might attract too much attention on the roads of northern Tehran. There were patrols to consider, maybe even bandits. No, an automobile would be far too conspicuous.

"Well," the minister countered, "maybe they could use bicycles." Her aides were taken aback. Surely she was joking. No, to their amazement, she was serious.

She returned to the maps, tracing a line with her finger down through the countryside toward a Persian Gulf port. "And then here aboard a ship." But the distance to be covered overland was far too great. Perhaps east, towards Pakistan, or Afghanistan. Who would suspect Americans of fleeing east, away from home?

She gravitated towards anyone — including newsmen — who might have specialized knowledge of conditions in Iran. She cornered Canadian journalist Duart Farquharson, just back from Tehran, and fired questions at him on everything from geography to his impressions of the Islamic militia. It was risky, she was flirting with exposure, but her need to know was compulsive. And as the hostage crisis dragged on

— no movement, no action, the stumbles and deceptions —
she began to worry constantly. She dreaded the red security
telephone she kept under the bed at her Kingston home. A
ringing in the middle of the night, she thought, would bring
the terrible truth that Taylor had been exposed and that she
had waited too long to fashion a getaway.

Another concern was her own ability to keep the secret.
"My God," she confided to David Elder, "if anybody should
ask me pointblank at a press conference about the houseguests, I'll have to lie. But I won't get away with it. They'll see
straight through me."

These were the fears that Flora MacDonald carried with
her to Paris on December 10. As she would say later, she felt
hopelessly out of her depth in the "grey world" of cloak-
and-dagger intrigue. The day-to-day exercise of politics came
naturally to her; she had even learned how to deal with the
convoluted and sometimes vindictive hierarchy at the Lester
B. Pearson Building. She understood force, and ruthlessness,
and how to deal from strength, when to speak out in cabinet
and when to swallow one's bile. Politics, after all, was her life.
But the clandestine operation in Tehran scared her. She felt
helpless in its murky netherworld.

On the evening of her first night in Paris, Flora attended
a formal dinner at the residence of the Canadian ambassador
to France, Gérard Pelletier. It was a sumptuous affair, with
sixty guests around a long, rectangular, candlelit table. The
talk was light and airy, and the minister momentarily put her
worries aside. Later, when the other guests had departed, she
spoke at length with the ambassador and his wife about
Ottawa and about world affairs, including, in general terms,
the hostage crisis.

They did not, however, talk about the ambassador's son
Jean in Washington, whose discovery was making pulses race
in Washington, Ottawa — and Tehran.

Ambassador Taylor was already pulling himself out of the
initial shock. For once, the cable from Ottawa had been

grimly serious. Events were moving down a one-way street, and the only thing that stood between the continued safety of the houseguests and their Canadian hosts and the violence of the street mobs was the discretion of a young reporter 7,000 miles away whom Taylor did not know.

"The guests must not learn about this," Taylor told John Sheardown, after showing him the cable. "If they do, they'll panic. They're already pressuring me and it'll become uncontrollable if they find out." The immigration officer didn't have to be told. The last thing he and Zena needed now was another dose of drama. Things were just beginning to settle down after a turbulent month in the Sheardown home.

"And we have to protect ourselves against the worst," the ambassador added. "We must assume that the story *will* surface, even though Towe in Washington is pretty sure that Pelletier will hold off publishing. Any ideas?"

Sheardown shrugged. He said he would give the problem all his attention. Taylor said the same. They broke off their conversation in a disconsolate mood.

The next morning Taylor had the approximation of an answer. It was a band-aid measure, but it would buy them and the houseguests a few precious days if the worst occurred. Taylor found, after some discreet investigation, a piece of real estate in the Shemiran district: a spacious villa, set well back from the main street amid trees and shrubbery, that was available for rent.

Taylor contacted Chris Beebe, the New Zealand ambassador and one of his closest friends in Tehran, and said he needed a favour. A big one. "It shouldn't involve any real risk," Taylor said.

He handed Beebe the newspaper advertisement offering a villa for rent in Shemiran. He told him about Pelletier, and the Canadians' need for a backup plan for their guests. "Now here's what I'd like you to do. Approach the landlord and pretend you're a British businessman. Say you're in the cement business, or something, and you need a temporary home in Tehran for members of your company."

Beebe started to laugh. It was the kind of oddball

stratagem so typical of Taylor. "Once he's interested," the ambassador continued, "you need not have anything more to do with him. Just say some people will be by to close the deal. You can leave that to me. Just sound properly businesslike, and tell the guy he'll get, say, three months' rent in advance."

For several minutes, they discussed details of the plan. It was straightforward and appropriately devious for both their liking.

The scheme worked with scarcely a hitch, but there was one small complication. The next day, after Beebe had laid out his proposal to the landlord, the Iranian began to show an unusual interest in the New Zealander's cement business. "Of course, of course, the house is yours," the man said. "You know, you are one of the first British businessmen I've met in Iran since the Revolution. That is a good sign. Now, maybe we can talk business. You have a cement company, do you?"

"Er...yes," Beebe said, concocting a corporate name.

"Well," the landlord said, "I would like to make a purchase of some cement, for building some home foundations. What kind of prices do you charge?"

Beebe was stunned. This wasn't part of the plan. "Well...er...you see, our production is pretty well tied up on building projects in the south. I'm afraid we only deal in very large volume and...well...I'm travelling south myself later this week. I'd like to help you but...well...you can understand my problem."

"Of course," the man said. "Regretful. Oh well, maybe we can do business some other time. Send your business colleagues to me, and we'll sign the rental papers."

When Beebe related this conversation to Taylor later in the day, they roared with laughter. "Good work," said the Canadian ambassador. "Now we can move ahead."

The next morning, Taylor advanced to Stage Two of his plan. He called in his security chief, Claude Gauthier, and told him he needed the services of two of his military police. "They are to dress in business suits. They will visit the landlord and tell him they represent a British business firm. They will be in Tehran for three months, and they would like the bungalow for that period. They will sign a lease and advance him three months' rent."

"What about papers?" Gauthier asked.

"We will provide them with letters that they can produce if asked. Now, the next part is important. At least one of them, and preferably both, must return to the bungalow every evening for at least a week, just to give the appearance that they are truly living there. They should be carrying briefcases. And make sure they don't stride around like military police."

Gauthier grinned, warming to the conspiracy. Taylor went on:

"Somehow, without arousing suspicion, I want them to get that bungalow stocked with emergency food and other provisions — you know, a lot of canned goods and bottled water and...oh...maybe some cigarettes and booze."

Taylor then called in an embassy staffer, and handed him a piece of paper with an address on it. "I want you to rustle up as much spare furniture as you can get your hands on, and arrange to have it moved to this address. Couches, chairs, at least four large beds, a few chests of drawers, even an old fridge and stove, tables, that kind of thing. Get a local moving truck to transport it there. And if anybody asks questions, refer them to me. Try and get this wrapped up within a week."

The staffer looked puzzled, and hesitated, as if waiting for an explanation. "That'll be all," Taylor said.

Having set the plan in motion, Taylor felt relieved. At the earliest opportunity he told the six guests about the villa, and outlined an emergency evacuation drill, which would be set in motion by a flash cable from Ottawa that Pelletier had published his story. He calculated that he would have two or three hours to have the guests driven to the safe house before the Revolutionary Guards came pounding on the embassy doors, demanding the six missing Americans.

After that, it would be bluff and bravado. With Roger Lucy, his first assistant, he rehearsed his lines if the militants should demand to search the embassy and his private residence. "On whose authority do you make this request?" he would bellow. "This is outrageous." He would rave about the Vienna Convention, and drop the names of officials in the Iranian Foreign Ministry. The militants would, of course, ignore his threats and search the buildings.

They would find nothing. Not a trace of the imaginary houseguests.

As he embellished this scenario, Taylor grew convinced that he could pull it off and dismiss the published reports from North America about the hidden Americans as just another example of Western fantasy.

But he hoped the plan was never put to the test.

When her commercial flight landed at Brussels Airport, Flora MacDonald was in a frazzled state. "How much time do we have?" she asked David Elder, her aide. Elder glanced at his wristwatch and shook his head. "Not much. In fact, we don't even have time to stop at the hotel. We'll have to race straight to NATO headquarters."

The minister cursed under her breath. "My God, I won't even have time to change."

A government limousine was awaiting the minister and her delegation after they had breezed through the special clearing area for diplomats. She politely asked the driver to hurry.

At the headquarters of the North Atlantic Treaty Organization, Flora MacDonald, carrying a small suitcase, dashed into the nearest ambassadorial washroom. In a stall, she quickly changed her dress, and then swept a brush through her hair. She peered into the mirror. "God, you look awful," she told herself.

Then, just enough time to dash into the conference room, where NATO Secretary-General Luns was beginning his opening address to the gathered foreign ministers. She spotted Allan Gotlieb, her undersecretary, already in his chair behind the desk allotted to the Canadian minister. She gave him a look of exasperation. Gotlieb smiled in sympathy, and Flora took her seat.

As Luns was speaking, a messenger in the hallway out-side approached David Elder and handed him a slip of paper. Would he please go immediately to the Canadian mission in the NATO building? There was an urgent message from Ottawa for the minister. Elder raced into the elevator. This was too much, he told himself. What could Ottawa possibly want now? At the offices of the Canadian mission, he intro-duced himself to the officer and produced his credentials. The man handed him a copy of the cable. Elder read the three or four sentences, and his face went white. He slipped the copy into an envelope, put the envelope into his inside jacket pocket, and hurried out the door.

The security guard at the conference room door shook his head when Elder demanded to get inside. "I have an urgent message for the Canadian minister," Elder said. "It cannot wait." The guard finally relented. Elder rushed to Flora MacDonald's seat, whispered into her ear, and passed her the envelope with the cable inside.

Her eyes scanned the words on the onionskin paper. Then she turned to Gotlieb and handed him the copy. The cable said only that a Canadian reporter in Washington, Jean Pelletier, had ferreted out the story of the houseguests in Tehran, and that Taylor had already been informed.

The minister huddled with Gotlieb, and she allowed the panic to creep into her soft voice. "Get in touch with Towe immediately," she said. "We've *got* to call this Pelletier in and make him realize how serious this is. This story has got to be stopped. My God, I was afraid something like this would happen. But why now? And why am I here?"

A quick meeting with Cyrus Vance was now of critical importance. It would have to override everything else. She instructed Elder to make the arrangements.

Her lunch hour was chaotic. The schedule called for a brief meeting with an Argentine official about the use of Canadian and West German equipment in the development of that country's nuclear program. Britain's Lord Carrington was next in line, for a review of the monitoring force that was being established to oversee the transition of government in Rhodesia. By mid afternoon, she was hopelessly behind schedule. But at least Vance was on his way. She would clear everything for a few minutes with the Secretary of State. Surely he would understand the urgency of the "house-guest" matter now that it had leaked to the press. She prepared her arguments for their meeting, confident that this day would be a watershed in the lingering crisis.

But Murphy's Law, the dictum that everything that can possibly go wrong will do so, had one more shock in store for her. Aide Hugh Hanson raced in to tell her that Prime Minister Clark was on the line — something about an upcoming non-confidence vote in the House of Commons on the recent budget.

The prime minister sounded like a man clinging to the side of a lifeboat in a hurricane. "You have to get back to Ottawa, Flora," he said. "The vote on the budget is set for a quarter to ten tonight. And it will be close. We need every available vote to beat a non-confidence motion. The NDP's after us and the Socreds are abstaining."

MacDonald was appalled by the vaulting opportunism of the Liberal and NDP opposition. Clark had been in power for little more than six months, and now he was about to be pilloried for energy proposals that made undeniable common sense. More personally, MacDonald was depressed about the possibility that her own dreams of a Canada intimately involved in key international crises might soon be dashed. She knew she must make every effort to get back to Ottawa in time for the critical vote.

The late hour and the capricious airline schedules conspired to frustrate her. She had her staff call airlines in a half-dozen European capitals, including Stockholm and Copenhagen, to see if they could patch up a flight for her to Ottawa. The vote in the House was scheduled for 9:45 p.m., Ottawa time. The closest available commercial flight, leaving London, would get her into Ottawa at 10:50 p.m. after a connection in New York. MacDonald cursed the fact that the government Boeing 707 had left for Canada the day before, carrying Defence Minister Allan McKinnon. Finally, in desperation, she asked her aides: "Hey, any chance of chartering a Concorde?" It was a crazy idea, but this was a time for drastic measures. She called the Paris headquarters of Concorde and explained her predicament. Could they rustle up one of the sleek jets at short notice to take her across the Atlantic? The Concorde executive sympathized, but regretted that, no, it would be impossible.

As she was bemoaning the vagaries of trans-Atlantic air schedules, Miss MacDonald suddenly realized that Cyrus Vance was waiting to see her outside. Thank God that Vance is a man of patience and civility, she thought, as she went out to meet him. She apologized for the delay, gave a brief outline of her problem, and then switched to the main reason for the meeting: the fate of the houseguests.

"A reporter in Washington, a Canadian, has come upon the story," she told him. "He knows about the six, and we have to get moving on a plan to get them out."

Vance listened, his brow furrowed.

"We are not moving forward on this nearly as fast as we should be. These people are just sitting there. They are in growing danger, our diplomats are in growing danger, and there doesn't seem any immediate way out." Flora spoke forcefully, trying to keep the mounting frustration out of her voice. She then unburdened herself of a politely stated but clear criticism. "There is a view in Ottawa that Washington is not demonstrating enough concern about what happens to the six. Obviously, your priority is the hostages, but Canada is sitting on a keg of dynamite. We need Washington's help."

Vance nodded. "Washington is as concerned as Ottawa about this," he assured her. "Believe me, we are." But he explained that the fate of the fifty-three hostages was such an overriding priority of the Carter administration, what with the efforts being made in the United Nations, the talk of sanctions, and the difficulty in gauging the intentions of Iranian leaders, that there was little opportunity to give a great deal of attention to the houseguests. "But when I get back to Washington, I'll see what I can do," he told the Canadian minister. "Then we'll talk again. Believe me, we appreciate what Canada is doing, and we really do have your interests at heart."

They then chatted briefly about the critical upcoming

vote in the House of Commons, and Flora's inability to get back in time to help install sandbags around the floundering Clark government. Vance gave his condolences. "If you absolutely can't get home tonight, I'd like to have you at the head table for the dinner I'm giving tonight for the foreign ministers."

It was a gracious gesture, and Flora thanked him warmly. But she knew she could not possibly sit at a head table and look out on a sea of faces while her world was collapsing.

It was her one failing as a politician: she could not disguise her misery with a brave smile.

15

M E R D E, at this rate we'll never publish," Jean Sisto said with exasperation, his right hand chopping the air over the debris of the dinner table. "Why don't we just forget about the whole thing?"

The conversation was going badly, Pelletier thought. Sisto, *La Presse*'s managing editor, had exhausted all his arguments for publishing the story immediately, but his Washington reporter was adamant. The time was not yet right. Publication now, in mid December, would jeopardize the entire "houseguest" operation in Tehran. No, Pelletier insisted, they would have to wait.

Sisto was not one for waiting. As the newspaper's second-in-command, he saw himself as a man of decision. His reputation at *La Presse* rested largely on the energy and imagination with which he had resuscitated the ailing newspaper after an eight-month strike in 1972. The reporters had a grudging admiration for Sisto's brusque, no-nonsense approach to news-gathering. They were also fond of his highly expressive personality; when he was excited, Sisto would bluster, blow air through his teeth, and emit a range of onomatopoeic noises to punctuate his staccato speech. He generally got his way.

Sisto, Pelletier, and their wives were sitting around the dining table at the home of news editor Claude Saint-Laurent in Montreal's South Shore region. Sisto and his wife had arrived with a bottle of Scotch and two bottles of wine, and the evening had started on a light note. As the group attacked the roast that Saint-Laurent's wife had placed on the table with a flourish, the conversation remained casual and friendly. It was Saint-Laurent who first broached the subject that was on everybody's mind.

"Jean," he asked Pelletier, "why don't you tell Sisto what we were discussing earlier today?" The group moved into the living room, and Pelletier positioned himself next to his managing editor on the sofa. He suspected this might become an emotional conversation, and he did not want to be shouting across the room.

Sisto, already familiar with the outline of his reporter's staggering scoop, kicked things off. "As far as I see it, and I've said this much to Claude, I think we should publish the story. Put it this way: I'm fifty-one per cent in favour of publishing, and forty-nine per cent against."

Pelletier was ready. "Do you mean that, regardless of the risks, you would have no qualms if *La Presse* came out with this story on page one next Monday?"

"That is exactly what I mean," said Sisto. "We are not in the business of covering up news. We don't keep information to ourselves, we don't make a practice of working hand in hand with governments. We are in the information business, dammit."

Pelletier suspected that Sisto was intentionally overstating his case for dramatic effect. That was his technique for quickly drawing out the most salient points of the argument at hand. Pelletier was convinced Sisto had a number of doubts, but he was playing the role of the intrepid, fearless editor. Pelletier knew he would have to refine his argument.

"We are in the business of reporting news," the reporter began, "but not at the price of common sense and judgment. You can't just simply apply your principle of publish-and-be-damned to each and every situation, regardless of circumstance. Hell, would you have called it freedom of the press to publish the names and addresses of Jews hiding in a foreign embassy in Paris in 1940?"

"Pfui," Sisto replied. "Come back to earth. Tehran is not occupied Paris. Who knows what the hell is really happening there? Besides, I could argue that by coming out with our story, we could even be contributing to a resolution of the crisis."

Sisto picked up his glass of Scotch with an air of finality. But Pelletier was not finished.

"I disagree entirely," he said. "We'd only be playing into the hands of the militants. Is there anything they'd enjoy more now than to expose yet another 'nest of spies'. No. I won't be a party to that."

"You're not convincing me," Sisto said.

The reporter leaned forward. "Look, we have the story. We sit tight. We watch. We wait a week, a month. We follow events carefully. Comes the time when the houseguests are safe, then we publish fast."

It was at this point that Sisto, feeling backed against the wall, suggested they drop the whole thing. His mood turned sullen. There was a long break in the conversation. "Here's another idea," Sisto said, breaking the embarrassed silence. "We publish the story with an editor's note explaining carefully why we feel the publication of this story might even accelerate the resolving of this hostage crisis. That way, we back you up fully. It doesn't leave *you* out in the cold."

Pelletier was tiring of the argument. It was becoming absurd. Did anyone care about a newspaper's rationale for printing such a story? Would it mitigate the effects of the story in the slightest? If the story blew up in their faces, could he point to an "editor's note" on page one as a defence? "I'd really have to think about that one," Pelletier said, convinced there would be no meeting of the minds tonight. Besides, his thinking had become dulled by the wine and the after-dinner drinks. At this rate, he would lose his temper, and that would really aggravate things.

"Look, we don't have to settle this thing tonight," Sisto said, backing away from a flare-up. "Tomorrow is Sunday. Think about what I have said, and we'll talk again Monday morning. We can't do anything without your agreement and your facts."

"How about some music?" said Saint-Laurent, playing the conciliatory host.

Pelletier had arrived in Montreal the day before, a Friday. Ostensibly, the reason for the trip was to discuss his story with his superiors. But there was a secondary, and more personal, reason. He had known about the houseguests for about a week, and the story had already become an agonizing obsession. Privately, he had made up his mind to hold the story in his back pocket, but he was still nagged by unresolved doubts. The pressure was building, and his small, lonely office in the National Press Building was not the best place to wrestle with his anxieties.

Maybe if he went home to Montreal for a weekend, he could see the story in better perspective. Thus, he met Saint-Laurent in the *La Presse* newsroom, and the news editor took him out for a drink at La Maison Beaujeux, a favourite haunt for the newspaper's night-shifters. They spent two hours trading small talk and shop gossip. Pelletier felt relaxed with Saint-Laurent, who never came on paternalistic. He was management, but he related well with his reporters. He did not know Washington, but he expressed sympathy with Pelletier's position. By evening's end, they were both feeling a mild and comfortable buzz from the alcohol.

They drove back to Saint-Laurent's home in suburban Boucherville, across the St. Lawrence River from Montreal. Winter was late in coming this year. Christmas was less than two weeks away, and there was no snow on the ground. To Pelletier, the city appeared stark and desolate.

Saint-Laurent probed his reporter gently, as if preparing him for the next night's meeting with Sisto. "Does anybody else know?" he asked. He could not believe that the heavyweight American press — the *New York Times*, the *Washington Post*, *Time* magazine, and the networks — had not yet fallen on the scent of the story. At any time, he warned, they could blow Pelletier's scoop right out of the water.

"Well, that's the way the game is played," Pelletier said,

his tone one of resignation. "They have their ethics, we have ours."

"But do you think anybody else has the story?"

Pelletier shrugged. The same question had been swirling through his mind for a week. "Well," he answered, "I have absolutely no way of knowing, and I'm not about to bang on the doors in the Press Building or the White House correspondents' room to find out. But you want my guess? I don't think so. And even if they did, the American State Department would be throwing a heavy net over them."

Saint-Laurent was unconvinced. He had no concept of how "the game" was played in Washington. He only knew Quebec City, where the rules changed every day and reporters on the trail of a story often behaved like reckless gunfighters. He saw correspondents as loners, who lived by their own opportunistic codes. In short, he was sceptical about altruism in the newspaper business. "Well," he said, "you better have your arguments ready for Sisto."

Pelletier caught his drift. Saint-Laurent was making it clear that he would suspend judgment on the wisdom of publication until Pelletier and Sisto had confronted one another. And may the best man win. He, Saint-Laurent, would side with the most persuasive argument.

"Christ, Claude," Pelletier said, his temper fraying. "If Sisto doesn't buy my position, he can run his damn story, but my name won't be on it."

Pelletier recalled an exchange he had had earlier that week with Tom Boehm at the Canadian embassy. He had told Boehm about the impending showdown with his bosses, and the young diplomat had grinned. "They're going to give you a hard time, aren't they? Need any help?"

Pelletier had answered with a categorical "No".

But now, forty-eight hours later, he needed all the moral support he could rally.

While Pelletier stared down his bosses in Montreal, Tom Boehm was sorting through copies of Taylor's most recent cables from Tehran at the Canadian embassy in Washington. Although he didn't have access to the traffic from Ottawa to Iran, the Taylor cables alone were enough to put him almost fully in the picture.

And what he read spelled DANGER, in flashing neon lights. Pelletier's discovery introduced an entirely new element into the problem, both for the Canadians and for the Americans. The two governments would have to find some common ground in solving this problem. And the opening move fell to Boehm himself.

He set up an appointment with a very senior offical at the U.S. State Department, a man named Henry Precht. Precht was head of the department's Iran Desk, and he reported directly to David Newsom, the highest foreign-service officer in State. Precht, Boehm reasoned, would have some answers. But he was known to be brusque and impatient, a man whose sense of graciousness had been dulled by the pounding pressure of a crisis that would not go away. Precht was not one for diplomatic niceties.

Boehm expected candour. But what he got far exceeded anything he anticipated. He began the conversation by noting that he knew Pelletier personally, and was confident that the reporter was not likely to publish while any lives were in danger. Still, he could not be ignored, and Ottawa was nervous as hell. What did the Americans have in mind?

"Well," Precht began, "you people are handling things pretty well. We are considering a number of contingencies, but there's nothing final on that score by any means."

"Forgive me," Boehm said, "but aren't we forgetting something?"

"Forgetting something?" Precht answered. "I can't imagine what."

Boehm was already irritated with the man's cavalier nonchalance. How could he reach this arrogant bastard? "Look, we appreciate that the priority here is the fifty-three hostages in the compound," he said. "But their fate is hand in hand with the six houseguests. How can we talk about one group and not the other?"

"Okay," Precht said, leaning forward in his chair. "How about this? Your man in Tehran, Ken Taylor. He seems to be a pretty competent guy. Do you think he might be able to do a little scouting around for us in the countryside? Maybe check out some sites where helicopters could land, for example?"

Boehm's eyes widened. The man's effrontery was incredible.

"Listen, Henry," Boehm said, bolting out of his chair. "I don't think we have anything more to discuss. If you seriously think that Ken Taylor has nothing better to do than wander around the Iranian desert helping you people put together some kind of rescue mission, then I think we'd better end this right here. You'll excuse me. I have to back to work. I think my people should be put into the picture about how you people here in State view Canada's role in all this."

Precht knew he'd gone too far. He came around his desk and tried to mollify Boehm, but the Canadian had already turned his back and was leaving the office.

As he stepped into a cab outside on C Street, Boehm was still fuming. But the question about the helicopter landing-sites confirmed what he had suspected for days: Washington was getting ready to call out the cavalry, and it was hungry for intelligence from Tehran.

Either that, or Precht was a practical joker, and stupid to boot.

Boehm's instincts told him the latter was unlikely.

16

*T**HERE IS NOTHING** in the world to rival rush-
hour traffic jams in Tehran—not in Manhattan, not
in London, not even in Rome. To Ken Taylor, they were a
good reflection of the state of the nation: anarchy, aimlessness, and aggression. So he always drove his Volvo through
the maze of Tehran's streets during off-hours. Taylor drove
slowly, choosing streets that passed by open spaces: stadia,
parking lots, wide-open city squares. A map of the city lay on
the passenger seat beside him, and he referred to it occasionally. Usually, he drove in late evening, and he would pay
careful attention to where people gathered at night—and
where they didn't. Occasionally, he would make small nota-
tions on the map.

The routes he followed were haphazard. Anyone following him would have been hard put to see any pattern. He
would take side streets, then turn onto wide boulevards. He
periodically checked the odometer on the dashboard and
marked the distances between points on the map. The markings he made with a felt-tip pen seemed innocent enough, but
whenever Taylor spotted an official-looking vehicle or a
patrol of Revolutionary Guards along the street, he would
throw his coat over the map, or fold it up and stow it in the
glove compartment.

For the most part, Taylor restricted his evening drives to
within a radius of a mile or two from the American embassy.
He avoided the wide perimeter roads that bordered the compound. There was nothing to learn there. He stuck to the

small tributary arteries, the lesser-known streets that fed into Taleghani Avenue and Ferdowsi Street and Sepah Road and, of course, the boulevard known as Roosevelt before Islamic authorities had changed the name to something more suitable. Occasionally, too, Taylor would leave the centre of the city and follow the main exit roads from Tehran, making mental notes of landmarks along the way, and where and when official patrols were likely to appear. He was certain that others in the city, men who passed as European businessmen in rented or borrowed cars, were also reconnoitring downtown Tehran, and also taking perfectly innocent drives out into the countryside to admire this or that natural phenomenon.

Taylor's primary interest, in these final days of December, was in compiling a list of what he called "bus stops" — areas in and around Tehran where large helicopters could land, and where they could be adequately protected while awaiting the passengers they had been sent in to collect. But there was more to it than that. The armed men that these helicopters disgorged would also have to find their way, in the least possible time, to their target area: the embassy compound. For this, they would need detailed road maps, and they would have to be guided along their route by familiar buildings and other landmarks.

Taylor also made it his business to learn everything he could about the organization of the militants within the compound, and where the hostages were kept. His exchanges of information with Western diplomats and newsmen provided scraps that he could amplify with his personal observations, his scrutiny of the local press, and his occasional contacts with middle-level Iranian bureaucrats. He also buttonholed diplomats from so-called neutral countries who had occasional access to the inner compound and the hostages, and quizzed them on their observations.

He watched, and he learned. The sandbag emplacements on the compound perimeter, for example, were absurd. "A ten-year-old could climb those bags and get over the top of the wall," he noted in one cable. Also significant was the non-military bearing of the Revolutionary Guards who patrolled outside the walls. They were sloppy and careless, even dragging their Belgian-made rifles in the dust. Taylor had heard stories about accidental shootings, guards cleaning their rifles and discharging the weapons into their feet or legs. He didn't put too much stock in these stories, but he reported them anyway.

Much of the information he gathered was more prosaic. John Neil, the economic expert at the Canadian embassy, was a useful source for data on just how badly Iran was suffering from the Western trade embargo. From his scrutiny of the Tehran bazaars, Neil noted that prices of such essential goods as rice and kerosene were skyrocketing. Meat was a luxury item and hoarding was rampant, as was the activity of the local black market. Neil also had lines of communication with people in the various Iranian ministries, and although they remained uncritical of Khomeini and his policies, he could sense a growing unease in what remained of the bureaucracy. Such information left Taylor with the conviction that if an attempt were made to topple Khomeini, either from within or from outside Iran, many middle-class Iranian bureaucrats would be secretly grateful.

But his immediate concern was an American military operation to free the hostages, and in his meetings both with Bruce Laingen and with the handful of American agents circulating throughout Tehran, the ambassador raised a number of salient questions.

First of all, he urged, Washington must be made to understand a critical point: "If you're going to stage an airlift with helicopters landing inside Tehran, you can only get away with it once. If you do it for the fifty-three hostages, you can't do it for the six we are protecting."

Taylor could imagine a gung-ho general in the Pentagon gloating over a successful evacuation of the hostages in the compound, and then telling the joint chiefs, "Okay, next Saturday let's do the same for the Canadians' houseguests." It wouldn't work, the ambassador said. That left two options: either the six would have to be included in the original chopper evacuation, or there would have to be a separate and simultaneous operation for them. Both these options entailed the most meticulous planning. What Taylor feared most, of course, was a commando strike that left out the houseguests altogether, on the presumption that they were safe and happy with the Canadians and would remain so indefinitely.

"Then there's the other question," Taylor said. "If the Americans do stage a military operation, what will they deem a success? Ten casualties among the hostages? Twenty? Heavy civilian losses in Tehran? Heavy military losses?"

He was convinced that whatever the loss of life the U.S. government would receive plaudits from Western countries for making the effort. The world would recognize that there really was one way to deal with the political primitivism of Khomeini's regime, and that was with force.

Taylor had become a confirmed hawk.

The weeks before Christmas were a heady time for Ambassador Taylor, as he expanded the scope of his information-gathering in Tehran. Most of the general material — politics, economic conditions, developments at the universities and among the social classes — went into the almost daily "sit-reps" (situation reports) he cabled to Ottawa and the embassy in Washington. The more sensitive material — information that would normally be outside the purview of a diplomat in a foreign capital, and that would compromise him if intercepted — was transmitted to American agents within Tehran. These agents had come to see Taylor as a valuable source of data, and while much of the material he provided only reinforced what they already knew, he was a useful channel to other sympathetic diplomats in the Iranian capital.

Taylor held regular informal meetings with a half-dozen other ambassadors in Tehran, and this loose "committee" was active in keeping pressure on Iranian authorities. They would seek out officials in the Iranian Foreign Ministry and lobby intensively on behalf of Washington. This pressure brought no real immediate results — Sadeq Ghotbzadeh dismissed their arguments with the official Iranian line — but it served to remind the regime that Embassy Row was by no means totally quiescent.

Taylor apparently did not feel it necessary to keep Ottawa up to date on the full extent of his activities in Tehran. In this regard he was probably wise, since security in the Canadian capital was by no means airtight on the question of the hostages.

One incident demonstrates this. In the third week of December, one of Taylor's sit-reps to Ottawa, which contained a specific reference to the houseguests, somehow found its way into a printed summary circulated among senior External Affairs bureaucrats. This summary of cables from embassies around the world is read by about 150 senior and upper-middle-level people, mostly in the Lester B. Pearson Building.

Since the houseguests had been given sanctuary in November, strict orders had been issued from on high that any cables from Tehran referring to the Americans were to be strictly excluded from the summary. But somebody slipped up. Furious senior officials, including Michael Shenstone, ordered a drastic cut in the circulation of the summary, even within the Middle East division. But it was too late. Presumably, in dozens of offices in the Pearson Building, bureaucrats read about Ken Taylor and his "guests" and scratched their heads in bewilderment. What in God's name was it talking about?

From that day onward, all of Taylor's cables from Tehran were restricted to three officials at the External Affairs department in Ottawa, including Michael Shenstone and a security officer, and to a small handful of upper-echelon people at the U.S. State Department in Washington and the Central Intelligence Agency in suburban Langley, Virginia. His situation-reports had become too sensitive for wider distribution.

There were other cracks in the dike of secrecy. At a Conservative Party caucus meeting in December, Prime Minister Joe Clark had hinted so broadly about the Tehran caper that at least two cabinet members — Jacques Flynn in

Justice and Sinclair Stevens at the Treasury Board — guessed the full story. And Senator Martial Asselin, government spokesman in the Senate on foreign affairs, personally asked his colleagues not to press him too strongly with questions about what was happening in Iran, because "lives are at stake". With this kind of "confidentiality", it seemed inevitable to people like Flora MacDonald that, in time, Jean Pelletier might not be the only threat to security.

TEHRAN December 25

"All is quiet in the little town of Tehran," Taylor cabled Ottawa on Christmas Eve. At the receiving end of the message, in the bowels of the Pearson Building, communications chief George Happy threw his head back and laughed, and then read on. The cable continued that a "strange airborne object" had been spotted in the western sky, pulled along by creatures with horns, with a large bearded person aboard. Could Ottawa advise who the strangely garbed visitor might be?

Taylor and Roger Lucy had more than puckish humour in mind when they drafted this cable to Michael Shenstone. The ambassador wanted Ottawa to know that the Canadian staff in Tehran and their six guests were in high spirits, after nearly seven weeks of Operation Houseguest.

To celebrate the holiday, Taylor and Sheardown had planned a feast at the latter's home. It would be a rousing, convivial get-together. The ambassador had prevailed on the British embassy to donate a Christmas pudding from Harrods, and Zena Sheardown had managed to find an immense turkey. The ambassador and his chief immigration officer set out a stock of wine and liquor that would have done justice to an army.

There was also a new person on the scene, fifteen-year-old Douglas Taylor, the ambassador's son, who had arrived six days earlier to spend Christmas with his parents. Douglas had two weeks off from his school in Paris, and when his father introduced him to Joe and Kathy Stafford, he was dumbstruck. Douglas and the Staffords quickly became close friends, and spent hours playing a game called Oil War, a Monopoly-like board game that featured oil gushers instead of real estate.

On the afternoon of Christmas Day, the Taylors and the Staffords climbed into the embassy car, with gaily wrapped presents under their arms, and were driven to the Sheardowns. Their hosts met them at the front door, and they greeted one another jokingly.

The drinks flowed freely, and by the time Zena signalled that dinner was ready, most of the group already had a mild buzz from the alcohol. A small but testy discussion was under way on the matter of how often the houseguests were permitted to send letters home to friends and relatives through the Canadian diplomatic pouch.

Taylor had heard it all before, and sympathized with the guests' complaints. He saw them as symptoms of the Americans' increasing cabin fever and edginess, and this worried him. "Try and understand," he said. "Every letter you send is a small security risk. The authorities at the airport would only have to open one pouch and they'd be knocking on the door so fast it would make your head spin."

"But they wouldn't open a diplomatic pouch," Lee Schatz said petulantly.

"Probably not," Taylor said, "but I'm responsible for the safety of several dozen people, and I just can't take the chance. Now c'mon, it's Christmas. Let's talk about more pleasant things."

At the dinner table there were half a dozen toasts as Taylor carved the turkey that had cost Zena $125 at Tehran's inflated prices. They even raised their glasses to President Carter, after a bit of playful grumbling. As Lee Schatz lifted his glass of Bordeaux, he stole a glance at Zena Sheardown, smiled, and intoned "To the president." It was something of a peace offering, for all the arguments they had had over things like American policy in Iran, and how Washington was treating the hostage crisis. Schatz chuckled inwardly; he had another surprise for Zena, his hostess. He hoped she would accept it in good humour.

The mood of levity was dampened somewhat as they discussed the latest crisis in Middle Eastern geopolitics. Taylor had picked up some details earlier in the day about Soviet moves against Afghanistan, Iran's eastern neighbour. The government of Afghan President Hafizullah Amin, the ambassador told them, appeared to be toppling. The Soviets had already begun airlifting troops into the country's mountainous regions on the pretext of helping the Afghans combat the provocation of external enemies.

"What will this mean for Iran, for us?" Cora Lijek asked, suddenly losing her appetite.

"Hard to say," Taylor replied. "I expect they'll have Kabul pretty quickly, but the resistance in the hills will be fierce. They're certain to install a puppet government. The Kremlin is worried about anti-Soviet Muslim forces taking control of the country. At least, that's going to be the rationale."

"But will they move west, against Iran?" Joe Stafford queried. He was expressing a fear that was prevalent in most world capitals — namely, that the Soviets had made the first move in their historic quest for a warm-water port, and Iran, with ports on both the Persian Gulf and the Indian Ocean, was an inviting target.

"Well, I don't think we have to worry about that just yet," Taylor said. "If and when that happens, you'll all be sitting safely at home in the States, watching it on the six-o'clock news. Now let's have some more of this turkey."

Talk turned to lighter subjects. Douglas was asked about life in Paris, and they kidded him about French girls. They teased Mark Lijek about the quality of the pizza he had baked recently, when his turn came up on a Sunday to cook a meal for the house.

Halfway through the pudding, Schatz announced: "Time for presents." With an exaggerated fuss, he guided everyone into the living room. "Now, I'd like to begin by giving something to Zena. Over the past weeks I've given her a pretty hard time. We haven't agreed on very much, and I fear I haven't been an ideal guest."

Lee picked up a parcel and placed it on Zena's lap. "So here is my peace offering." Zena pulled off the tape, unwrapped the bundle, and saw a folded-up scatter rug. "Oh, Lee, that's gorg — *omigod*." The design on the rug was a full face of the Ayatollah Khomeini! There was an explosion of laughter from everyone in the room. Schatz's voice cut through the merriment: "You can use it as a wall-hanging, or a doormat. An all-purpose Khomeini rug."

John Sheardown wore an ear-to-ear grin. He had picked up the rug at a downtown bazaar after Lee had asked him to find something appropriately goofy. It was a hit.

Schatz wasn't finished. He distributed a half-dozen smaller parcels to Zena and the other houseguests. "Something else to mark the occasion." Bob Anders was the first to unwrap his gift: a chain of "worry beads" that fit around the hand. Muslims used the beads to say their prayers, but Schatz felt they would serve another purpose for his nervous confreres.

Cora Lijek said she had something special to open. "Mark and I got boxes from our parents, delivered through the State Department. I've been dying to see what's in them, but we decided to wait until we were all together."

Mark's box from his folks contained a handbag for Cora and a tie and tie-clip for him. Underneath lay a large salami and some cheese. There was a groan from the group. "Just what you always wanted," Joe Stafford said. Cora's box had a supply of socks and underwear. There were tears in her eyes as she handled the simple gifts.

Mark said it was time they paused to reflect on their colleagues inside the American compound, whose Christmas celebration wasn't such a joyful one. Four Western clergymen had been allowed access to the hostages, and they led solemn services for small groups.

"I think we should thank God for our good fortune," Mark said. "And our hosts."

In the moment of silence that followed, the six fugitives

did not put their thoughts into words. They didn't want to put a pall on the celebrations. But they realized they were captives just like the rest, their collective future as uncertain as that of their colleagues in the compound.

"Should we begin to make plans for Easter?" Schatz finally joked, breaking the ice.

But no one laughed.

17

THE OVERTHROW of Afghanistan President Amin two days after Christmas, in a coup backed by thirty thousand invading Soviet troops, rocked the Carter White House. Amin was summarily executed and replaced by a Soviet puppet, Babrak Karmal, who made one public declaration. All subsequent statements were issued on behalf of the new Afghan "government" by the Soviet news media, in line with Kremlin policy. Meanwhile, in the country's northern regions, poorly armed Muslim rebels began a long and costly guerrilla campaign against the invaders, striking in mountain passes with old U.S.- and Russian-made rifles. But it was marginal action, with little impact on Soviet strategy.

President Carter blasted his counterpart, Leonid Brezhnev, with one of the most memorable — and controversial — remarks of his administration. "My opinion of the Russians," he said in a speech, "has changed more drastically in the last year than even the previous two and a half years." The statement, hardly a rousing call to arms by the most powerful man in the world, drew sneering editorial catcalls from across the country, and from Carter's political opponents, who were already racing their motors for the 1980 presidential campaign.

The invasion's impact on the Iranian crisis was also significant. Now that the Soviets were perched on two of Iran's flanks, Washington felt a compulsion to deal more cautiously with Khomeini. The stepping-stone theory — that the Soviets planned to hopscotch to the oilfields and Persian

Gulf ports of Iran — became increasingly popular. The Carter administration had to weigh its policy of isolating Iran against the threat of Khomeini swinging over to the Soviet camp. In the White House situation room and at the State Department, the lights burned long into the night.

The United States sponsored a resolution in the Security Council of the United Nations that threatened Iran with a series of sanctions, but gave the government a week to comply with a demand for the release of the hostages. Meanwhile, Secretary-General Kurt Waldheim was to visit Iran to negotiate for their release and report back to the Council on January 7. If he failed to secure the release, the sanctions would go into effect. To further soften the package for the Iranians, Waldheim dissociated his trip from the American sanctions plan. He announced that Tehran's willingness to allow him into Iran was tied to "contacts" he himself had established with government authorities there.

Into all this diplomatic chaos strode Flora MacDonald, feeling a bit out of her depth, like a supplicant with a begging bowl in a bustling bazaar. It had been decided that Canada would lend its voice to the sanctions and deplore the Afghanistan invasion alongside the Americans. But no less important for its own interests, Canada once again had to catch Vance's ear to plead the case of the houseguests.

On December 30, Flora flew to the United Nations to observe the Security Council debate on the sanctions. She sensed that the Clark government, which had lost the crucial non-confidence vote on the budget seventeen days earlier, faced defeat in the upcoming February election. The Canadian public had already tired of Joe Clark; he had been unable to shake his image as a fumbler and the Liberal Opposition took full advantage of every misstep. Flora feared that this trip could well be her final important act as a cabinet minister.

But once again she had to steel herself and push these gloomy thoughts from her mind. This time Secretary of State Vance had to be persuaded, once and for all, of the need to evacuate the houseguests from Iran. Canada would not be able to fashion such an operation entirely on her own. And

Ottawa was now convinced that the Americans were planning a military operation to free the hostages.

Still, it was a bad time to put the heat on Vance. As Michael Shenstone had put it: "The invasion of Afghanistan has terrified the U.S. like nothing in years. It'll make it harder than ever for us to get their attention with the houseguests."

Arriving in New York, Flora MacDonald picked up another piece of worrying news. The *New York Times*, apparently, had also uncovered the houseguests story, using resources and contacts in the State Department that far exceeded anything available to Jean Pelletier working alone in Washington. Vance had been forced to meet personally with *Times* management to plead that the story be kept under wraps. "My God," she told her aide, David Elder, "the whole thing is coming unravelled."

Miss MacDonald's meeting with Vance, in the corridor outside the Security Council chamber, was brief and succinct. She sympathized with Washington's concern over Afghanistan, but Canada's position had become perilous.

More than two weeks had gone by since their meeting in Brussels, she said, and there had been no progress. "We absolutely cannot delay any longer," she said. "Washington and Ottawa have got to get together on a plan to evacuate the six. I have nightmares about reading the headlines in the morning papers, exposing the guests. Really, Mr. Secretary, I can't argue our case any more strongly."

Vance, to her surprise, agreed without hesitation. "I'll send someone to Ottawa from my office next week. He'll report directly to me. I'm confident we'll come up with something." Vance gave Miss MacDonald the name of his emissary, and said he would carry with him the full authority of the U.S. State Department.

MacDonald thanked him warmly. Finally, there was movement. She hoped it was not too late.

TEHRAN   *Early January 1980*

Ambassador Taylor read the piece of paper a second time. It

had been brought to him by John Sheardown. The proposed cable had been drafted by Lee Schatz and Mark Lijek. Dammit, Taylor said to himself, they have gone too far.

In the days after New Year's, the houseguests had decided to draft a cable to the State Department in Washington, demanding to know what was being done to secure their freedom. They were growing impatient, and the tone of the message was, to Taylor's mind, rather abrupt. Sheardown had brought it to the ambassador, and said: "They would like you to cable this to Washington as soon as possible. They think it might do some good, both for them and for us."

Taylor was furious. "What does this mean, anyway? That they don't believe we're doing everything we can for them? Dammit, John, I don't like this at all."

The ambassador had no intention of sending the cable. After all, the six had put themselves into his hands, and they would have to trust him explicitly to do what he felt was right. Furthermore, all cable traffic from the Canadian embassy had to carry what, in effect, was the ambassador's signature. And he was not about to authorize an appeal to the State Department, which had already clearly shown that it considered the six to be low priority.

"What should I tell them?" Sheardown asked, after Taylor had reread the paper.

"Tell them nothing. Nothing at all. Tell them you delivered it to me, and that's it."

In a roundabout way, however, the proposed cable from the houseguests had been effective. It was an oblique message to Taylor himself that said: "Get us out of here, we have overstayed our welcome."

Taylor crumpled up the paper and hurled it into the wastebasket. But it had ruined his morning. He made a luncheon appointment with Beebe and Munk, the New Zealand and Danish ambassadors, and before leaving, he retrieved the paper and smoothed it out. He slipped it into his inside jacket pocket.

Over the third round of drinks, Taylor pulled out the paper and showed it to his colleagues. They understood his rage, and told him he had done the right thing by refusing to forward it to Washington. Several drinks later, Taylor had pushed the incident well back into his mind.

OTTAWA   *January 3*

Cyrus Vance was as good as his word. On January 3, an official from the State Department arrived in Ottawa and presented himself to Flora MacDonald. The minister made it immediately clear that she wanted to get to work.

"We'll get together tonight in my apartment," she said, giving him the address. "I'll be there with my aides, a couple of senior people from External, and someone from the department's security division."

"Intelligence?" the American asked.

'That's right. Oh, and another thing. The prime minister is on this very day asking the cabinet to issue six Canadian passports, no questions asked. We don't expect any problems. The names are meaningless, but the houseguests will have an identity. We can start from there."

They shook hands. "Until tonight, then."

While the plans were set in motion for what would become known as the "exfiltration", the security people in External Affairs had quietly launched another operation that centred on Pelletier himself.

The word went out quietly to the Canadian embassy in Washington: had Pelletier been fed his story from someone on the embassy staff, and, if so, who was the culprit? Suspicion fell on a political officer who knew Pelletier socially, an aide to Ambassador Peter Towe named Georges Léger. Léger had reason to worry, since his relationship with Pelletier was well known, and they were often seen together at embassy functions. But Léger noted that he was out of the country at the time that Pelletier had contacted the embassy with his information. For the moment at least, Léger was off the hook. Within External Affairs, many of the officials who knew about the houseguests suspected that Pelletier's source was nobody in Washington, but rather his father, the Canadian ambassador to Paris and a close friend of Pierre Trudeau.

And then there was the strange incident of the Curious Warning, an incident that dramatized just how nervous Ottawa was about Pelletier's intentions. In late December, an editorial writer for *La Presse*, Marcel Adam, was approached by an External Affairs undersecretary while on a visit to Ottawa. The undersecretary gave Adam this message: "Tell Pelletier that, whatever he knows, he should not publish." Adam was baffled. He didn't know what the bureaucrat was talking about, and the man refused to elaborate. So Adam shrugged, and forgot the incident.

Several days later, Pelletier, who was holidaying in Paris over the Christmas season, received a cable through the Canadian embassy there. The cable asked the reporter to get in touch with one of his colleagues, Marcel Adam.

Pelletier placed a trans-Atlantic call.

"Marcel, I have a message here that you want to talk to me. It sounds urgent."

"A message? I don't know what you're talking about."

"The message came from External Affairs in Ottawa," said Pelletier. "They said you were trying to get hold of me."

"Oh, yes," Adam said. "Now I remember. Somebody approached me in Ottawa and said you were not to publish your story. Jean, what the hell was he talking about, anyway?"

Pelletier hesitated. "Er...oh, nothing much really. Just your typical Ottawa screw-up. Listen, forget it. It's already been taken care of."

Pelletier hung up, and laughed to himself. The mandarins at External Affairs were obviously getting twitchy.

In Flora MacDonald's eleventh-floor apartment, overlooking Ottawa's Rideau Canal, maps and notepads were strewn over the living-room table amid glasses of Scotch and cups of coffee. The men huddling with the minister had their shirtsleeves rolled up, and two or three of them were smoking furiously.

On Ken Taylor's advice, it had already been agreed that the best, indeed the only, avenue of escape for the six was through Tehran's Mehrabad Airport and onto a flight to Europe.

Initially, an escape via the airport had been considered far too bold, too direct a challenge of Iranian immigration security. Taylor, in consultation with Roger Lucy, had studied a number of more surreptitious plans.

One of them involved a dash for the Turkish frontier. Taylor had envisioned driving the houseguests north, to the Iranian city of Tabriz. There, they would be within range of a helicopter launched from inside Turkey. The plan had a number of advantages, but the disadvantages were much greater.

As Lucy had pointed out, they would need a network of safe houses along the highway route to Tabriz. They would also need a Farsi guide, and probably some kind of communications setup. "It might take two, two and a half, months to set this up properly," Lucy had said. Far too long, they agreed. Flora MacDonald had been keen on the "Turkish option" herself, but she recognized the pitfalls.

Another scheme had been a drive west, to the port city of Khorramshahr, near the Iraq border and on a waterway issuing into the Persian Gulf. There, they could be spirited onto an oil tanker carrying the British flag. Indeed, the British themselves had evacuated some of their own personnel by this route during the revolution. But this plan, too, involved too long an automobile ride through unknown and potentially dangerous terrain.

So, through a painful process of elimination, Mehrabad Airport had become the most logical staging point for the exfiltration.

"Any problem with the passports?" the American liaison man (whom we will call Edward) asked the minister.

"No," said Flora, "the prime minister requested an act of faith, and no one in cabinet argued." Miss MacDonald did not feel it necessary to mention that she disagreed with Clark's decision not to take the cabinet into his confidence. She was

A charred body and wreckage are strewn in the Dasht-e Kavir desert after the tragic failure of an American commando raid to free the embassy hostages in April 1980.

Sergeant Claude ''Sledge'' Gauthier, chief of security at the Canadian embassy in Tehran.

Michael Shenstone, director of the Bureau of African and Middle Eastern Affairs, Department of External Affairs in Ottawa, was in constant communication with Ken Taylor during the entire houseguest operation.

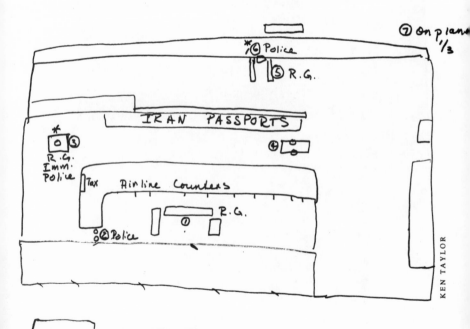

KEN TAYLOR

For his heroic rescue of the six Americans, Ken Taylor was made an Officer of the Order of Canada in a presentation by Governor General Ed Schreyer, July 25, 1980.

◁ *On the evening before the exfiltration, Ken Taylor drew a sketch of the interior of Mehrabad Airport terminal to guide the six Americans through the seven checkpoints they had to pass before reaching safety. Checkpoint Number 3 was the most critical; here the six came under the scrutiny of the Revolutionary Guard, the immigration authorities, and the national police. Taylor also warned them that there was a one-in-three chance that a further check could occur on the plane before takeoff.*

State Department employees in Washington gave the six freed diplomats an exuberant welcome. Lee Schatz at right; Bob Anders in a joyful embrace.

Five of the six escapees visited the Canadian embassy in Washington to thank the staff for their role in the Canadian Caper. From left to right: Bob Anders, Cora Lijek, Canadian embassy political counsellor Tom Boehm, Joe Stafford, Mark Lijek, Kathy Stafford.

"Merci Canada — Thanks Canada" signs decorate the stage at the press conference given by the six escaped Americans at the State Department on February 1, 1980.

Looking happy and relieved to be home, the six "houseguests" pose for the world press after telling the story of their three months in hiding in Tehran. From left to right: Bob Anders, Joe Stafford, Kathy Stafford, Lee Schatz, Cora Lijek, and Mark Lijek.

Jean Pelletier receives a grateful handshake from Lee Schatz at the State Department reception for the six Canadian "houseguests". Deputy Undersecretary of State, Hodding Carter, III, looks on.

External Affairs Minister Flora MacDonald received hundreds of thank-you letters from grateful Americans when news of the Canadian Caper broke. As Canada's first woman minister of External Affairs, Ms. MacDonald found herself overseeing her country's most daring diplomatic exploit.

◁*In one of hundreds of "Thanks Canada" demonstrations across the United States, four thousand residents of Biloxi, Mississippi, turned out to express their gratitude to their northern neighbours.*

"We get letters . . . ." Canadian embassy staff in Washington sort through thousands of thank-you letters from around the world. No incident in recent memory has done so much to enhance Canada's image abroad.

convinced it would only prompt them to ask questions and conjure up wild speculations. Furthermore, she thought it was unwise and unfair to leave the cabinet in the dark, when the Opposition leader, Pierre Trudeau, had already been let in on the secret. But Clark had been adamant. "No," he had told Flora, "security is already enough of a problem. Don't worry, they'll trust me."

"So what identities will they have?" Edward asked.

Here again a number of ideas had been generated by Taylor and Lucy, and subsequently rejected. They could attempt to leave under their own names, but with a cover as American businessmen — part of the slow but steady exodus that had been underway since the fall of 1979. This was abandoned, however, because Iranian officials could have had their names on file.

They had discussed passing the six off as a delegation of Canadians, sympathetic to the revolution, but leaving Iran after unsuccessful efforts to meet with militant leaders. Roger Lucy had thrown out an even more farfetched idea: they could be a group of Canadian anthropologists, leaving after working on some digs in the east.

One of the more provocative ideas had been to pass them off as departing U.S. reporters, but after hearing how some newsmen were treated at the airport when they had been expelled in December, Taylor scotched that idea.

"They will be a delegation of business men and women from Canada," Flora said. "In the oil industry. We thought their cover should be that they entered Iran in early January, spent two or three weeks with Taylor conducting their business, and were returning home."

The security man from External Affairs broke in: "We are in the process of putting together any other documents they might need: driver's licences, business cards, social-security cards, credit cards, medicare cards, the normal contents of any wallet. Plus documentation to prove they work for the company they claim to work for."

"Sounds pretty straightforward," Edward said. "So what do you need from us?"

"Probably the most important thing," the security man answered. "Forged entry and exit visas, and passport stamps. We don't have the CIA's...er...expertise in this area."

Edward wondered if this were an allusion to the ease with which the CIA had slipped agents into Iran since the embassy takeover. How much did the Canadians know, he asked himself.

"I think we could arrange that without too much problem. And what kind of timetable are you thinking of?"

"We'd like to have the completed passports over there, in Taylor's hands, by mid January. We're looking tentatively at the end of the month for an exfiltration."

Flora MacDonald realized full well the implications of issuing the false passports. Should the houseguests be stopped and apprehended at the airport during the exfiltration, the Canadian government would have no choice but to come to their aid openly and unequivocally, defending them as legitimate Canadian citizens. The "adoption" of the six would be a total commitment, carrying with it the full force of the Canadian government. There could be no turning back, no abandonment of the foster children. Prime Minister Clark also appreciated this fact fully, the External Affairs minister told the meeting. If the fugitives were arrested, it would be Ambassador Taylor himself, their host for three months, who would be required to plead their case at the Foreign Ministry in Tehran.

The preparation and delivery of the travel documents was, in a sense, the simplest part of the operation, participants at the meeting agreed. That could all be done in Ottawa and Washington. Far trickier was the question of how the documents would stand up under actual scrutiny as the bearers made their way through the airport checkpoints. "We need to know everything, absolutely everything, about the procedure at the airport," Miss MacDonald said. "What kinds of questions are asked, what is the sequence of checkpoints, are there any random checks? We have to develop a complete scenario of the process of boarding an airplane at Mehrabad."

The Canadian security man said that the procedure

could easily be nailed down. Several Canadians would be leaving Tehran during the month of January — embassy officers and their families and security people who rotated regularly. "Everybody who passes through Mehrabad Airport must be quizzed in minute detail. Where did you stop? What were you asked? Where was the scrutiny the most severe? What are the placements of the various immigration and customs people and police? Who are the most officious and the least officious? What is the best time of the day to pass through the terminal?"

Everybody at the meeting was taking notes, raising small points, quibbling, arguing, trying to find holes in the evolving plan. So far, in theory, the exfiltration was shaping up well. But it was only a paper structure.

A crucial question was the phasing out of the Canadian embassy personnel, whose safety was being imperilled daily in Tehran. When Flora MacDonald later described the mood of these three months as having been like "living under the gallows", it was this staff of twenty men and women on the front lines that she was referring to — the people who would feel the heat of the Ayatollah's retribution if the Canadian operation was exposed. "We have to start pulling them out as soon as possible, with as little fuss as possible," she told the strategy meeting as it proceeded into the night.

It was decided that the staff would be pulled out in groups of two or three, at intervals of several days, over a period of three weeks. The least vital personnel, the clerks and secretaries, would go first, and the remaining staff would take up the slack as best they could. In a sense, it was like the evacuation of a sinking ship, with the first lifeboats being filled with non-essential crew members. The trade and immigration people would trickle out next, followed by the economic and political aides.

Throughout the exodus, however, it was crucial that the embassy not give the appearance of shutting down. The staff that remained — Taylor, the senior officers, the communicators, and the security people — would have to go through the motions of normal activity. Cable traffic would continue: Ottawa had even dispatched a second communicator to Tehran to assist Mary O'Flaherty, whose workload had mushroomed during the past two months. As a partial disguise for the slow exodus, fresh security people would be flown in periodically from bases in Europe. If there were any official inquiries about the hustle and bustle, the explanation would be staff turnovers and holidays.

"So when do we exfiltrate the houseguests?" the Vance aide finally asked. "It's my thinking that we should take advantage of the Iranian presidential elections which will be held at month's end."

The Canadians agreed, but it was made clear the Ken Taylor, the field commander of the operation, would have to select the specific day and the time. The ambassador, so well attuned to the flux of the revolution, must be given full control over tactics.

The planners stood up and stretched their legs, turning away from the clutter of cups and glasses and ashtrays and notepaper around the living room. One more matter had to be broached; it was indirectly related to the exfiltration plan, and in an ideal world, it would not even have appeared on the agenda. The matter was politics. The Conservative party was about to enter a painfully difficult election campaign after only eight months in office. The Liberal party, uncomfortable in the Opposition seats in the House of Commons, would be hitting Joe Clark hard on Canadian foreign policy. There would be a mounting temptation to puff out the chest and boast that Canada, under a Clark administration, had indeed assumed a role of courage and leadership in the most important foreign-policy issue of the day.

But the Conservative party would have to swallow the bile and turn the other cheek if Trudeau pummelled them and Canada's support of the United States in the Iranian crisis. There would be a price to pay for discretion. Perhaps, before the election, the story might come out once the houseguests were back home and all the embassy staff were safe. Then the Conservative party could bluster and strut a bit. But Miss MacDonald told the meeting that the prime minister had no intention of cashing in on the "Canadian caper" for political laurels; nor, for that matter, did she. Indeed, the story of the exfiltration might well have to be kept under wraps indefinitely, or at least until the remaining fifty-three hostages were released. The Ottawa bureaucracy felt itself capable of muzzling the embassy team coming back from Tehran, if this was judged necessary. But would reporters like Pelletier cooperate with this policy of silence? Privately, the people in the room doubted it. The meeting ended after several more minutes of desultory conversation.

The following day, Michael Shenstone drafted the cable to Taylor in Tehran, outlining the main points of agreement reached at the meeting with "Edward". It was a pleasant task for a man who had undergone nearly two months of excruciating worry. At last, an end to the crisis was in sight.

"There's just one small thing that disturbs me," he said.

His deputy, John Fraser, sitting across from him, asked, "And what's that, Michael?"

"The staff is not going to like the order to leave Tehran," Shenstone said. "It's always the same. Trouble breaks out, and they all suddenly develop a sense of purpose, of importance. They want to stick it out. You remember Beirut last year? The gunfire and the shelling start, and they want to man the barricades. They accuse *us* of over-reacting. We can expect some bitching from Tehran. Oh, well, I suppose we shouldn't criticize them for it. But they know the drill."

Shenstone signed the cable and called in his secretary. "Would you take this downstairs to communications," he said. "It's time Taylor got some really good news."

*T*HE PASSPORTS ARRIVED in Tehran, crisp and new and almost without a flaw. They were delivered by a Canadian diplomatic courier who had flown into Mehrabad Airport with a pouch under his arm. The pouch bore the red markings of privilege: it would not be searched even in this country where diplomatic protocol had little currency. As he made his way through the terminal complex, the courier kept an unhurried pace. He made mental notes of guard placements and customs checkpoints and how the immigration officials did their work. He counted the numbers of National Police and Revolutionary Guards in the terminal. Oustide, a car with diplomatic plates was waiting. He slid into the rear seat.

Resting alongside the half-dozen passports in the pouch were other items of personal identification. They were also new: credit cards, driver's licences, social-security cards. All the plastic detritus that the average citizen carries in his wallet when he ventures abroad.

The courier was deposited at the Canadian chancery, where he presented his pouch to Ambassador Ken Taylor. Taylor emptied the bag onto his desk. He made a cursory inspection of the items, and remarked, "Yes, good. It's all here."

While the courier sat and waited, Taylor and Roger Lucy flipped through the passports, admiring the handiwork of the visas that had been prepared by the CIA forgers. Superficially, at least, everything was in order. The visas had a slightly worn look, with subtle little folds and creases that one would expect after being carried about for three weeks.

The photographs of the houseguests were sharp. "A fine-looking bunch of Canadians, if ever I saw one," Taylor joked. "I'm sure Ottawa would be proud to have them."

The ambassador handed the batch to Lucy, and told him to study them carefully, verifying the dates and the Farsi writing on the official-looking customs-and-immigration stamps. "Take your time, Roger. Compare them with as many genuine passports from our staff people as you can get your hands on. I don't want a single mistake, a single discrepancy. And take all the credit cards and other documentation with you. We can't be too careful.

"Now," Taylor said, turning to the courier, "tell me everything you can remember about passing through the airport terminal. Don't leave anything out...."

January 18

As Taylor sat in the car with John and Zena Sheardown, bound for Mehrabad Airport, he could feel the couple's despondency. John's face was drawn, and his lips were curled down. Zena was staring vacantly out the car window.

"It's not right," Sheardown finally said. "We shouldn't be leaving now. Dammit, we have a job to do, and we're leaving it unfinished. It's not right. I feel like a quitter."

"John, don't be so concerned," Taylor said. "And you're selling yourself short. You and Zena have done a helluva job. The rest will be easy. Anyway, despite what we might feel, Ottawa says we have an evacuation schedule to follow, and I must say I agree."

"Ken," Zena said, "I feel responsible for those people."

Taylor could well understand her feelings. For more than two months, Zena had been a self-imposed prisoner in her own home, taking on the burden of worry for her four guests.

An incident a few days earlier had terrified her, and had almost taken her over the edge. It was around midday, and

Bob Anders was outside doing his daily exercises in the yard. Suddenly, he heard a chopping sound in the sky, the unmistakable sound of an approaching helicopter. He rushed inside, where Zena was standing, near-frozen in shock. As they listened, the helicopter seemed to be circling above the house. She grabbed Anders' hand and breathed, "Oh my God, we've been discovered." Her face was a portrait of terror.

"No, wait," Anders said. "I think it's going away. Yes. It is." He peered up, out through the living-room window, and saw the helicopter leaving. "It's okay, Zena. It was nothing. Just a military helicopter on patrol." But he could feel his heart beating double-time. It had taken hours to calm Zena down. (Later, they learned that the 'copter had been searching for an Iranian gunman believed to be in the area.)

Nevertheless, as he reflected on that scare, Taylor could still understand her reluctance to leave. Both she and John had been through so much, it *was* unfair to pull them out of Tehran now, just days before the successful conclusion of the operation in which they had been so instrumental.

Inside the airport terminal, they glanced back at Taylor as they passed through the required checks. The ambassador waved goodbye, both relieved and sad to see them go.

January 20

Roger Lucy couldn't believe his eyes. No, it was impossible. He looked at the date on the passport visa one more time. He'd been through the passports as least half a dozen times, and he'd never noticed this. But there it was. Holy Jesus in heaven.

"Jesus Christ, goddam incredible, of all the bloody..." He leapt up from his desk, and, clutching the passport, ran into Taylor's office. "You won't believe this," he told the ambassador. "They screwed up a goddam entry date in this visa. The CIA screwed up! Can you beat that, those assholes fucked up."

"Settle down, Roger," Taylor said, astonished at Lucy's rage. "Here, let me see."

Lucy moved around the desk and pointed at a page in the passport. "There. That date. It's February. They have one of the houseguests entering the country in February. That's *next* month, for Christ's sake. Holy shit, somebody in Langley is going to get his ass roasted for this."

Taylor had never seen his first secretary so fired up. A skinny bachelor who'd been posted in a succession of trouble spots — from Beirut to Baghdad to Tehran — since 1972, Lucy had come to terms with his fate as a foreign-service officer who was moved from one "hot" city to another. He took the postings in stride, and compared himself to the character in the L'il Abner cartoon strip who brought trouble along everywhere he went.

"Well," Taylor said calmly, "it seems we have a problem. Now, the question is: Can we fix it?" Lucy said he had the necessary equipment to doctor the visa; it would take him but a few minutes. "Good, then go ahead," the ambassador said. "And check all the other dates."

Lucy stalked out, muttering about having to wet-nurse the "greatest intelligence organization" in the world. By afternoon's end, the error was corrected.

The telephone rang in the Taylor residence, and Pat Taylor picked it up. The voice bore a soft, North American accent. She guessed that it belonged to a man in his early thirties.

"Hello, who is this?"

"It's Pat Taylor. Who is this speaking, please?"

"I'd like to speak with Joe or Kathy Stafford, please. It's important."

Pat Taylor felt an icy hand seize her heart. She could barely sputter out the next words.

"Is this some kind of joke? Who is speaking, please?"

"Look, I know that the Staffords are there; they're staying with you. Can you put one of them on the phone, please."

Pat Taylor fought to steady her voice. "There is no one here by that name. I don't know anybody named Stafford. Maybe you should speak to the ambassador. He's at the embassy." She gave the caller the number, and he rang off abruptly.

She dialled the ambassador's office and told him about the conversation. "Could it have been a joke?" Taylor asked. "Mark Lijek maybe, some kind of prank?"

"I don't know," Pat said. "Maybe you should check. But Ken, I'm worried. Really worried."

"I'll be right home," Taylor said.

That same day, Taylor booked an airline reservation for his wife on a Paris-bound flight for Friday, January 25. The houseguests would be leaving on the twenty-eighth.

Every minute's delay now increased the risk of capture. The countdown had started.

January 26

The weather intervened to delay Pat Taylor's departure until the 27th. A massive snowstorm struck the city on Friday, and all outgoing flights were cancelled.

Taylor had his secretary make six reservations on a 7:35 Swissair flight Monday morning, January 28, destination Frankfurt, West Germany, with a stopover in Zurich. He also told her to book six seats on subsequent flights with KLM, Air France, and British Airways, all leaving Mehrabad Airport for various European destinations.

The tickets were paid for in Canadian-embassy funds. The total bill came to nearly $25,000. From his office, Taylor then telephoned Roger Lucy, who had moved into the Sheardown home when John and Zena left.

"Okay, Roger. We have the tickets. All clear for Monday morning, if the weather holds. Keep your fingers crossed. The last supper will be Sunday night. You can tell the guests when they'll be leaving, and get ready for a full dress rehearsal. I'm afraid they're not going to get much sleep."

"Sleep? What's that?" Lucy said with a laugh.

sal. I'm afraid they're not going to get much sleep."

"Sleep? What's that?" Lucy said with a laugh.

They sat around the dinner table and on nearby chairs. They numbered twelve: the remaining Canadian embassy staff— Taylor, Lucy, Claude Gauthier, and communicator Mary O'Flaherty, the six houseguests, and Taylor's closest diplomatic friends, ambassadors Beebe and Munk. Lucy was dressed in a military camouflage jacket and high boots. "My interrogation uniform," he quipped, and the houseguests laughed nervously.

Taylor handed out the six passports and, for the first time, the houseguests were allowed to see the documents that would get them out of the country. They flipped through the pages, and it was obvious to Taylor that they were impressed with the forgeries.

Lee Schatz read aloud from page one of the passport, which was printed in English and French: "The bearer of this passport is a Canadian citizen." And farther down: "It may be used only by the rightful bearer and accompanying children whose names are included in it."

On the inside front cover, under the Canadian coat of arms, appeared these words in golden script: "The Secretary of State for External Affairs of Canada requests in the name of her Majesty the Queen, all those whom it may concern to allow the bearer to pass freely without let or hindrance, and to afford the bearer such assistance and protection as may be necessary."

"Without let or hindrance," Schatz repeated. "I like that. Hope it impresses the folks at customs and immigration. So this makes us all loyal subjects of the Queen."

"Exactly," Taylor said. "While you carry those passports, you are legally Canadian citizens, under the protection of the Crown. Of course, you'll be surrendering the passports when you get home."

Lucy broke in. "But check out the visas inside. Those are

your real passports to freedom. Courtesy of the CIA, with a little help from yours truly."

Taylor said it was time they familiarized themselves with their respective aliases. He had them recite their new names one by one, and their hometowns. "You are members of a business group, visiting a project in Iran. You have been staying with members of the Canadian embassy staff."

He then handed out the rest of their "cover" documentation and told them to study the plastic cards and papers carefully. He gave them small maple-leaf lapel pins, and warned them that, before they went to bed that night, they should make sure that all labels were removed from their suitcases and carry-bags.

"It's details, little details, that'll get you through safely," Roger Lucy said. "And it's details that'll trip you up....Now, let's see how you will bear up under questioning. Lee, you're first."

Lucy and Claude Gauthier put on their most menacing faces, and stood side by side. Schatz approached them, grinning. "Jesus, Roger," he said. "You'd make a terrific Gestapo agent."

"*Achtung!*" Roger shouted. "Mr. Schatz, where was your visa issued?"

Schatz looked at him blankly. "Er...God, I forgot."

"Ottawa, Ottawa, dammit," Lucy roared. "Guards, arrest this man. He is an American spy." He was joking, but there was anger in his voice. "Listen, Lee, this is vital. One slip-up like that and they've got you."

One by one, they were submitted to an interrogation by Lucy and Gauthier. They made few mistakes. They even remembered to use the Canadian interpolation "eh" every sentence or two.

"Good, good," said Taylor, when Lucy and Gauthier had exhausted their questions. "Now gather round, and I'll draw you a map of the airport terminal, with all the checkpoints. I want you to memorize this map, and every one of the points where you may be stopped and questioned, and whom you will be questioned by."

He sketched a layout of the terminal on yellow legal paper and numbered the critical checkpoints, repeating over and over again: "Here are the guards, here are the National Police, here are guards, police, and immigration. This is where the visa slips are inspected. This is the waiting area; don't believe for a minute that this is the end.

"Here, point number 7, you're on the airplane, and the Revolutionary Guards occasionally come down the aisles and demand your papers. So you don't let out a hoot until you're off the ground. Remember that."

Over and over again, Taylor took them through the route. "Oh, I almost forgot. This window here is where they check your tax forms. Don't worry about that, it's only for Iranian nationals. Just remember what it is."

When he was finished, Taylor asked them one by one, "Any questions? If there's anything worrying you, say it now." He looked at his watch. It was nearly midnight. "Less than eight hours before takeoff."

He searched their faces, and stopped at Joe Stafford. "Joe," he asked, "you look disturbed. Anything wrong?"

"Do you really think this will work?" Stafford said. "I mean, the whole thing looks so chancy. I just don't know. The crisis could be over in a week, and this whole thing would be unnecessary——"

"No, Joe," Taylor interrupted. "It won't be over in a week, or two weeks. We have to move you now. And even if they do let the hostages go, how would you feel marching down to the Foreign Ministry and saying, 'Here I am. I've been hiding for three months with the Canadians, and I'd like to go home now,' No. Joe, we have to do this tomorrow."

Stafford seemed unconvinced, but he didn't raise any more objections. Shortly after midnight, Taylor shook their hands one by one and wished them luck. "I won't be there tomorrow morning, so I'll say so long now. And remember, the two cars will stay outside the terminal in case anything goes wrong.

"If any one of you is stopped at a checkpoint and arrested, the others are to walk slowly towards the exit and get into the cars. Don't try to interfere. Remember, we still have other options. Now, the best of luck and try to get a few hours' sleep. You should be on your way to the airport by four o'clock. See you in Frankfurt."

They saw Taylor and his two colleagues to the door, and returned to the living room. Lee Schatz, who'd been drinking heavily all night, picked up a bottle of Cointreau and two clean glasses and sat down beside Joe Stafford.

"Now listen, Joe," he began, "we've got to be together on this thing...."

As he spoke, often slurring his words, Joe Stafford listened anxiously. By 2 a.m., he'd grudgingly given Schatz his word that he would go through with the plan.

Then they both went to bed, leaving the mess for Lucy to clean up the next day.

19

*T*HE FALSE DAWN. The mosques of Tehran were faintly etched against a cloudless sky. The city of three million people was sleeping. Within the American compound, a dozen militants, their Belgian rifles held carelessly at their sides, kept a drowsy watch. Some wandered the well-paced grounds, smoking and reflecting dreamily on the ten-month-old revolution. In a few hours, the morning prayer call would ring across the city. They would mutter the prayers and crawl into their cots. It was a chilly night. There would be some squabbling about blankets in the morning, and some arguing about the guard shifts.

Four a.m., Tehran time. In Shemiran, to the north of the city, six people stirred out of a restless sleep, their mouths dry. Lee Schatz, his head pounding with a hangover, dragged himself out of bed and marched down the hallway on the way to the bathroom, moaning and cursing the Cointreau that he had consumed. "Coffee," he groaned. "Black coffee." Other voices in nearby bedrooms yelled at him to shut up.

Back in his room, Schatz, still in his undershorts, hefted the suitcase that was sitting at the end of his bed. Inside were bundles of clothing, much of it left behind by departing Canadian embassy staffers earlier in the month.

On the dresser, neatly arranged, were his travel documents. He leafed through them one final time.

In his room Bob Anders stared into the mirror. He parted his hair on the opposite side, and darkened his eyebrows with some makeup borrowed from Cora Lijek. Today he would wear dark glasses and try not to worry about meeting an Iranian whose papers he might have processed while working in the American consular office. Today he would be the stereotypical Western businessman, open-mouthed and innocent and obsequious if need be.

In the Sheardowns' bedroom, Joe and Kathy Stafford dressed quietly, keeping conversation to a minimum. There was little to say that had not already been said. Like Anders, they were obsessed with fears of the "fluke factor"—an accidental meeting with someone who recognized them and shouted out: "Hey, I've seen you before. At the American embassy? Yes, I remember." Would they be able to bluff their way out, insist in a surprised voice that they were Canadians, that all North Americans looked alike? Stafford doubted he could pull it off. And despite last night's pep talk from Taylor and Schatz, he was still terrified that the exfiltration scheme would fail.

The Lijeks, Mark and Cora, on the other hand, were anxious to get under way. As they dressed, they continued to coach themselves. "Remember what Taylor said," Mark told Cora as he brushed his hair. "The airport guards are more interested in Iranian nationals leaving the country than in foreigners. They're on the lookout for tax-evaders and people smuggling money, and they don't often do careful searches of Westerners, as long as the papers are in order. And, if anything goes wrong with the flight, there'll be someone at the airport to give us tickets on the next one."

But the anxious questions, the doubts, were never entirely dispelled. "What if we're missing a document that is crucial, something we didn't know about?" Joe Stafford had asked the night before. They all knew that if there was any weak link in the chain of the operation, it lay here. Insufficient documents. Records lost or destroyed. An over-conscientious officer who'd had a bad morning and would take his irritation out on a foreigner. All it took was one bloody-minded official, one stickler for following the book, one eager young clerk with a grudge, and all could be lost.

And then there was the dicey matter of the "yellow

slips". Whenever a foreigner enters Iran, he is required to fill out a form with his name, citizenship, anticipated length of stay, and purpose of visit. An original of the paper remains with the immigration officials. The visitor keeps his carbon of the yellow slip, which he must produce when he leaves the country. The houseguests were all carrying expertly forged yellow slips; the problem was that there were no original white slips to match them with if an official decided to stage a search. It had been determined by Taylor and Lucy that the immigration officials rarely bothered to plough through their files in search of one slip of paper. It was one of those bureaucratic chores that was dutifully ignored. However, in the event that a zealous official did decide to go hunting for a matching white slip, and not find it, the "Canadians" were to display outrage and bluster. If they were challenged, they were to insist: "You must have lost the documents. Why should innocent Canadians be blamed for administrative problems? Here, look at all these other documents I am carrying." In all likelihood, the official would give up his questioning as a waste of time.

At 4:30 a.m., after a hurried cup of coffee, the six were collected in two Canadian diplomatic cars for the forty-five-minute drive to the airport. Tehran had not yet awoken in earnest, although a few cars and bicycles straggled through the streets. Despite their edginess, the Americans were euphoric at being in the open air again. They strained their eyes in the dim light for a last look at the city that had been so hostile to their compatriots: the mosques, the narrow streets with their open-sewer gutters, the mammoth inverted Y of the Shahyad monument, an extravagant concrete tribute to the Pahlavi dynasty built by the exiled Shah. They spoke little among themselves; after three months of captivity, of terror and frustration, of jokes and arguments, there was now little left to say.

By North American standards, Mehrabad International Airport is anything but a model of jet-age splendour. The terminal buildings are cramped and ill-suited to the streamlined needs of a major airport. An adjacent military base further clutters up the scenery. To the six Americans, however, the airport was the focus of all their dreams of freedom and safety, and it could not have been a more welcome sight as the cars pulled up to the terminal doors and discharged their passengers. The six collected their bags from the trunks, gave winks and hopeful smiles to their drivers, and strolled casually through the open doors into the airport lobby. In a ragged file, they sauntered over to a checkpoint, where a clutch of Revolutionary Guards asked them to open their suitcases. The guards rummaged through the clothes, eyed them carefully, and waved them on. The bags were checked, labelled and taken away. "One down," Schatz whispered to himself, walking past the airline counters towards the second checkpoint, where a uniformed policeman asked to see his papers. No problem here. It was only a cursory check, and the policeman barely nodded as he checked them through.

They turned, and directly ahead was checkpoint Number 3. This, they recalled Taylor telling them, was the major hurdle—the main immigration barrier, manned by civil servants, National Police, and the ever-present Revolutionary Guards. If they could pass through there, they were halfway home.

"Good luck and keep cool," they whispered to one another as they approached the gate, opening up the distance between them. They watched as Bob Anders, nodding and smiling politely, steered his way through without difficulty.

Lee Schatz was next, his face set. The immigration official asked for his passport, and Schatz casually placed it on the desk. The official picked it up, looked at the photograph carefully, and then stared into Schatz's face. Lee's stomach churned, and he could feel his heart thumping. "Wait here," the official said, and walked into a nearby office.

Schatz glanced behind him, and noticed the Staffords and the Lijeks watching the doorway of the immigration office, wide-eyed and obviously scared.

Within a minute, the immigration man came out again

and pointed at Schatz's passport photograph. "The moustache," he said, "it's different." Schatz assumed a serious expression to match that in the photo, and pulled down the edges of the moustache. "I trimmed it a little since the picture was taken. See?"

The official grunted and waved him through. Schatz could feel the sweat trickling down his forehead. And his hangover headache was throbbing, drum-like, in his temple.

About a hundred feet away, another problem arose, the most baffling of the day. As Mark and Cora Lijek approached a booth where their visas were once again to be checked, they noticed that the official was not at his post.

"Why, we could walk right through," Cora whispered. Mark huddled briefly with Bob Anders, and Anders decided that it was not worth the risk. If someone should see them passing through, it might attract unwelcome attention.

"I'll go and find him," Anders said, and buttonholed a nearby guard. The guard nodded, and went off to find the official, who came striding out of his office, apologizing for the delay. He cleared the six "Canadians" with great dispatch.

KINGSTON, ONTARIO January 28, 1 a.m.

The telephone rang on Flora MacDonald's bedside table. She awoke from a light sleep and looked at her wristwatch, momentarily disoriented.

"Hello," she said groggily.

It was an official of External Affairs, calling from Ottawa. "The operation is on," the man said.

"Where are they now?" the minister asked.

"They are at the airport, going through the checkpoints. There have been no problems."

"Thank God," she said. "Keep me informed, please." She hung up the phone and lay back on the pillow. But she was fully awake. She made a quick mental calculation. By 11 a.m. that morning, the last Canadian would be safely out of Iran.

TEHRAN   January 29, 7 a.m.

Claude Gauthier and Roger Lucy had stationed themselves at strategic spots in the terminal to monitor the progress of the six and report back to Taylor. One would go to the telephone, while the other maintained the vigil.

But, unknown to them, the progress of the six was being watched by another group of men, American agents standing in shaded corners and near telephone booths. They jokingly called themselves "mother hens", and they were ready to spring out at a moment's notice, to create a distraction in the terminal that would cover the escape of the six if trouble arose.

The "mother hens" did not anticipate trouble, and were confident they would not have to expose themselves in any way. They had more pressing things to do, and when they saw the six pass through a checkpoint into the passenger waiting area, they nodded to one another, and prepared to leave.

At roughly 7 a.m., Taylor received a call from Gauthier —his second of the morning. "They are in the lounge. No serious problems," the security chief reported.

"Thank you, Claude," Taylor said. "I think the worst is over."

In the Mehrabad passenger lounge, the bogus Canadians continued to play their roles with growing confidence. Mark and Cora Lijek splurged their remaining rials on jars of high-quality caviar at the delicacy shop. As they made their purchases, they uttered all the right noises: "Wow, what a bargain! Imagine what these would cost in Canada!" The salesman eagerly pressed a few more jars into their hands.

The other four strolled through the tacky souvenir shops and the coffee shop, wandering with an aimlessness designed to remove any official suspicion. At about 7:15, a delay was announced on their Swissair flight. The six conferred hastily about whether they should attempt to board one of the other flights for which they held tickets. They agreed that this might attract suspicion and decided to wait it out. Over an hour later, it was announced that the Swissair plane was ready for boarding.

Stepping lightly, they walked past the Revolutionary Guard at the gate and filed into the airplane. Lee Schatz found it hard to hold back a grin, a big toothy smile of victory, as the stewardess pointed him to his seat. Goddam, he thought, we fooled the bastards!

The jetliner taxied down the runway, engines screaming, and the nose lifted to a forty-five-degree angle. The rear wheels left the earth. Banking slightly, the liner fought for altitude. Observing the takeoff, Claude Gauthier was tempted to wait until the plane was no more than a speck on the horizon before calling in to Taylor. But his orders were explicit. He picked up the public telephone and dialled the embassy. "They are in the air," he cheered. "We did it!"

Later that afternoon, for more than a half-hour, the resounding crash of a blunt instrument striking metal echoed through the third floor of the nearly deserted Canadian chancery building. Sergeant Gauthier was relishing his last official job. Taylor could visualize his powerful arms swinging the massive hammer, from the ground up in a big arc, and bringing it down on the cipher machine. The metal box, as big as a large typewriter, was surprisingly solid. It would require nearly forty minutes of pounding to destroy it.

The standard embassy "comm room" comes equipped with an array of wrecking gear, including a wood-handled axe on the wall behind the cipher machine. Early in January, Gauthier had inspected the tools, and decided that the axe would be too flimsy. "That handle will break like a splinter," he told a bemused Taylor with a shake of his head. So Gauthier went shopping. He found a metal shop in Tehran and placed an order for a custom-made sledgehammer weighing about fifty pounds.

Hefting it into the chancery, Gauthier, as jaunty as a

lumberjack, had shown the ambassador his new toy. Taylor tried to lift it and went red-faced. Gauthier laughed. "If this doesn't do the trick, nothing will," he said.

And now, with the embassy about to close its doors indefinitely, the broad-shouldered sergeant was enjoying his act of demolition. With a grin, Ambassador Taylor walked down the hall to the comm room and hailed his security chief. "Just about finished, sergeant?" he asked. "We have a few other things to clean up."

"Just one more, sir," Gauthier replied, bringing the hammer down in a final swing. "Almost through." Then he gathered up the twisted bits of metal in a cloth bag for disposal. "Should I break up the telex machine, too?" he asked, nodding at the device outside the vault that linked the chancery with Ottawa.

"No, leave that," the ambassador said. "We'll probably be using it again someday."

Elsewhere in the chancery, the New Zealand officials were collecting the Canadian-embassy documents that they would be caring for. These were non-classified papers — the mission's administrative files. All other files would be passed through the electric shredder today — the final act of "house cleaning" before the evacuation.

Taylor's last telex to Ottawa, co-drafted with Roger Lucy, paid homage to Gauthier's special weapon. "Hammer in hand," the telex said, "we are prepared to leave Festung Iran and break out to the West." The term "Festung" was Lucy's idea. It was the German for "fortress" and was used by the Nazi hierarchy to describe the last stand of the Third Reich in Berlin.

The Canadians hoped Shenstone would forgive the schoolboyish glee in the final communiqué, the touch of vaunting bravado and high drama. The cable was also a subtle chuckle at themselves, at the Iranians, and at those poor, hand-wringing officials and politicians in Ottawa, sweating out the final hours. The reply from Ottawa came quickly by return telex: "Good luck, *bonne chance*. See you later, exfiltrator."

OTTAWA   January 28, 8 p.m.

It was a courtesy call. Margaret Herman, Flora MacDonald's secretary, had located Opposition Leader Pierre Elliott Trudeau in Montreal, at the Four Seasons Hotel, where he was making a campaign appearance.

"I have Mr. Trudeau," the secretary told her boss.

"Thank you, Margaret. Hello, Mr. Trudeau. This is Flora MacDonald. I thought you should know. All our people are out of Tehran. Ken Taylor should be in Paris by now. And the houseguests are in Frankfurt."

"Congratulations, Madame Minister."

"And tomorrow morning," the minister continued, "I will officially announce the closing of our embassy in Tehran, for reasons of security. And the prime minister has made it clear that he does not intend to use the successful conclusion of this operation as a campaign issue."

"Thank you for telling me," Trudeau said. Not a campaign issue, he thought. Clark was incredible!

20

*I**T WAS ONE** of those bleak and chilly Washington D.C.days, when the news is as leaden as the winter sky and the press corps yearns for the Florida presidential primary. The Iranian hostage drama was in its third month, and the capital's attention was on Edward Kennedy and Ronald Reagan. It was also State of the Union week.

At Georgetown University, Ted Kennedy shifted his campaign into a higher gear with a sweeping speech that damned Carter for his domestic and foreign policies. In his National Press Club office, Pelletier thumbed through the Kennedy text and yawned. To relieve the tedium, he flipped through the pages of a *New Yorker* magazine and chain-smoked his Madison little cigars.

He stiffened slightly at the ringing of the two bells from his UPI teletype. Two bells signalled an upcoming "urgent" item. On any day, the bells trigger a Pavlovian response in all correspondents. On a slow day, the bells are the sweetest music.

The story carried an Ottawa placeline. Pelletier made a mental note of the time: 1:32 p.m. The teletype spat out a half-dozen paragraphs. The Canadian government had closed its embassy in Tehran and recalled its personnel. Ottawa was worried about the safety of its diplomatic staff. So went the official line.

Pelletier stood frozen over the machine. Later, he would recall the slight trembling of his hands as he dialled the number of his editor in Montreal, Claude Saint-Laurent.

"Claude," he said, "they've evacuated the embassy. You know what that means."

Indeed he did. Operation Rescue had climaxed. The "houseguests" had fled, under the cover of an embassy closure. It had to be. Dammit, this was it. "So, we finally go with your story?" Saint-Laurent asked. He sounded relieved.

But Pelletier wasn't sure. After seven weeks of patience, he didn't want to jump the gun now, and possibly jeopardize any Canadian or American diplomats who might not yet have evacuated. "Let's not blow it now," he said. "Give me a few more hours, just to be sure."

Pelletier then asked if Canadian prime minister Joe Clark, whose Progressive Conservative government was facing a gruelling general election, had given any explanation of the embassy closing at his campaign stops. But Clark, he was told, was playing it close to the chest. Pelletier could well imagine the nervous jitters that must have seized official Ottawa.

His suspicion was confirmed when he dialled the Canadian embassy in Washington and was put through to the office of Gilles Mathieu. "I was expecting your call," Mathieu said, with a nervous chuckle. Pelletier voiced his fear that "The Story" was about to break wide open. "I don't think they can keep the lid on this for long," he said. Mathieu, ever cautious, disagreed. "But, Jean," Mathieu said, "we would much prefer you wait until the entire crisis is over. We don't know yet, but we fear repercussions on the fifty-three. *Vous me comprenez....*"

Pelletier did *not* understand. His instincts were now shouting that it was time to go. Cracks were opening; he could almost feel the story seeping through his fingers. He choked back an impatient outburst. "What is Ottawa planning to say about the embassy closing?" he asked. "Surely they have to go beyond a simple security reason." Mathieu told him that Flora MacDonald would give an explanation at a meeting with the Ottawa press corps that very evening.

Pelletier turned back to the Kennedy piece in his typewriter. He punched the keys listlessly, stopping every five minutes to scan the UPI wire. His careful and secret cultivation of the story of his life was now a house of cards. Five bells from the UPI wire — announcing a bulletin — could topple the structure. It was that simple. Oh sure, his integrity and reputation would survive, probably even be enhanced. But he would forever be remembered by his colleagues as the guy who lost the big one. Pushing this gloomy thought aside, he telexed his Kennedy story to head office.

Driving home in rush hour, Pelletier twirled the dials of his car radio. The Canadian embassy closing was one of those "meanwhile" items in the hourly newscasts: "Meanwhile in Tehran, the Canadian embassy, etc...." Nothing new or startling.

In Montreal, the *La Presse* senior editors, Saint-Laurent and Jean Sisto, were equally nervous. Intuitively, they sensed that the story might hold for a day or two, but Ottawa was certain to spring a leak somewhere. At 7:30 p.m., Saint-Laurent called Pelletier at his home. "Okay, Jean. File the story. Give us everything. If the story breaks tonight, at least we'll be able to throw a page together. Let's play this safe."

Pelletier, his half-digested supper churning in his stomach, agreed and mumbled a question about his Kennedy story. Saint-Laurent laughed. "Good stuff," he joked. "We'll try to find a hole for it tomorrow." The tension broken, Pelletier joined in the laughter and rang off with a familiar salutation: "*Bon, à plus tard.*"

When he returned to his office, Pelletier attacked his Olympia portable with vigour, referring only to sketchy notes from his diary and his recollections of past conversations. Halfway through the story, the cleaning woman came in, apologized for the interruption, and began to vacuum the carpet. She politely asked him to move his chair while she vacuumed under his desk. She emptied the ashtray filled with cigar butts.

Pelletier, welcoming the break, toyed with the idea of telling her the whole story and recording the reaction. "Listen, can you keep something secret for a day...?" he would say to her. It might be fun to entrust this story to a complete stranger, to swear her to secrecy, to note her exclamations and congratulations. Maybe she could read his copy, suggest changes. What a half-baked scheme, he thought. Might make a good sidebar for a future book, a footnote in his memoirs of this day. And maybe she wouldn't believe a word of it.

Chuckling to himself, Pelletier continued typing. He particularly enjoyed a paragraph quoting Iran's ambassador to Canada as saying that he couldn't understand why Ottawa was pulling its people out of Tehran.

By 9:30 he was finished. The story ran four double-spaced typed pages. The copy was straightforward, without any speculation or commentary. The Canadians had closed their embassy and withdrawn their diplomats as a cover to spirit out the Americans. The escape of the six was effected with false passports and visas as part of a meticulously planned Canadian-masterminded operation.

Pelletier knew that the third paragraph might give him some trouble with his editors. But it was central to the article: "*La Presse* has been aware of the Canadian role in this drama since December 10, but withheld publication at the request of the United States and Canadian governments."

By 10:30, Pelletier knew that the story would have to run the next day. Further delay would be indefensible by any standards of the profession. In Ottawa, Saint-Laurent told him by phone Flora MacDonald had told an audience of newsmen that U.S. Secretary of State Cyrus Vance had personally thanked the Canadian government for its "good offices" in Tehran.

This was not in her briefing notes. The minister had apparently gone beyond her "script" in a moment of enthusiasm. Surely, Pelletier thought, this comment would beg the question: "What exactly did Canada do for the United States in Tehran?" Was MacDonald deliberately teasing the press with this tidbit? After all, the Conservative government was in the thick of a general election, and its staging of the Canadian Caper could be a powerful vote-getter.

Pelletier saw this as a green light. He made one more call to the Canadian embassy. An informed source told him that "as far as we are concerned, the story is still under wraps." Pelletier dismissed this as a normal bureaucratic reflex, and told the source he would be filing the story for publication the next day. "At this stage," the embassy staffer told him, "we have no advice to give one way or another."

Pelletier sat in front of his telex keyboard and began punching in the story, making slight alterations along the way. The editor receiving the copy at the other end was warned that it must not be shown to anyone in the newsroom, other than Sisto and Saint-Laurent.

At sunrise the next day in Montreal, a fleet of trucks pulled out of the *La Presse* garages with 165,000 still-moist copies of that day's newspaper. A blazing red headline announced the success of a daring Canadian diplomatic caper in Tehran.

Within an hour, the wire services had picked up the story, and the message recorder in Pelletier's office at the National Press Building was filled to capacity.

By then Pelletier was sleeping soundly.

21

*T*HE SUCCESSFUL CONCLUSION of the Canadian Caper, as it quickly came to be known, brought
an outpouring of gratitude so extravagant that Canadians
were almost embarrassed. The news broke on the early
morning radio and television newscasts throughout North
America, even as *La Presse*'s early edition was hitting the
streets.

Ottawa had managed to keep the secret for a bare few
hours, saying that it had closed its embassy in Tehran for
vague reasons of security. But Pelletier's scoop quickly shattered that story.

To the embassy staff's heroism was added a typically
Canadian touch of modesty. "It was important," said Ken
Taylor, in an interview later, "for Americans to say thank
you."

They did more than that. They went wild. It was the first
good news after three months of national trauma.

In San Francisco, a man walked into the offices of the
Canadian consulate, steadied himself against a wall, whistled
a ragged version of "O Canada", gave a drunken salute, and
ran out the door before the security guard could get his name.
In West Virginia, a service station along Highway 81 offered
to tow, without charge, any cars with Canadian licence plates
that happened to break down.

The maple leaf was flown in Oklahoma City, in Livonia,
Michigan, and in a hundred other American towns and cities.
Canadian expatriates in the United States were embraced by
friends and neighbours, many with tears in their eyes. Callers

to radio stations wept freely as they tried to express their gratitude to their northern neighbours. Billboards sprang up throughout the American countryside, with giant letters that spelled "Thank you, Canada." A major U.S. bank bought a full-page ad in the *New York Times* to commemorate the Canadian deed.

At thirteen Canadian consulate offices in the major American cities, extra staff was brought in to answer the flood of telephone calls and postcards that poured in.

President Carter in Washington telephoned Joe Clark in Ottawa, with effusive thanks for an act that cemented the American–Canadian alliance like nothing before. Privately, External Affairs officials in Ottawa grumbled about the fact that the story had broken, even now that the lives of the six fugitives and the Tehran embassy staff were not in danger. They worried about possible retribution against the remaining American hostages, a fear that was unwarranted. But they remained silent, and let the waves of gratitude wash over them.

Tehran, naturally, let loose with a blast, but for once, it was laughed off. Canada would "pay" for its skulduggery, threatened Sadeq Ghotbzadeh. The Iranian government said Ottawa had broken international law by assisting "spies" with forged passports. The North American press had a field day with this outrageous posturing, but political analysts in Ottawa and Washington recognized it for what it was: a bone thrown to the Iranian militants. Secretly, the Iranian government was pleased that the six Americans had escaped. It was one less complication to worry about. But, of course, the spokesmen for the revolutionary regime could not admit their relief publicly.

And what about Ken Taylor, the man who had pulled off Canada's greatest cloak-and-dagger coup? He was an instant, certified hero. The press caught up with him in Paris, and laid siege to the Canadian embassy there. Canadian officials tried to persuade Taylor to keep a low profile, but he rejected the advice and consented to brief interviews. In spite of this, the cordon of newsmen around the embassy were hungry for more, and finally Ambassador Gérard Pelletier, exasperated by their persistence, had to flee the building by a rear window. The irony of his situation was beyond the scope of even the craziest Hollywood script: the father of the man who had broken the story of the Canadian Caper was now giving haven to his fellow ambassador who had harboured the six Americans.

Taylor played his role well, accepting the praise, indulging himself in it, and flashing the toothy smile that would become famous overnight. He made occasional diplomatic disclaimers — "I was only doing my job, after all" — but for the most part, he wore his laurels with flair. America needed a hero then, and even if he was not one of their own, he was still dashing, handsome, and gracious. Taylor cringed a bit when he heard himself described as the "Scarlet Pimpernel" of diplomacy, but he knew that the outpouring of enthusiasm was a kind of therapy for the discouraged Americans. In the months ahead would come more agony, more outrage, more frustration, and more defeat over the hostage crisis. But for the moment, Americans were in the mood for a party.

As Taylor headed home to Ottawa, covered in glory, the six Americans had their own exuberant homecoming. After a stopover in Delaware, they were flown to Washington, where, on Friday, February 1, the staff of the U.S. State Department rolled out the welcome mat. In the high-ceilinged lobby of the building, decorated with the flags of the world, hundreds of workers abandoned their desks for an hour to shout themselves hoarse. "Welcome Bob Anders, and Welcome Canada" read a huge banner that spanned the balconies of the lobby. Friends and relatives of the six embraced them unabashedly, and then applauded when they shook hands with a representative of the Canadian embassy, First Minister Gilles Mathieu. (Canada's ambassador to Washington, Peter Towe, was conspicuous by his absence: he chose not to cut short a visit to Hawaii to return to the U.S. capital. While not strictly a breach of protocol, his absence did raise some questions. Was he being petulant, or even a touch envious of Taylor's celebrity?)

Later, in a packed auditorium of newsmen, Bob Anders read a statement of thanks to Taylor, his staff, and the Canadian government, and related how the six houseguests had kept themselves busy with a marathon game of Scrabble during their period of hiding. At a more private function, the six then shook hands with Jean Pelletier, and told him how much they appreciated his discretion in holding the story until they had fled Iran.

Pelletier was moved, as he had never before been in his career. He had feared that the six would have preferred to return to the United States in anonymity, lest the story of their escape enrage the militants still holding their fifty-three colleagues in Tehran, and thus place them in danger. But their meeting was warm, and untarnished by any resentment.

At that very moment, six hundred miles away in Ottawa, Taylor appeared at his first formal press conference, before a jostling mob of newsmen at the National Press Building. Camera crews from a score of countries jockeyed for space in the room, and a squad of Royal Canadian Mounted Police was kept busy inspecting dozens of floral bouquets that had been sent to Taylor. They were sniffing for bombs.

Taylor was as candid as his superiors would allow him to be. He told how he and John Sheardown had harboured the six, he told of some of the anxious moments, and he related, in a necessarily sketchy way, the clandestine circumstances of the exfiltration. He said nothing about his intelligence-gathering forays for the Americans. He said nothing about the CIA, about the agents and the Iranian "friendlies" still active inside that country.

Nor was this the time to unburden himself of what Taylor saw as the most profound lesson of those three dramatic months in Tehran: the tragic failure of diplomacy. When the historians delved into the early months of the hostage crisis, that breakdown, he believed, would fill several chapters. In a sense, he, Taylor, was a hero because his government had dared to stand apart from other Western governments who had shied away from extraordinary action. Canada alone had taken that extra step into the unknown. And God knows, that kind of grittiness was not characteristic of Ottawa.

It is easy to say (and many Canadians would say) that the Canadian government, through its envoy in Tehran, did what it had to do, what any *civilized* government would have done, in the same circumstances. After all, what embassy would have turned away six diplomats, blameless of any specific crime, but on the run in a hostile foreign capital? True enough. The British, Swedes, Danes, New Zealanders, Germans, French, and a host of others would likely have opened their doors, in a humanitarian gesture, and hidden the six — at great risk.

But Canada put a special premium on their safety. It not only hid the fugitives, but it spirited them out of the country, knowing full well that the price would be a complete break in diplomatic relations with Iran. That was the cost of success; the cost of failure would have been far greater. And while Canada safeguarded the six houseguests, Taylor continued in his efforts to have Western diplomats in Tehran light a fire under the Iranian government. Supported by Flora Mac-Donald and Prime Minister Joe Clark, he aligned himself with Washington's stand in the crisis. The Iranians were outlaws, and the world should have condemned them as such, and acted from this conviction. Had Embassy Row in Tehran mounted a campaign of unrelenting pressure on the Iranian government, drawn a line in the sand, then perhaps Ken Taylor would not have had to play the role of hero to its dramatic conclusion.

The headlines trumpeting Canada's bit of derring-do flashed around the globe, leaving an impact in every world capital. At the U.S. compound in Tehran, a sympathetic "jailer" showed hostage Kathryn Koob a newspaper article about the Canadian Caper. As she read about the escape of her six colleagues, her mood brightened. "It was the greatest thing I ever read," she would say months later. Koob passed the word to other hostages, and the exhilaration spread. It was a small victory, but it was sweet.

From Canada's point of view, the months that followed the Caper were perplexing ones. For one thing, Prime Minister Joe Clark was ingloriously dumped by Canadian voters in a spring election. It is one of the enduring mysteries of modern Canadian politics that Clark never used the incident for personal political gain. Not since Lester Pearson and his intervention in the Suez Crisis had Canada made such a thunderous impact on the international stage, but Joe Clark treated his government's coup like yesterday's stale headline. He was too busy courting obscurity.

Nor did the Canadian Caper yield any tangible benefits for Canada in its relations with the United States. The goodwill failed to move the United States Senate to approve, for example, a fisheries treaty with Canada that Ottawa dearly wanted. Canada's act of friendship did not provoke Congress to repeal a number of "Buy-American" laws that hurt Canada's trade balance. And a small-scale water-diversion project in North Dakota that threatened rivers and farmland in Manitoba and Saskatchewan went ahead, despite appeals from the Canadian government. To be sure, Ottawa never openly asked for a *quid pro quo* from Washington. But it did expect something more than a golden handshake in gratitude for its role in creating the one ray of hope in the long months of America's deepening crisis.

Ken Taylor, however, found that the currency of heroism was more lasting. He went on the road as an unofficial ambassador-at-large and reaped the rewards of the American euphoria. Over the next eleven months, he made 108 appearances in virtually every major city in the United States and Canada. He was given the ceremonial keys to New York City and sixteen other communities. He addressed the World

Affairs Council, the Detroit Freedom Festival, the International Association of Firefighters, the U.S. Veterans of Foreign Wars, the Marine Corps League, the Ancient and Honorable Artillery Company of Massachusetts, the Buffalo MS Dinner of Champions, and the International Association of Chiefs of Police.

Ken and Pat Taylor opened exhibitions all over the continent. They rode on horseback, in black police cars, in red fire-chief cars, in antique cars, aboard sailboats and destroyers, in open carriages, and even in a hot-air balloon.

Taylor was cheered by 80,000 football fans in Seattle, and 30,000 baseball fans in Yankee Stadium. At the Terry Fox telethon for cancer research, a lock of Taylor's hair was knocked down for $80. In Toronto, a musician wrote a song in his honour, entitled "I love you Kenny Taylor, the Gold Medal man". He was made an Officer of the Order of Canada, received the Congressional Medal of Honor from the United States, and was awarded several honorary degrees. A national newsmagazine characterized him as "a new champion, noble and pure as Luke Skywalker".

One hundred and eleven resolutions and proclamations were issued in his honour. He collected plaques and citations like other men collect stamps. The Girl Scout Troop 671 of Manteca, California, sent him their Walnut Tree Plaque. Governor Bob Graham of Florida sent him a framed picture of the state capital building, the president of the Rotary Club in Red Bank, New Jersey, sent a plaque. So did Inspector Steven Hardkopp of United States Customs at Port Huron, Michigan. Sixteen ladies from Chelsea, Oklahoma, sent him a hand-stitched maple-leaf quilt. Mr. Peter Bizzigotti of Mount Pocono, Pennsylvania, sent a poem about Niagara Falls.

For ten months, Ken Taylor was a blur, skipping time zones and digesting more testimonial dinners than any man should have to in a lifetime.

But there were some dissenting voices, and ironically, they were mostly Canadian. The Montreal newspaper *Le Devoir*, for example, boldly suggested that while Taylor had done the proper thing, he had also breached international law in spiriting the six Americans out of Iran.

In May 1980, Canadian Ambassador to Washington Peter Towe instructed his staff not to accept an invitation from the management of the New York Yankees baseball team to attend a function honouring Taylor, the Tehran embassy staff, and the six Americans. But one staffer, Pelletier's contact, Tom Boehm, disobeyed the order and sat in Yankee Stadium while the crowds cheered Canada and Taylor, its emissary.

In an interview at the External Affairs Department in Ottawa, Michael Shenstone tried to shrug off questions from two reporters about the Canadian Caper by saying: "Can't we tell this story without getting into personalities?" Privately, officials resented the adulation that was heaped upon Taylor, arguing that perhaps a little modesty and humility were in order. One of Taylor's "failings", his colleagues muttered, was that he had a commercial rather than a diplomatic background. What was he doing, revelling in all the adulation when he should be at his desk, issuing memos and planning diplomatic cocktail parties?

Despite all his globe-trotting, Taylor was aware of the petty carping and backbiting at home. But as best he could, he ignored it. He was dealing, after all, with that Canadian syndrome that reduces its national achievers to scale, so that they can be scrutinized back and front, top and bottom, and then tossed aside. Canada has little love for its homegrown heroes. Thus, John A. Macdonald is remembered as a gin sot, Mike Pearson is remembered for his stammer, and Billy Bishop is a Canadian play that survived a week or two on Broadway.

When Taylor had run his course as a goodwill ambassador late last year, Ottawa put him back to work, as consul general in New York City.

On Wednesday, January 21, 1981, Bruce Laingen, the American chargé d'affaires in Tehran, who had been held hostage with fifty-one other Americans for 444 days, alighted from the jetliner Freedom One in Wiesbaden, West Germany, a free man again. He made a number of telephone calls. One of them was to Ken Taylor in New York. "Thank you, Ken," he said. "We're coming home."

Within days after stepping back onto American soil, Laingen was in bed with a fever — a relatively minor ailment resulting from his prolonged captivity. The other returning hostages suffered from varying degrees of psychological and physical stress. They told stories of humiliation and despair, of torture and terror at the hands of their captors. They told of being subjected to games of Russian roulette, of being beaten and interrogated, of being stood up against a wall to undergo mock executions, and of being told that their countrymen had forgotten about them. They were alive, but scarred.

A week after they were liberated, the returning Americans were led out of the White House by President Reagan onto an elevated stage before the television cameras of the world.

The cameras panned across their faces. After the speeches and the military music, the TV cameras shifted to the crowds on the White House lawn. They found Ken Taylor in a small cluster of ambassadors. In time, they found the faces of Bob Anders, Mark and Cora Lijek, Joe and Kathy Stafford, and Lee Schatz.

They were all craning their necks over the sea of heads for a last look at the ex-hostages up on the stage. They seemed wistful. This was not their moment.

But they too were survivors.

At the time of this writing, Ken Taylor is Canadian consul-general in New York City.

Robert Anders is a senior consular officer in Stockholm, Sweden.

Joe and Kathy Stafford are consular officers in Palermo, Sicily.

Mark and Cora Lijek are consular officers in Hong Kong.

Lee Schatz is with the agricultural department in Washington, D.C.

John Sheardown is an official with the Department of Immigration in Ottawa.

Roger Lucy is with the security division of the Department of External Affairs in Ottawa.

Tom Boehm is a political counsellor with the Canadian High Commission in Nairobi, Kenya.

Ambassador Peter Towe and Gilles Mathieu are still with the Canadian embassy in Washington, D.C.

Joe Clark and Flora MacDonald occupy Opposition benches in the House of Commons in Ottawa.

Sadeq Ghotbzadeh is a newspaper publisher in Tehran, and has no official connection with the Iranian government.

Abolhassan Bani-Sadr is President of the Islamic Republic of Iran and commander-in-chief of the Iranian military in the war against Iraq.

The Ayatollah Khomeini, reportedly in failing health at his residence in Qom, remains the head of the Islamic Republic of Iran.

Jimmy Carter is a private citizen in Plains, Georgia.

238

Of the many sources consulted, the authors are especially indebted to the following for information that was invaluable to the writing of *The Canadian Caper*:

BOOKS

American University, *Iran, a Country Study*, Foreign Area Studies Series, Washington, D.C., 1978.

Hoveyda, Fereydoun, *The Fall of the Shah*, New York: Simon & Shuster, 1980.

Rubin, Barry, *Paved with Good Intentions: The American Experience in Iran*, New York: Oxford University Press, 1980.

Troyer, Warner, *200 Days: Joe Clark in Power*, Toronto: Personal Library Publishers, 1980.

Facts on File, 1976, 1977, 1978, 1979, 1980 editions.

MAGAZINES
Newsweek
The New Yorker
Time

NEWSPAPERS
La Presse (Montreal)
Le Devoir (Montreal)
Le Monde (Paris)
The Globe and Mail (Toronto)
Toronto Star
The New York Times
The Washington Post

ACKNOWLEDGEMENTS

We are grateful to the following people who, as politicians, diplomats, colleagues, and friends, donated their time and knowledge to help us write *The Canadian Caper*: from the Department of External Affairs, Ken and Pat Taylor, Tom Boehm, Michael Shenstone, David Elder, Gilles Mathieu, Roger Lucy, Yves Margraff, Allan Gotlieb, Peter Lawless, Ruth Francis, George Happy, and Rejeanne Dodd; from *La Presse*, Jean Sisto, Robert Pouliot, Claude Saint-Laurent, Roger Lemelin, and Pierre McCann; from the United States State Department, Carl Clement, Henry Precht, and Bill Crawford; the Honourable Flora MacDonald; Richard Lelé; Christian Bourguet; Les Harris; Anne Holloway, our editor at Macmillan; and our wives, Dianne Proulx and Rowan Marsh.

We wish to thank also the Canada Council for their financial assistance.